W9-AOE-325

Goodnight Sweetheart, Goodnight:
The Story of the Spaniels

Goodnight Sweetheart, Goodnight: The Story of the Spaniels

Richard G. Carter

August Press
Sicklerville, N.J.

Design by Rob King

ISBN 0-9635720-2-4

Library of Congress 94-78836

First edition

10 9 8 7 6 5 4 3 2 1

*To Susan, for coming into
my life at just the right time.*

Contents

Preface

"Do do do do dooo . . . Goodnight sweetheart, well it's time to go . . ." – The Spaniels, Vee-Jay Records (1954).

June 8, 1991, was a hot and humid Saturday in New York City. By the time 7 p.m. rolled around, the hundreds of people in line outside Radio City Music Hall were rocking back and forth, trying to stay cool. But there was something atypical about this otherwise typical New York gaggle of music lovers waiting to enter a theater to listen, tap their feet and sing along to black music. Most were in their 40s and 50s and most were white.

Inside the storied home of the Rockettes – a place were countless show business legends have strutted their stuff – the near capacity crowd sat in quiet anticipation. They were awaiting the appearance of another show business legend – albeit a sadly unheralded one in mainstream America. It was a black vocal group from Gary, Ind., whose breakthrough recording of "Goodnight Sweetheart, Goodnight," was more responsible than any other song for bringing black rhythm and blues to whites.

After an hour of serviceable, feel-good doo-wop by a local group from the Bronx and several vaguely familiar aggregations from elsewhere the time had arrived. And the well-dressed crowd of devotees of the original R&B was buzzing to beat the band.

New York radio disk jockey Bobby Jay – himself a former member of several black R&B vocal groups – took the stage to introduce the singers everyone had come for. And as he mentioned the names of Gerald Gregory, the boom-boom bass who had been his inspiration, and James (Pookie) Hudson, the phenomenal lead voice and songwriter extraordinaire, it was clear the "25th Royal New York Doo-Wop Show" had reached its climax.

Four of the original Spaniels were there – including Willie C. Jackson and Opal Courtney Jr. – with only Ernest Warren missing. And although far removed from the talented teen-agers who burst upon the scene in 1953 with the haunting "Baby, It's You," they still displayed that splendid mix of rollicking emotion that put them at the top of the black music heap in the '50s – the formative years of a musical art form that began as rhythm and blues, became rock 'n' roll and changed the nation for all time.

Yes, it was still there. Pookie's incredible phrasing and tonal quality on the slow stuff – bringing to mind the perfectionist work of Frank Sinatra and the silky smoothness of the Ink Spots' Bill Kenny. Along with Gerald's booming, bouncing, walking bass rivaling the sounds of a tenor sax and the mellow background harmonies of Willie C., Opal and their old Gary singing pal Billy Shelton, the Spaniels – now in their mid-to-late 50s – were as always, a real treat.

This is the unique vocal group that introduced "doo-wah" which became "doo-wop" to this unique American music. Which is one reason three busloads of people from Connecticut waited outside the stage door after the show – many having left the hall after the Spaniels finished singing – for them to sign autographs.

But even before that, and before Gerald brought on "Goodnight, Sweetheart" "Do, do, do, do doooo" – the most famous five notes in the history of our country's pop music – I once again was entralled. And I realized that as one of the few blacks in the Radio City audience that night, I could really identify with the sounds I was hearing. I went home very happy that night.

Two months later, as part of a mostly black crowd at the world-famous Apollo in Harlem, I watched the born-again Spaniels in an R&B reunion of some of the famous acts that played the theater in the '40s, '50s and '60s.

Opening their set with "Baby, It's You," electricity filled the hall by the time the Spaniels gave out with their classic a capella version of "Danny Boy," amidst audience cries of "do it, Pookie" and "get down, Gerald."

The Spaniels were the only act among the likes of the Coasters, Shirelles, Harptones, Hank Ballard and the Midnighters, Bobbettes and Chuck Jackson – to name a few – called back for an encore. At the conclusion of "Goodnight Sweetheart" in both shows, the resounding shouts of "more, more, more" simply couldn't be ignored, so Pookie led them on stage for "You're Gonna Cry," and the crowd went wild. The Spaniels, indeed, were back.

* * * *

I grew up on original black R&B and saw the Spaniels perform a number of times in my hometown of Milwaukee in the '50s. "Baby, It's You" – their first record and, I feel, their best – shaped my musical tastes. Since 1979, I've written many newspaper columns on the music and was present in New York on Feb. 21, 1991, when the Spaniels were honored by the Smithsonian Institution's Rhythm and Blues Foundation with a Pioneer Award recognizing their lifetime contribution to the art form.

On that memorable evening I decided I wanted to tell the story of how it all began, fell apart, and came together again for the Spaniels:

How and why they never got the credit or the millions in royalties they deserve for "Goodnight Sweetheart" – a song featured in hit movies such as *Three Men and a Baby, Diner* and *American Graffiti,* adapted by Sha Na Na as part of its act, and heard on television commercials. And why the original members are singing again.

And how three background singer replacements – James (Dimples) Cochran, Carl Rainge and Donald (Duck) Porter – made such great contributions during the group's multihit heyday from 1956-60. These young men rocked the nation with "You Gave Me Peace of Mind," "Everyone's Laughing," "You're Gonna Cry," "I.O.U.," and a dazzling, up-tempo version of "Stormy Weather."

That's what *Goodnight, Sweetheart, Goodnight: The Story of the Spaniels* is about. It's a true story of a gifted group of young African-Americans who came of age the hard way. And what a story!

* * * *

Nearly 40 years after joining the Spaniels, Willie C. Jackson, the group's affable second tenor, still lives in Gary, Ind. in a large brick and frame home at 4321 Jefferson St. he shares with his wife Zola. Willie C's rec room is one of the places today's Spaniels often gather to rehearse – a daily routine for them. Belief that practice does, indeed, make perfect is a thread that runs through the group. And it's one reason, aside from awesome individual talent, that these singers actually sound better than ever.

In this refreshingly cool basement, on a summer day of record-breaking 100-plus-degree heat in Gary, I sat down to learn first-hand the true tale of this great black vocal group. It was the first time in more than three decades the original Spaniels came together as one to talk to an outsider, honestly and openly – no holds barred.

At the end of the long day, the Spaniels sang a cappella 1958's "Heart and Soul" – featuring Gerald Gregory's gutteral bass lead – and "Baby, It's You," which launched the group way back in 1953, while they were still teen-agers. And what a thrill it was. The great Spaniels were singing for an audience of one. Me. And I'll always remember – and cherish – the experience.

But before the Spaniels sang for me, they talked to me – and to each other. All day. Pookie, Gerald, Willie C., Opal and Billy. Teddy Shelton, Billy's son – the group's guitarist and musical director – also sat in. The only missing original member was baritone Ernest Warren, now a preacher, to whom I talked at a later time. This was to be the first of several group and many individual interviews I conducted with the Spaniels. And what they told me – their own way and their own words – is the way it was and is.

Richard G. Carter
Milwaukee
November 1994

ONE
The Beginning

"Our first venture into singing was doing gospel. And we got to be pretty good. We were darn good, as a matter of fact. I think it was Pookie and I that leaned toward trying to sing what was more popular. You know, rhythm and blues at that time." – Calvin Fossett, an original member of the Three Bees, forerunner of the Spaniels.

Among his blood relatives, Thornton James (Pookie) Hudson was fortunate to be able to include cousins Josephine Baker and Fats Waller. In the late 1930s and early '40s, these internationally renowned entertainers – along with the phenomenal Ink Spots – while touring often stopped over at the home of Pookie's aunt, Audrey Stephens, in Davernport, Iowa, where the youngster visited every summer.

Meeting such dedicated, talented people – hearing them rehearse and talking with them while listening to their easy kind of sound – helped peak Pookie's interest in singing. That, and constantly playing his grandmother's "stack of records."

Another catalyst was a jukebox in his grandfather's tavern in Cedar Rapids, Iowa – along with machines that showed pictures of performers. Among his favorites were the Charioteers gospel group, led by Billy Williams – later to appear regularly with his quartet on television's "Your Show of Shows," starring Sid Caesar and Imogene Coca.

Pookie, whose relaxed vocal quality and precise phrasing became instantly recognizable as the Spaniels' sound in years to come, always felt Williams and the Ink Spots' Bill

Kenny had the most beautiful voices he'd ever heard among lead singers. These two men, more than anyone, were his seminal influences in the world of music.

In 1941, when he was 7, the musically precocious native of Des Moines, Iowa, was in the habit of listening to the rehearsal of a gospel group run by his cousin's husband. One day, the lead singer took sick and since Pookie had learned the part, he asked if he could take over. The flabbergasted group laughingly agreed. Pookie did so well, the cousin insisted they take him along to sing on their rounds of the churches in Davenport. This vocalizing in church at an age when most kids were playing cowboys and Indians, was to provide invaluable early practice in developing the distinctive style that was to serve him so well.

But Pookie – a name bestowed by an aunt for his early childhood habit of messing his pants with regularity – didn't get the idea that he really wanted to sing until later in Gary, Ind., where his mother moved when he was 2 years old. When he was 9, he and his cousin Lloyd, who lived with them in the Delaney public housing project, listened to music on the radio as they washed dishes. Pookie would imitate the bass fiddle and Lloyd would invariably tell him: "Man, you can't sing, so why don't you shut up."

Prior to getting their two-bedroom apartment in the projects – single-story, brick buildings populated mainly by low-income female-headed households – Pookie and his mother lived in a small frame house a couple of blocks away on 24th Avenue. His most vivid recollections are of the smelly outhouse in back, having to bathe in a galvanized tub and bedding down in the front room.

Thus, the move into newly constructed Delaney was like a godsend to him. For the first time since coming to Gary, he had his own bedroom – which lasted until his cousin and some of his mother's friends moved in. Best of all, he was able to go to the bathroom and get cleaned up in the same place inside. Across the street was all-black Roosevelt High School, where his musical talents later burst into full bloom.

World War II was going full-force and uniforms were everywhere, especially those of sailors on leave from the nearby Great Lakes Training Station near Chicago. And the regular blackout drills run by neighborhood air raid wardens kept everyone on their toes, even if it was only practice.

Despite Lloyd's bad-mouthing, Pookie persevered in his singing doing his thing in talent shows.

He and his young friends put on shows in unlikely places like the building's coal bin. Most were won by a kid named T'deorice Young, who sang the blues. Undaunted, Pookie continued to sing and listen to the radio. Because he had a knack for remembering the words, he was able to sing most of the songs his friends couldn't, since they could only remember the melodies.

At that time, in the mid-1940s, so-called "popular music" was out front while the black sound was called "race music." And Pookie listened intently to all of it. He cut his teeth on pop hits such as "All the Things You Are" and "Bewildered" – pleasing only himself in the process. Although he felt he sang well enough to please others, he didn't know for sure until the ninth grade, when he entered a talent show at Roosevelt High School.

An older neighborhood kid, Sylvester Harris, who used to play piano in the shows, let Pookie sing along when he practiced at home. Knowing a good thing when he heard it, Sylvester convinced Pookie to go on the talent show himself.

He did, singing something called "Sloppy Drunk" – a tune he wrote and sang at his grandmother's house in Davenport. And even though listeners never could understand the words, they liked the way he sang it, and the melody. So after surprising himself by taking first place in the show, Pookie began to sing around the school whenever he could – in the halls, lavatories and the gym.

Part of one of his classes consisted of an "auditorium" period in which teachers would insist that everyone sing along. Pookie was quick to notice that one teacher, Miss Simms, was always walking up and down the aisles and listening closely. Finally, she picked out his as the voice she was hearing above all the other students.

Miss Simms, who also was in charge of the Girls' Glee

Club, advised Pookie to join the Boys' Glee Club to exercise his talent. She liked his singing so much she also invited him to come in and sing to her girls.

This expression of encouragement turned out to be the push Pookie needed to get started on what would blossom into a full-fledged career as a singer.

By 1952, the tall, reed-thin Pookie had established himself in the black neighborhoods of Gary as a young man with a unique singing voice, style and delivery. Then 18, he was part of a quartet at First Baptist Church, where his voice was admired by Spaniels' top tenor to-be, Ernest Warren, and was regularly sought out by other churches to sing in their choirs. Often, members would come to his home on Sunday mornings and take him to church to make sure he'd be there.

At that time, Pookie also was part of a teen-age vocal group called the Three Bees. The other, slightly older members were Calvin Fossett, a boyhood chum who'd visited him in Iowa and got a chance to hear his uncle's gospel group sing, and founder Billy Shelton.

Billy, more than anyone, mentored Pookie in the fine points of group harmony.

(There are two versions of how this very important vocal group was named. One claims Three Bees was chosen by Gary's Vivian Carter, of Vee-Jay Records, because they sang bop, ballads and blues. The other says the name stemmed from the group's harmony, which approximated the tuneful, airborne humming of those busy little insects.)

The musically mature Billy first met Pookie and Calvin in the Boys' Glee Club in 1949, the year after his family moved to Gary from Chicago. In Chicago, Billy grew up on Oakwood Boulevard – a block from the year-younger Sam Cooke, with whom he would "get together and sing all night a lot of times." This neighborhood also was home to Nat (King) Cole, the Flamingos, Lou Rawls and Minnie Ripperton. And Thomas A. Dorsey, the "father of gospel music," lived just two doors from Billy.

The boys sang together for the first time in a 10th grade skit written by Calvin for the drama portion of the"auditorium" period. Billy, to whom Calvin had been introduced by Pookie, asked to join their singing part. They agreed and were happy with the results.

The Three Bees then began to seriously try their wings on Ink Spots and barbershop-type things, featuring light harmonies. Their numbers included gospel songs as well as "Straighten Up and Fly Right," "I Know" and "I Only Have Eyes for You" before the Flamingos hit record.

Billy had been astute at putting harmonies together as early as age 14 or 15. Working with his arrangements, the boys would wail away in the hallways at school, causing teachers to come out of classrooms and make them stop. Singing on the first floor, the trio's melodic, adult-sounding, echo-enhanced a capella voices interfered with kids trying to concentrate in the study hall on the third floor – a tribute to the tonsils of this very good, very powerful young vocal group.

The Three Bees from time to time became the Four Bees when a fellow named William Dooley sang bass.

Joe Jackson – father of Michael, Janet, Jermaine and the rest of the famed singing Jackson clan, also from Gary – claimed to have joined on occasion.

After a while, flush with youthful exhuberance and promise, they approached Vivian Carter, then a 29-year-old radio disk jockey with a popular late night show on WWCA-FM called "Livin' with Vivian." This ambitious young woman was trying to form a record company and looking for talent with her husband, Jimmy Bracken. But incredibly, the pair felt the boys sang too well – sounding too much like the established Orioles. And Vivian was looking for something different.

About that time, glee club and mixed chorus members Willie C. Jackson and Gerald Gregory happened upon Billy "training" Calvin and Pookie in group harmonies in a school hallway. And they liked what they heard.

This proved to be yet another accidental, albeit providential event in the creation of the Spaniels.

The graduation from high school later in 1953 of Billy, Calvin and William proved the undoing of the youthful trio/quartet of dynamic vocalizers. Thus the Bees – which may have developed into the Spaniels themselves had they hung in – didn't last. Although Billy had singing in his blood, and would become a Spaniel years later, he lacked Pookie's foresight and didn't think they'd make it. Calvin went into the Army and in subsequent years was Gary's long-time housing commissioner under Richard Hatcher – its first black mayor.

Yet, the Three Bees had a profound effect on original black rhythm and blues music. It provided Pookie Hudson his very first shot at doing his stellar vocalizing in close concert with other talented singers.

And then, as if by magic, the real thing happened a few months later. Pookie was preparing to compete as a solo in a Christmas talent show at school. The musically inclined Willie C. and Gerald had the same idea, but backed-off when they realized they'd have to compete against him. Althought they didn't know Pookie personally, they certainly knew of him.

Yet, Willie C. and Gerald were big talents in their own rights. The recipient of countless compliments for his soaring tenor in his church choir, Willie C. was also interested in performing in high school plays. His flair for comedy later surfaced with the Spaniels on several novelty hits, most notably, his signature "Play it Cool."

The short, compactly built Willie C. auditioned for the plays by doing a variety of songs – singing different parts – which led to a fortunate friendship with Gerald, the ultimate bass man. But Gerald didn't always have the deep voice – belied by his average physical stature – that helped change the sound of American pop music.

A tenor until a sophomore in high school, Gerald's dulcet tones deserted him for an entire year, during which he "sounded funny." But at the end of that time, the future "boom, boom band" of the Spaniels had emerged, once and for all. Along with Pookie, colorful, fun-loving Gerald would become the best known of the group.

An archetypal pop music historian, Gerald always admired bass singers of old – whom he called his "grandparents" – and learned a little from every one. He loved the Golden Gates, a spiritual group, and idolized the great Jimmy Ricks of the Ravens.

Thus, figuring that three voices might be better than one, Willie C. and Gerald decided to try to join forces with Pookie. They approached him at his locker and asked if they could sing in the show with him.

"Let's get a group," Gerald requested.

Their timing was perfect, owing to the departure of the the other Bees.

Although Pookie didn't really want to become involved with another vocal group, he reluctantly agreed.

Arriving backstage, the three new compadres literally picked up the slender, baby-faced Ernest, another glee clubber and member of the mixed chorus, who was waiting around hoping to be in the show himself.

A minister's son, Ernest loved singing, although his family disapproved because of his calling even then as a "Holiness" preacher. Yet, he had known he was blessed with a good voice since his days in the church choir. He also had long known Pookie.

So the newly formed quartet – with no time to practice what they were going to do – went on. They sang "I Will Wait," a song made popular by the Four Buddies, and won the talent show hands-down.

Afterwards, with their heads held high and chests stuck out as they basked in triumph, the boys got together in the gym for a little "after set." But they fell short of their performance onstage, making them wish that they'd left well-enough alone. That night, however, they went out and sang "I Will Wait" on the street. And dozens of kids who gathered around to listen "went crazy" – responding with thunderous applause.

Without knowing it then, the Spaniels – dubbing themselves "Pookie Hudson and the Hudsonnaires" – were born. And as Gerald recalled, they grew so close "we didn't feel right without seeing each other every day" – even singing together in Willie C.'s little blue Ford.

Ironically, the actual first name chosen was "Hudsonettes" until somebody realized "nettes" meant girls. But Gerald, ever the historian, had a thing about naming groups.

Since he was not satisfied with "Hudsonnaires," his first choice was the name of an obscure plant. Then he discovered it was a poison plant. So that name was out. And he eschewed bird names, what with groups such as the Orioles, Ravens, Cardinals, Larks, Swallows, Crows and Flamingos already on the scene.

It developed at the time that Gerald's young wife, Faye, used to joke about the group sounding like "a bunch of dogs" when rehearsing at the Gregory home. So Gerald came up with four "dog" names – among them "Cocker Spaniels." With everyone agreeing that the "cocker" part would leave them open to ridicule – or worse – the vivacious Mrs. Gregory suggested they shorten it to "Spaniels." She simply liked the way it sounded.

And music history was made.

Thus, the newly birthed Spaniels had its nonpareil lead singer (Pookie), its dynamite bass (Gerald), its top tenor (Ernest) and its second tenor (Willie C.). But they were still missing a real good baritone, which is where the youngest original member – 16-year-old Opal Courtney Jr. – entered the picture.

The bookwormish Opal was an honor student from an academically inclined family – and an unlikely addition to the group. His brother was a high school valedictorian, his sister a salutatorian and his mother always felt he'd become a preacher. Opal's father, Shag Courtney, a phenomenal basketball player and original member of the world-famous Harlem Globtrotters, stressed the value of education.

So Opal primarily was interested in athletics and preparing himself for college by reading and studying. And although he also sang in the mixed chorus and the Boys' Glee Club at Roosevelt, he had no intention of involving himself with any organized vocalizing outside of school.

Nonetheless, one day while playing basketball at Campbell Friendship House, Opal happened to walk by a room in which the group – including Willie C.'s piano-playing nephew, Junior Coleman – was practicing. He stopped to listen. And although he knew them only slightly, Opal, who'd always had a good ear for music and could sing baritone or tenor, sensed something was missing. He began humming along – adding his silky smooth voice to the old standards they were doing.

As time wore on, the five boys started to rehearse regularly – on street corners, in the park, at one another's homes, at Gerald's father's candy store, in cars – putting new songs together as they went. Soon, their vocal talents became the talk of the school. After embarking on a round of appearances at talent shows and small club functions in the area, a female schoolmate who worked with Vivian Carter at her record shop and brand-new Vee-Jay Records, heard them and suggested they be signed up.

Thus, in 1953, the Spaniels became the first artists put under contract by Vee-Jay at its original location at a record store at 1640 Broadway in Gary – although noted Chicago belter Jimmy Reed made the first record under its auspices.

And while the inexperienced youngsters didn't aspire to be songwriters, events continued to dictate their fortunes.

In their naivete, the Spaniels thought writing your own songs was something you had to do – with everyone singing what they alone wrote. Lacking proper advice and counsel, the boys simply were not aware that composing was a different occupation – a separate, distinct discipline. So when they were told by Vivian that they needed material to record, they dutifully began coming up with their own music and their own words.

Their first effort was "Baby, It's You," its melody, words and background written by Pookie and refined by the group. This was paired with another collaboration – "Bounce" – which became Gerald's nickname and signature bass lead. Doing these early tunes without really knowing how to sing – only what sounded good – the Spaniels created a close-knit, bluesy effect that was the sensation in the nation's musically tuned-in black communities, where R&B ruled.

The distinctive opening of "Baby, It's You" began with Coleman as "Da dom da dom da dom . . ." from a hit record by Shirley and Lee called "I'm Gone." The line was altered by piano player "Count" Morris Wilkerson to "Dom, dom da dom da dom . . ." from a down-and-dirty beat that had been successfully used in a lot of black music over the years.

The group rehearsed in a Gary garage behind Vivian's

mother's home on Connecticut Street before finally entering a recording studio for the first time – Universal Studios on Ontario Street in Chicago – to make "Baby, It's You." They also recorded "Bounce," "Since I Feel for You" (which wasn't released until 1956) and Pookie's "Sloppy Drunk" which was never released.

Also present for this historic session – May 5, 1953 – was gospel singer Maceo Woods, who recorded a spiritual, "Garden of Prayer." A good omen if there ever was one, for the talented teen-agers from tough, nearby Gary.

Accompanied by Wilkerson on piano, tenor sax man Leon Washington and drummer Red Saunders, they did it on the cheap – nervously working with a single microphone set up between all five singers. But the resulting togetherness made the sound stronger – emphasizing a tight background – and produced a unity that remains to this day as a Spaniels' trademark.

The result of the session was a two-sided smash hit on the nation's black R&B charts. "Baby, It's You" was a classic blend of natural, seat of the pants harmony and feeling, and "Bounce" was a rollicking, good-time musical story about drinking to excess. The record was released in June 1953 by Vee-Jay after everyone except Opal had graduated from Roosevelt High.

Sales of "Baby, It's You" were so strong as Vee-Jay 101 on its way to the Top 10 on the R&B charts, that it was leased by Vivian to Chance Records – an established Chicago R&B label, which she felt could do a better distribution job. It came out on Chance in July and soared.

But the Spaniels – individually and as a group – had no idea their first record would be so successful. Thus, their mini-celebrity status in Gary, where they began to be recognized in public if they went together to dances or places like the skating rink, didn't change them. Their lives remained essentially the same. Although they were able to hold up their heads with pride while walking the street, they still hung out on the corners with the same old guys.

And they saw precious little money – a heartbreaking harbinger or things to come.

Except for Opal, who was still in school, each of the

boys now had to go out and get jobs to make a living. And they did – to the steel mills and boxcar plants of their tough-as-nails, blue-collar home town. And they were glad to get the work.

Things weren't all that different from 10 years earlier when Pookie first moved into the projects. His modest neighborhood remained home to all classes of black folks – including those who achieved success in business, as well as doctors, lawyers and schoolteachers. Mom-and-Pop grocery stores were within easy walking.

However, most adults – white and black – toiled in the mills of U.S. Steel, which employed some 50,000 people in working-class Gary, where blacks accounted for about 40 percent of the population. For the most part, black people continued to live in the same inner city area and steered clear of the white parts of town – including some ostensibly public facilities such as Glenn Park.

Pookie clearly recalls an occasion when a black policeman known as "St. Louis," shot down "Colored" and "White" signs in the Greyhound Bus Depot waiting rooms. In another instance, Opal's father, "Shag" Courtney, was brutally beaten by whites while "integrating" the park one bright Sunday afternoon.

In addition to Roosevelt, some blacks attended mostly white Froebel High School in a mixed-race area, about two miles away. One of its main features, Pookie recalls, was a big swimming pool used by white kids Monday to Thursday and blacks on Friday. But before the whites swam again on Monday, the pool was drained and refilled.

Pookie, himself, was unaware of the existence of the best "white" beach in town until he was 18 years old. He and many other blacks frequented, instead, beaches in East Chicago or Chicago proper.

The Korean War, which claimed the lives of many young men from 1951 and '52 graduating classes at Roosevelt, was responsible for another proliferation of military uniforms on the streets. Sailors, again, were out in force competing with local boys for teen-age girls.

But through it all, Pookie's low-income, almost totally black Mid-Town area in Gary was safe and free from crime. Kids played in the streets without incident, nobody locked the doors to their houses and there rarely was heard anything about someone getting shot, stabbed or even robbed. Drug use was almost unheard of and the near proximity of a "Red Light" district offered ample diversion for those interested.

The group was back on Vee-Jay when their second record came out in September 1953 – "The Bells Ring Out" backed by "Housecleaning" – but it remained business as usual. There still weren't many live singing gigs available for them. Most of those were to come later in the wake of "Goodnight Sweetheart." At that point, however, the Spaniels were just five local kids who sang pretty good and had been lucky enough to get a chance to make a couple of records. No more, no less.

But all that was soon to change. The names Pookie Hudson, Gerald Gregory, Opal Courtney Jr., Willie C. Jackson and Ernest Warren were to transcend the black part of Gary, Ind. They were about to become the nationally renowned Spaniels – known on 125th Street in New York, Pennsylvania Avenue in Baltimore, Euclid Avenue in Cleveland, Walnut Street in Milwaukee, Woodward Avenue in Detroit, Auburn Avenue in Atlanta, Central Avenue in Los Angeles – and all points north and south – in black America.

All because of one song out of some 200 written by Pookie Hudson. But what a song!

TWO
The Song

"What's so nice about singing is, your low points, you get rid of them when you're on stage. All my problems I ever had, when I went on stage they were released. It's funny, too, that singers usually sing better when they are sad, when they have someone in mind, something in your heart. It comes out really sincere." – Gerald Gregory

"Do do do do do . . . Goodnight sweetheart, well it's time to go – oh; Do do do do do . . . Goodnight sweetheart, well it's time to go – oh; Do do do doooo . . . I hate to leave you but I really must say, oh – oh goodnight sweetheart, goodnight.

"Do do do do do . . . Goodnight sweetheart, well it's time to go – oh; Do do do do do . . . Goodnight sweetheart, well it's time to go – oh; Do do do doooo . . . I hate to leave you but I really must say, oh – oh goodnight sweetheart, goodnight.

"Well, it's three o'clock in the morning. Baby, I just can't get right. Well, I hate to leave you baby; don't mean maybe, because I love you so.

"Do do do do do do do do do do doooo. . . Goodnight sweetheart, well it's time to go – oh; Do do do do dooo . . . Goodnight sweetheart, well it's time to go – oh; Do do do doooo . . . I hate to leave you, I really must say, oh – oh goodnight sweetheart, goodnight.

"Mother, oh and your father, won't like it if I stay here too long. One kiss in the dark, and I'll be going; you know I hate to go.

"Do do do do do do do do do do doooo . . . Goodnight sweetheart, well it's time to go – oh; Do do do do do . . . Goodnight sweetheart, well it's time to go – oh; Do do do doooo . . . I hate to leave you, I really must say, oh – oh goodnight sweetheart, goodnight."

The Spaniels – Vee-Jay Records (recorded Sept. 23, 1953).

Lead: James (Pookie) Hudson (age 19)
Top Tenor: Ernest Warren   (18)
Second Tenor: Willie C. Jackson (19)
Baritone: Opal Courtney Jr. (17)
Bass: Gerald Gregory (19)

What can you say about a song that means so many things to so many people? You could say that never in the field of popular music have so many Americans owed so much listening and dancing and humming pleasure to so few whose only desire was to sing. And they sang to perfection.

"Goodnight Sweetheart, Goodnight" – as written and originally performed by the Spaniels – was vintage black rhythm and blues. It had all the attributes: A slow, danceable beat, romantic lyrics and a simple, easy-to-follow melody set off by muted, yet viscerally appealing harmony.

Perhaps best of all, "Goodnight Sweetheart" featured Gerald's famous five booming bass notes as a lead-in, and melodic, meticulous phrasing by Pookie that was every bit the equal of Frank Sinatra at his peak. Their unique combination of talent has never been equaled in black R&B – or by any of the copycat white singers they spawned.

* * * *

Pookie's reputation as the highly visible lead singer occasionally presented him with problems. On one occasion in 1953 following the release of "Baby, It's You" – the very night he wrote "Goodnight Sweetheart" walking home after visiting Bonnie Jean Davis in the projects – he was recognized and stopped in the schoolyard by a gang called the

"Poor Devils." And it was an event that sticks in his mind to this day.

Deciding they wanted a private concert, the tough youths forced him to sing and "rewarded" him with a gallon of very dark port wine. To please them – and avoid trouble – Pookie sat there and sang and consumed almost the entire bottle.

This resulted in what Pookie still refers to as an "out of body experience" – an alcohol-induced condition in which he doesn't remember how he got back home. However, the singer's eerie description of what took place in his subconscious is truly the stuff of dreams – and weird old TV shows such as "The Outer Limits" – are made of:

"I saw myself on the ceiling. I saw a white light at the end of a long, white narrow way with all these people sitting around wearing white. And at the end, I could see this real bright light that kept beckoning me, and kept beckoning me and kept beckoning me. I turned around and saw myself on a bed and I saw this big purple spot around me – where I had thrown-up all this wine.

"My mother was trying to wake me up. First I saw her and she was cooking in the kitchen. She was cooking pancakes and eggs and ham. I could smell it, too. Then I saw her come into the room and try to wake me up, try to wake me up. And then just like that I was back in my body, and I woke up. I've always felt that I think I died for a few seconds at one time, and it was my choice to either go to the light or come back. And I think the choice I made was to come back."

Pookie came back, all right. And how. And although the individual Spaniels – himself included – found themselves working as common laborers despite clicking with a big hit record on their first try, they began to hear how good they were from Vivian Carter and her people at Vee-Jay. Vivan's radio show was the biggest black record program in the Chicago-Gary area, and she gave their career a big boost by giving prominent play to "Baby, It's You" and "Bounce," right along with songs by the top black recording artists of the day. Of course, she had an understandable ulterior motive. She was their boss.

But it wasn't until "Goodnight Sweetheart, Goodnight" burst upon the national music scene the following year – and the Spaniels became a household name in black America – that the full implications of this blue-collar, black success story turned-tragedy, began to unfold.

Unfortunately, "Goodnight Sweetheart" – the farewell song of a generation of black and white Americans looking for just the right way to end an evening of love – was not to be the start of something particularly big for its creators, the talented Spaniels.

When Pookie first presented the song to his fellow singers – a tune he'd written "in his head" that night after visiting Bonnie Jean – it was greeted with a collective yawn. And even though he agreed with the general assessment, the onus was on the group to come up with new stuff to record, so they began practicing it.

One particular day, the group rehearsed "Goodnight Sweetheart" – the song they had to learn to love – in Opal's basement. This was alright with Opal's family since the boys were doing only talent shows and small club functions in the immediate area, and he understood he was expected to attend college like his five brothers and a sister. His interest in singing notwithstanding.

After a while, Opal's mother came to the top of the stairs and called for the group to come up and sing it for the family's relatives visiting from Knoxville, Tenn. This was the first time they'd done it for someone other than themselves, and they were pleasantly surprised at the compliments they received.

Nonetheless, Pookie recalls that Vivian and her people at Vee-Jay literally "had to make us do 'Goodnight Sweetheart,'" which the group simply was not sold on. Not yet, that is.

It developed that recording this song – what may have been the single most important element in the evolution of rock 'n' roll music that changed America forever – was part of another day's work for the Spaniels. That's how good these five young men were at what they did. It happened on Sept. 23, 1953.

The group still used only two vocal mikes – the studio

standard of the day – to make the record that was to become the Spaniels' lasting claim to fame. One mike was for the background singers and one was for the lead singer. A third was used by Red Saunders' band, again comprised of Saunders on drums, Wilkerson on piano and Washington on tenor sax. And, limited to only two recording tracks, they had to begin again whenever someone messed up.

"And if you're not really sure of what you're doing – which we weren't" – Pookie recalled, "somebody was bound to mess up. And there was no such thing as cutting out bad parts."

So, owing to nervousness, false starts and general goofs – a singer would make a mistake, an instrumentalist would stub his toe, someone would drop something, sneeze, cough or crumple a piece of paper – it took all night to record "Goodnight Sweetheart, Goodnight" before they got it right. As Willie C. said, "We had to do that thing almost a hundred times," recalling the marathon 9 p.m. to 9 a.m. session.

And yet, despite recording a tune none of them really wanted to do because they felt "it sounded stupid" (and later were surprised that anyone actually liked it) and the relatively primitive set-up, the result was pure magic. Much of the perfection was due to Gerald's booming bass – his first five notes which, he likes to say, "came to me out of nowhere," adding, "I just wish I knew how I did that."

Paired with Pookie's clear-as-a-bell answering lead which so identified the Spaniels, and a velvet smooth background by Opal, Ernest and Willie C., the song became memorable to millions the very first time they heard it. And the Spaniels' recording technique – invented for "Baby, It's You" and perfected for "Goodnight Sweetheart" – remains the standard by which all rhythm and blues, rock 'n' roll and soul groups are measured.

The night after the recording session, "Goodnight Sweetheart, Goodnight" had its premiere on "Livin' With Vivian" – in the form of an acetate of the record she'd spirited out of the room. And she took great pride in using it to introduce what was no more than a working albeit dynamite version of the blockbuster-to-be.

When the Spaniels' breakthrough record was released as "Goodnight Sweetheart, Goodnight" in the spring of 1954 as Vee-Jay 107, it took off instantly. The next thing people on the home turf in Gary knew, it was being played by loudspeaker at a popular skating rink. A few miles west, the South Side of Chicago was going wild for the tune. Which meant that in their own area, at least, because of this song, the Spaniels seemed to be big time.

If you were black, everywhere you turned – North, South, East or West – you could hear someone going "Do do do do doooo . . . Goodnight sweetheart, well it's time to go . . ." There was little doubt the record was a humongous hit for the boys from Indiana.

*   *   *   *

The Spaniels' signature song brought black music into mainstream white America two years before Elvis Presley's widely ballyhooed crossover, and a dozen years before the Beatles. But they were not to enjoy what should have been the fruits of their success. "Goodnight Sweetheart, Goodnight" was ripped-off – "covered" is the industry term – and made popular for whites in a syrupy, inferior fashion by a white female vocal group, the McGuire Sisters, who had vaulted to prominence on the old Arthur Godfrey Talent Scouts TV show.

Meanwhile, the black teen-agers who brought "Goodnight Sweetheart" to life, were ignored by millions of white record buyers to whom they were all but unknown. They were left for dead by a white-dominated record business. They were left in the white dust, so to speak, of the song they wrote and recorded – becoming unwitting victims of their own creativity and talent.

But if the truth be known, with dozens of fine R&B records in their future, the Spaniels were to suffer even more at the hands of the black entrepreneur in whom they put their trust – Vivian Carter. And in 1954, they embarked on a near 40-year odyssey of despair and disillusion. It was a destiny definitely not to be desired.

In the real world – monster record or not – Pookie, Gerald, Willie C., Ernest and Opal could do little besides poke out their chests in self-satisfaction. Because believe it or not, the fruits of their musical efforts had put no money in their pockets.

Once "Goodnight Sweetheart" started to make noise – rising to fifth on the R&B charts and 24th on the pop charts – the Spaniels became a hot property. Opal was so enthused he quit high school two weeks before graduation. In so doing, he gave up a basketball scholarship to Tennessee State University – to the consternation of his parents. But the youngster saw what was happening and wanted to be a part of it.

The group then began to tour the country for the first time – along the way making the big five stops on the black "chitlins" circuit: the Regal in Chicago, the Howard in Washington, the Royal in Baltimore, the Uptown in Philadelphia and the Apollo on 125th Street in Harlem. Popular black artists in those days would hit all five within a month-and-a-half – doing four and five shows a day.

But before that initial trip, they needed a booking agent. So they drove to New York City and met with the Gale Agency. And hit record or not, the fellows found they had to audition in the agent's office to secure dates. Since they knew no different, they dutifully obliged.

One of the tunes they did at the session was their sensational, a capella version of "Danny Boy," which they mainly sang for practice. And it went over like a lead balloon. "If you sing 'Danny Boy' on stage," the booker told them straight out, "they'll kill you." He said it's "an Irish tune that blacks have no business singing," adding that he "was dead-set against them doing it." And since they wanted to work, they again obliged.

They auditioned four of their six recorded tunes – all of which the man liked. As a result, the group's first big tour was arranged – climaxing with their appearance at the Apollo.

What's more, the Spaniels headlined the Apollo show over Big Joe Turner, a tremendous tribute to their professionalism, poise and quality of the youngsters from Gary.

But they experienced a profound, unexpected negative, resentful reaction for the first, but not the last time, from older, more famous performers.

Big Joe, an established star riding high with "Shake, Rattle and Roll," simply freaked out. Unaccustomed to sharing the spotlight with young upstarts like the Spaniels, Turner "was so pissed he acted very rude," according to Pookie. "Down the line, he became alright, but in that first encounter, he really wasn't happy about the situation."

Later in Washington, where the group was big, it was hit-maker Etta James ("Roll With Me Henry"). Pookie said she told the manager "don't you ever again in your life put me after these boys." And she wasn't alone. Owing to their astounding effect on audiences as well as other performers, the Spaniels became the closing act in most places.

The Apollo gig, in the fall of 1954, culminated the Spaniels' first tour outside the Illinois-Michigan area, except for a trip to Bill & Lou's in Philadelphia. And it was a memorable experience – from staying at the storied Theresa Hotel to gracing the Apollo stage – although the fresh-faced young men didn't really grasp the meaning. They thought of the Apollo simply "as a place for us to work." Its history – and what it stood for as the international mecca of black show business – was, in effect, lost on them at the time.

One thing that wasn't lost on them was a memorable lesson learned the hard way. After wowing the sophisticated, all-black audience with "Baby, It's You" and ending with "Goodnight Sweetheart" the sellout crowd screamed for more. So they returned and did their unusual, unreleased version of "Since I Fell For You," with Willie C. talking in 1954-style rap.

Needless to say they bombed out. And when you bomb out at the Apollo, you really bomb out. Those uptown audiences can't stand subpar work and if you give it to them they want you off-stage – and fast.

When the Spaniels finished, Opal spotted Bobby Schiffman, who ran the Apollo, standing in the wings. He could tell by how the big boss stared at them that this wasn't going to be pleasant. And it wasn't, as they listened to the law being laid down:

"I want you guys to know that as long as you live, never go back behind your hit song. Let 'em pay for the next show." In effect, he told them you always leave with your best – unless you can come back with something better – even if they're begging for more.

Opal calls this, performing-wise, the Spaniels' "biggest mistake." And they vowed never to make it again – especially at the Apollo.

As Pookie so colorfully put it: "We were just a bunch of young dudes out of Gary, Ind., who wanted to sing, and we were singing. We weren't hip to what was going on – as far as being at the Apollo, or the Howard or the Royal. It didn't mean that much to us."

But the Spaniels' live shows – in which they were often decked out in green suits – meant a lot to the overflow, paying crowds of black fans who ate up their incredibly smooth, energetic performances as they took their lilting brand of music all over the country.

THREE
Touring South and Learning

"When we came out in 1953, we did some harmony, but our basic thing was the answering, where the group would answer the lead singer. Most of the other groups at that time – like the Orioles, Flamingos and Five Keys – were singing that straight, pretty harmony. The thing that made 'Baby, It's You' so different was the answering and the channel." – Pookie Hudson

By the summer of 1954, it appeared that the Spaniels had, indeed, arrived. Confidence oozed from each member of the group. Bound and determined to play the Apollo, Opal quit high school, left home and hearth and moved into a house with Pookie on Harrison Street – just across the road from Roosevelt High where it all began. The sky seemed to be the limit.

Yet, not a single one of the Spaniels in those early days ever considered himself anything special, much less a celebrity. They continued to hang out with the same people in Gary and go to the same places. Through the years, they remained regular guys.

"We never carried ourselves that way," Pookie said. "We never put ourselves above people, and they liked us. Maybe that's why we didn't succeed as well as we should have, because we were always intermingling. People were just people to us – not someone you shun because of who you are.

"If you saw us in a crowd, if you didn't know us personally, you'd never know we were the Spaniels."

As if to reinforce their lack of celebrity status at home,

the Spaniels first out-of-state, close-to-home tours were made in rented vehicles as well as a 1946 finless, black Cadillac limo that closely resembled a hearse. The latter was provided by Vee-Jay, which, obviously, didn't know how to treat the hired help.

On one of the Midwest trips, Opal was driving a rented van when the steering wheel came off in his hands and they came to an abrupt halt in a cornfield. But the workhorse – while it lasted – was the old Caddy, in which the boys drove to New York for the audition at the Gale Agency. And, as usually seemed to be the case, money was involved.

Approaching the big city, someone spotted a sign touting gasoline for 18 cents a gallon and diesel fuel for 6 cents a gallon. "We were young and dumb," said Willie C., as well as low on dough and gas, so they stopped and put in a few gallons of diesel. And it didn't take long for the worst to happen.

"After a while, the motor started smoking," he said, "so we stopped to see what was wrong. Courtney opened the hood and the pipes were red hot. All we could do was jump back in and get as far as we could.

"Since the old Cadillac had one of those hoods that opened on both sides, Count Morris, who knew something about cars, rode on the hood while Courtney drove. He had to keep his head down and a screwdriver in contact with some gizmo on the engine. That way, we made it to a service station and filled-up on gasoline."

At that point, Pookie got on the pay phone to Vee-Jay, now at 1449 S. Michigan Ave. in Chicago, reversed the charges and explained their predicament. Vivian arranged for a brand-new 1954 Buick station wagon to be delivered to them in New York – one of the few times she seemed to appreciate the difficulties her young singers were facing.

But things got interesting once again on the drive back to Gary. With Willie C. at the wheel of the new car, the Spaniels crossed the Ohio line just as the daylight was fading, and stopped to buy gas. Then, unsure of their way – except that they should be on U.S. Route 30 near Canton – they decided to sack out in the car overnight.

With everyone else still asleep, Willie C. took it upon himself to start off again in the pre-dawn dark. The only problem was, he somehow missed Route 30 – confusing it with the Bypass Route 30 sign. A few hours later, when the others began to awaken, Pookie noticed that they were right back were they'd started. Willie C. had followed Bypass 30 in a circle all night long!

"Plus, I was supposed to go on 30 and I thought the speed limit was 30," Willie sheepishly recollected.

Such youthful misadventures notwithstanding, the Spaniels were big in R&B circles. But before they were able to cash-in on their new-found popularity as singers, before they were to become a national household name among music fans – black and white – the Gary teen-agers had to hit the road big-time. And whenever that road was traveled, it always seemed to naturally climax at the magic Apollo Theater in New York's Harlem – their ultimate proving ground before their peers.

Of course, the big-time road throughout the '50s included the Deep South. There, the fresh-faced, wet-behind-the-ears youngsters learned what it really was like to be black in America in the old days, even for celebrities, which to whites, at least, they admittedly were not. Hit records or not. Not yet.

In big, reasonably progressive Southern cities such as Atlanta, there were a few downtown hotels that catered exclusively to black people. So bed and board was available to travelers in urban areas. On the street, however, it was business as usual. That meant if you wanted a drink of water, you used water fountains marked "Colored." To eat out, you chose a black restaurant. If you wanted a cab, you had to wait for a black cab or call the black cab company.

Everything was separate and unequal for black and white.

But out on the road below the Mason-Dixon line, it was much, much worse. Although booked on a number of occasions to appear with white performers such as Paul Anka, the Diamonds, Buddy Holly, the Everly Brothers, Bobby Rydell and the Hispanic Richie Valens, the Spaniels weren't permitted to share their accommodations. Star quality meant nothing. If you were black. you were black. Period.

Since there were no hotels or motels that accepted them, or any black guests, travelers seeking overnight lodging had two choices – look for a house with friendly black residents who would agree to put you up, or sleep in the car. And the Spaniels did plenty of both.

Finding food was even more onerous. Howard Johnson's, which was all over the map much like Holiday Inns today, was out of the question for lodging or dining. And you could forget about eating in roadside restaurants or diners. Some might permit blacks to order and pay for food at the cash register up front, but it was strictly take-out.

The standard quotes were: "Ya'll git your food and git on outta' here."

Many establishments wouldn't even go that far, simply dropping the food down a chute outside in the back – without warning. If you missed it, that was your problem. Others would say, "Naw, we don't have a back door, so git goin'." More often than not, the Spaniels found themselves trying to buy something to eat at filling stations on side roads that sold groceries like lunch meat and bread along with gasoline.

As Willie C. recalled, "A lot of times, we'd make do with eating beans, or whatever, out of a can."

But the biggest concern faced by black folks traveling by car in the South in the mid-to-late 1950s, was, simply, their safety. Black motorists and their passengers – especially those from the North unaccustomed to "down home" ways – ventured forth at their own risk. And it made no difference who you were, how you were dressed or the kind of car you drove.

When the Spaniels left Gary in the steamy hot days of that first "Goodnight Sweetheart" summer, they were driving that new 1954 Buick wagon. Of course, station wagons are big, which plays into the stereotypical notion some whites have of blacks: fondness for big cars.

On both sides of the car, logo-style, was a painted picture of four dogs – Cocker Spaniels – along with the group's name. This distinctive identification, which always facinated onlookers, was to be the focal point of a number of run-ins with whites in several Southern states throughout the '50s.

For example, there was the time while stopped at a service station for gas and food, one of the "good old boys" who was sitting around asked, "What are you? What's that dog on your car? You got dogs or what? I see you got Spaniels. You trainin' dogs?"

After identifying themselves as a "singing group," someone said, "What do you sing?" Pookie responded: Rhythm and blues." To which one man replied, "Oh yeah? Then sing for us."

"We can't do that," Willie C. remembers answering. "We sing professionally and we're trying to make our destination." The man then said, "You gon' sing for us today before you leave," and locked the door behind them.

"So we sang 'Baby, It's You' and 'Bounce,' and they finally let us go," Willie C. said. "We had been raised in the North and been hearing about these things, and now we were experiencing them."

On another occasion, in Atlanta, Pookie went into a drugstore to buy cigarets. He said he wanted a package of Camels "if you got 'em."

Not realizing he also was supposed to say "if you please," the female clerk threatened to call the police, adding "you must be one of those up-North niggers." And the normally placid Pookie was visibly shaken.

Another time, state troopers stopped the group's car on the way to Chattanooga, Tenn., at the bottom of Lookout Mountain. The cops made them get out, searched them and then ordered them to do what they called a "buck dance" – the shuffling, loose-limbed, stereotypical kind of steps at which blacks were supposed to excel – on the side of the road. Then the cops brought some watermelon from a nearby stand and made the boys eat and sing for them.

"Sing, niggers, sing," Pookie recalls them saying. "All the while, they just sat there and had a good laugh at our expense – just because we were black and had our name on on the side of a brand-new car."

Mississippi was the scene of another flagrant case of racist behavior by police when the Spaniels were stopped by state cops who demanded they give them copies of "Goodnight Sweetheart." Then the officers took their picture and made them sign autographs. This, after calling them "a bunch of uppity, singin' niggers."

Once in Texas, the group pulled into a one-pump service station and a little white boy of 5 or 6 came running out with a real surprised look on his face. He yelped, "Hey, Mommy, Mommy, come quick. There's a car full of niggers." A woman came outside and tried to hush him, but obviously the child was simply saying what he had been trained to say or parroting his parents.

"This is one thing I never will forget," recalls Willie C.

On a lighter note, Pookie was at the center of an incident in North Carolina on a tour with the sensational Dells vocal group, that could have ended in disaster.

As the vehicle in their two-car motorcade crossed the top of a mountain, the Dells' car stopped. But the Spaniels – with Pookie, Gerald and Ernest playing poker in the back seat – decided to try and make it all the way down the steep incline. As they began their descent, Pookie, who had been the big loser, got four aces. Just then, the car began sliding and came to a stop at the edge of a cliff. As a result, they were hung-up in a scene reminiscent of a comedy movie.

The other fellows gingerly began to try to get out, but Pookie refused to let go until they finished the hand. So they stayed there – hanging off the edge of a mountain until a tow truck arrived.

"I didn't think of it at the time," Pookie said, "but we could all have been killed."

Perhaps the most infamous, albeit memorable incident in which the group was involved while touring the South began early one hot Sunday morning in 1955 outside the tiny town of Hollyanne, Miss., in the northeast corner near the Alabama border. The Spaniels, with Gerald tooling along "at about 80" were leading a two-car motorcade followed by the Drifters – including David Baughn who'd just replaced the legendary Clyde McPhatter – with bass Bill Pinkney at the the wheel.

As the cars zoomed through Hollyanne, a town Pookie described as "about the size of my front room," Ernest tossed an empty pop bottle out of the window – breaking with a sound loud enough to be heard in the next state. Two or three miles out of town, a Mississippi state police car "shot right by us," according to Gerald, stopping the singers about 10 miles from the Alabama line.

After harshly questioning the occupants of both cars (four Spaniels and five Drifters), and declining to merely hand out speeding tickets, the two troopers, learning that they were "singing niggers from up North," ordered them to precede the police car back to Hollyanne.

Upon arrival, the troopers demanded that Gerald hand over the keys to the Spaniels' car, which he refused to do. They then took the keys, threw Gerald and Pinkney into jail and impounded the cars.

With the two great bassmen jammed into a hot, basement cell some 10-feet wide and 100-feet long with about 100 other black men, the seven remaining singers stood in a courtyard outside pondering their next move.

At that juncture, the cop running the jail strongly advised them to find a place to stay before nightfall "or ya'll gon' be locked up too, because the judge ain't gon' preside over no niggers on Sunday." The next day, he said, they could watch their drivers face the local magistrate in court.

With Gerald's cries of "Get me out of this hole" ringing in their ears from a barred window below sidewalk level, the young men began walking the couple blocks to the black part of town in search of help.

As they approached, doors and windows started to be closed and locked in graphic testimony to the fact that the local blacks had no desire to put themselves in jeopardy by giving aid and comfort to "a bunch of Northern niggers."

Retracing their steps, they encountered the jail's cook – an older black man Pookie heard referred to as an "Uncle Tom." After learning of their predicament, the man offered to help. He went into the countryside where the judge was on a picnic with his family, and begged him to come to town and hear the case so the young singers could leave town that day. Although annoyed at having his outing interrupted, the magistrate agreed.

When he got to the jail, the judge ordered that Gerald

and Pinkney be released and brought to where the cars were – about five miles outside town, off the main road. Then he proceeded to hold court at the side of the road.

Casting an admiring eye on the Spaniels' wagon, he said, "Boy, I bet that thing can ride, won't it?"

He then smilingly imposed fines of $75 on each driver and $65 on each occupant for "disturbing my Sunday dinner," and sent them on their way.

Luckily for the Spaniels – who were accustomed to being broke on the road – it was pay day and they had some money. Both groups then sped off to Birmingham, where they were to perform that night. The Drifters, scheduled for mid-show, had time to get ready. But the Spaniels, who were to open the show, had to get dressed in the car and just made it in time to appear on stage.

But had it not been for that black cook at that small-town Mississippi jail, chances are both these great vocal groups would have been no-shows at the gig in Birmingham – spending the night in Mississippi behind bars instead.

Putting the experience in its proper perspective, Pookie said: "I guess that old man just didn't want to see some dumb, young black dudes from the North in trouble. I'll never forget what he did for us, and I'll always be grateful to him."

The youthfully exuberant Spaniels weren't always on the side of the angels. For instance, on one all-black southern tour – when they and the McPhatter-led Drifters drove their own cars while the other performers rode buses – it was considered great fun to toss exploding cherry bombs out of windows. Pookie's explanation? "We were young and dumb. Just think, pulling that stuff down South in 1954!"

One time in Memphis, appearing with the Lloyd Price band, the yellow-suited Spaniels – each with straightened and waved processed hair – were made to sit in front of the bandstand at an all-white dance. Pookie recalls that they were told to "look straight ahead as white girls came up and ran their hands through our hair. We were sweatin' and shit, knowing we were getting ready to go to hell."

But when it came time to get paid, "the man got to counting the money and I was there counting with him. He said,

'Nigger, you counting behind the white man?' But he forgot he gave us a check. Next morning the bank opened, we cashed the check and took his money too, and left."

On another humorous-in-retrospect occasion, the Spaniels were on their way to Charleston, W.Va., when they spotted a long line of cars on the road. Not wanting to be held up, Gerald, who was driving, darted into an opening in the procession and tried to forge on ahead on the left.

The next thing they heard was a loudspeaker, which blared: "You are in the middle of the Ku Klux Klan . . ." Then they all noticed a cross burning on top of a hill.

"You ain't never seen no niggers drive so fast," Pookie recalled.

But what may have been the closest the group came to physical harm was the time near a beach in Bilaxie, Tenn., when while in their car the Spaniels encountered some young, bikini-clad white girls crossing the road.

As the fellows took in the scene – as any normal young men would – two cops drove up and told them to look straight ahead or we'll blow your brains out."

Once in New York state enroute to Connecticut, they were stopped on the highway by state cops who made them empty their wallets on the ground.

"I don't know if it was for speeding or what, but Courtney had a rubber (condom)," Pookie said, "and they wanted to know how come he had a rubber. They took us to the police station and gave us a hard time. I really don't know why we were there, but they let us go."

Perhaps the most horrendous experience the Spaniels lived through as a group while they should have been basking in the glory of their success with "Goodnight Sweetheart," took place in Newark, N.J., while touring the East Coast in 1954. They nearly starved to death.

Recalls Opal: "Back then, we were glad to get money – and we got some – but people in New York didn't see us in New York, eating a hot dog and soup. That was our dinner. On the corner of 125th Street and Eighth Avenue. A hot dog joint. That's all we ate then. It got so bad that we moved to the Coleman Hotel, in Newark, and stayed there a long time – more than three weeks. Screamin' Jay Hawkins was around there, too.

"If it wasn't for Father Divine's Hotel down the block, where they served meals – the Divine Loraine Hotel – we'd have starved. He charged 50 cents a day to eat. After we ran out of money, the man who owned the Coleman Hotel gave us each a bowl of beans a day and one room. And we all stayed together in that one room."

Said Pookie: "We weren't getting no money from the company. The company wasn't doing nothing for us. They wasn't getting us no bookings. We were just stuck. We had no money to get back home. Then Gerald went out and got a job for us in a small club and we survived."

Any doubts the Spaniels had about how they were being ripped off by Vivian and Vee-Jay were dispelled by the Coleman Hotel experience.

But this was only the beginning of their travails.

FOUR
Working With the Stars

"At that time, Gerald was the only one who really knew
he had one job of singing. We used to change up. Ernest
would sing tenor a while, then Courtney would go up to
fifth. Then I would sing low tenor and then I would go up.
It was just switching around. That's really what doo-wop is
all about." – Willie C. Jackson

Not that everything that happened on the Spaniels' road
trips was bad. Not by a long shot. And it wasn't only because much of their traveling was outside the South.

Still, Willie C. said he "had been raised to know that
black people were treated secondary, and that you would
always respect the white people because you would stay
out of trouble."

As the group worked its way to the Apollo, their experiences ran the gamut from great artistic triumphs to taking
part in, and witnessing backstage and offstage hijinks, to
gracious co-stars, to those who were mean-spirited and jealous. And much of the time, they went unpaid.

Willie C. recalled in astonishing detail performing in
those early days – a singular testimonial to an incredible
time in his life and the life of the Spaniels:

He began with a particularly memorable auditorium
dance in Kansas City in 1954, in which the Spaniels appeared on the same bill with superstar Nat "King" Cole.
The boys were singing up a storm – to the tumultuous appreciation of the audience – and enjoying every minute of
it. But returning to their dressing room after taking several

page 32

curtain calls, they encountered a livid Cole, apparently upset at having to share the applause. He told them the people came to see him, "so after you do your little act, get on off the stage."

"This was very discouraging" Willie C. said. "I know we weren't a threat to him. Maybe it was because the music was changing and the group thing was coming in. I thought he'd say we're helping the show by the people applauding like that. I looked up to him ever since I first heard him sing. I lost a lot of respect for him. But we overcame it."

Another legendary musician whose demonstrated attitude left something to be desired was the late, nonpareil trumpet man, Miles Davis. According to Pookie, Miles – the jazzman who epitomized the word "cool" – once played a gig with the Spaniels in his pre-legend days. But he didn't want his band to back-up the Spaniels after he did his set. As a result, the promoter had to threaten not to pay him.

"Jazz musicians, especially in that period, at that time, they were really deep into jazz," Pookie said. "And they always had a problem about playing with our kind of group because No. 1, our music was unorthodox. We did not sing what people learned in college. They had beginnings and endings and things and we had bridges and things where they weren't supposed to be, and we had notes where they weren't supposed to be.

"As far as they were concerned they said, 'Man, I went to school all these years trying to be a musician and get across and you walk out here and sing some unorthodox shit and all the girls fall on you. You're getting all the glory.' And they resented it."

On a lighter note, Gerald recalls when a young James Brown – riding high with The Famous Flames on the blockbuster, "Please, Please, Please" – burst into the Spaniels dressing room in Philadelphia and "wanted to wrestle everybody. James was a boxer. He was always an athletic dude and liked horsing around. But he found no takers."

Willie C. went on to say that "everything on stage is not really what's happening. A lot of people get backstage, and, well, they have their own personality. Some are not very pleasant."

He said jealousy was rampant, with individual performers as well as members of groups disliking one another. Some groups they appeared with – including the Drifters and the Nutmegs – used to get in a lot of arguments among themselves, he recalled.

"Something would happen in the street, or someone didn't look right when they got to the show. Or someone didn't like the way someone else was dressed. They'd get on stage and be right back to the same old arguments and bickering."

Of the Nutmegs, who hit it big with "Story Untold," Willie C. said: "I mean those guys would actually have fistfights backstage."

He said alcohol had a lot to do with the problems many groups encountered. "People used to do a lot of drinking. Being on the road a long time, with all the one-nighters, you get frustrated and tired and get on each other's nerves. Sometimes, people turned to drinking and other things to sort of relax and cool them out so they could perform. This is something that really brought a lot of people down. Drugs and alcohol and women, too. I would say 90 percent of the arguments among groups backstage was because of tiredness, one-nighters, alcohol and drugs.

"I learned a lot through this," Willie C. said. "One thing I like about the Spaniels. We were a very disciplined group and always said we wouldn't get into this when we saw how other groups were affected. We've got a slogan 'all for one and one for all.' And even though we were singing R&B, we always said a little prayer before we went on stage. And still do today."

Willie C. said performers often went on stage under the influence, "and although some people can perform drunk, they'd get on stage and barely could make it off. I saw Larry Darnell get so high one time at the Howard in Washington that he started laughing while he was singing and couldn't stop for his whole performance."

Among the Spaniels, Pookie, who admits to "drinking wine by the gallon," recalls being "so drunk sometimes they had to hold me up on stage." But he quickly boasted: "And I never missed a beat."

"In those days, in the southern states," said Willie C., "they once had us in the wrong place – more like a country and western or hillbilly joint. They didn't understand our music" and, in a scene reminiscent of the movie "The Blues Brothers" many years later, "they started throwing thngs."

Willie C. continued: "We were playing a dance in Jackson, Miss. in 1955, the night before Emmett Till got killed. When we got to the gig there was a rope in the middle of the hall and the blacks would be on one side and the whites on the other side for the dancing. Something happened; somebody threw a bottle and they cleared the place.

"The next night, the whites would come in first, about 7 to 10 or something like that, and they danced. Then the blacks would come in at 10 o'clock. The blacks were restricted to going to the bar, and everything they got had to be in paper cups, even whiskey. They couldn't get a bottle of beer. Now what was strange about this to me is, the first night nobody really knew who threw the bottle; we never did find out. It started something like a little riot but it was under control.

"Well, it was a normal thing at that time, I guess."

What also was normal on southern tours, was the Spaniels doing two separate shows each night – for blacks and for whites. This meant working twice as much for the same money. Although doing as many as three or more shows a night was the norm for the times, integrated audiences in the North would have meant doing half the number of shows for the same pay.

"As a group for a gig then, we would get about $1,500 a week. But half the time we weren't getting no money no way. We were talking to the Drifters and they were telling us that, well, 'we get a salary, we don't get royalties, don't get paid for touring shows. We get a certain amount of money every week whether we work or not.' And we thought about this and it sounded good.

"Our manager (Vivian Carter) wasn't giving us any money. On our touring, we might have a payday, and most times you're on tour with other artists you would get paid. But a lot of times we were booked on our own, did our own shows. We'd get there and the money would come out of

Chicago and then have to come back to us and a lot of times it didn't get back. So whatever we got at that time it was nice, because starting off, the money didn't matter. It was the glory. And with all this attention, you really thought nothing about the money. Just people wanting to hear you sing and you wanted to sing for them.

"Of course, we had so much fun before we went to the South, and we kind of knew what to expect, so it wasn't really a surprise to me. But you still had some of those white people that did treat you nice, that gave you respect, that liked the music. A lot of times they'd come back and try to offer us things, while in another place another type of person would come back and be cussing you out, you know. They just didn't like black people. Most trouble was on the highways and the streets, not in the places we were singing."

In those days – 1953-55 – Spaniels' audiences in the North were mostly black. But in the South, they were mixed, except for local dances where they played for blacks. At most of the auditorium shows, blacks would sit in the balcony and whites downstairs.

Pookie recalled a night in Augusta, Ga., when the Spaniels were playing in a hall with the stage between the black and white audiences, which meant they had to sing to the wall to keep from directing their attention to either group.

"People got disturbed about it and started throwing bottles and eggs because they thought we should turn one way or the other. But we couldn't. The only ones to get hit were in the band. We left when they started throwing things down. We just got off the stage."

According to Willie C., most of the missiles came from blacks in the balcony. He said the next night they changed it around and had the blacks sit downstairs.

"That way, if anything was thrown, it would be down on the blacks," he laughed.

"It was real low down a lot of times," Pookie said.

The Spaniels were one of the first black R&B vocal groups to appear in Las Vegas – in the wake of "Goodnight Sweetheart." But they weren't booked into one of the big casinos. That's the way Vegas was in 1954-55. They played instead in an auditorium setting. And just like down South, they were forced to find lodging in the private homes of black residents. The hotels weren't open to them to perform or to stay.

"Those were the days of 'blacks across the tracks,'" Pookie said.

Despite this lack of respect for their humanity – owing to their race – the Spaniels received nothing but respect for their talent. As a result, when they played their gigs, they were in the best company.

For example, in addition to the Drifters, Nutmegs, Dells, Buddy Holly, Everly Brothers, Richie Valens, Diamonds, Big Joe Turner, Bobby Rydell, the Erskine Hawkins band, Nat "King" Cole, Sammy Davis Jr., Miles Davis and a 90-day tour with Paul Anka, the group appeared and toured with a host of other big names of the period.

Included were the Clovers, LaVern Baker, Sonny Til and the Orioles, Flamingos, Platters, James Brown, Roy Hamilton, Faye Adams, Chuck Berry, Frankie Lymon (without the Teenagers), Sam Cooke, Big Maybelle and the towering tenor sax man, Illinois Jacquet, among many, many more – white and black.

Like most artists, Willie C. had his own personal favorites – especially among those who sang the Spaniels' kind of music. "I always did like the Drifters," he said. "They were my favorite group. Clyde McPhatter had just left and they had a guy named David (Baughn). He sung very well. I also liked the Five Keys. I loved them, and the Dells. And the Flamingos were my favorites, too.

"The Moonglows were fantastic. I liked them. And the El Dorados had their sound, too, with Percy (Pirkle Lee Moses Jr.). They were a very good group. They also recorded on Vee-Jay and came along right after we got started."

Of the Spaniels' dance routines, which augmented the group's classy stage presence, Willie C. said: "We got a hold of a guy named James Derringer, who was a good choreographer. He was a cheerleader at our school and a dance teacher and was very, very creative. He taught us some dance staps which were very simple at the time to us because we were at that young age. It just took a few practices and everyone caught on pretty well."

Everyone that is, but Pookie, and, to an extent, Opal. Pookie maintains to this day that he has "two left feet." Said Willie C.: "Pookie said he couldn't dance and he wasn't going to try to dance. So it was left up to us.

"We had one act where I used to be like a clown. I had to dance in a lot of the songs by myself. And everyone asked me how did I learn the steps. I really didn't. I just got out there and my legs would go where they wanted to go and never did the same thing twice. I just got out there and started dancing. I didn't realize anything; just let my legs go and my arms go and it was a lot of fun."

Willie C. said that white audiences down South knew the Spaniels songs as well as blacks and "really liked what we were doing. Those that came, I guess they came because they liked us. A lot of them would try to talk to you and sometimes try to get autographs – but not too often.

"But the most disappointing and heartbreaking and disgusting thing about those days was when we traveled and we didn't get paid. You're on the road and singing at the time and you're out there and you ain't got no money. The money didn't come in for us to get paid. Vee-Jay – Vivian Carter and Jimmy Bracken – they were the managers. They were supposed to pay us.

"Sometimes, when we traveled by ourselves, the money was sent from the booking agency out of New York at the time, Gale Booking Agency. They would send money to Vee-Jay and forward it to us. Sometime they'd send it and sometime they wouldn't. Vee-Jay would come up with excuses like, 'Well, you know, we bought that car and we have to pick up the payment on your car.' All kind of different excuses, knowing you're out there. And sometime we had to go and get a little gig for ourselves to get money to get back home.

"These would be gigs at nightclubs unbeknownst to them (Vee-Jay) and underpriced. We'd approach the owners and tell them what we would give them for so many days and most times they'd be glad because they were getting you for little or nothing. Where if they had to go through the agency, it would have been a high expense on them."

But since the group was on the hook for their own expenses on the road, the little money they did see usually went for travel, food, clothes, uniforms and personal needs – the necessities of life.

"It really hurt," said Willie C., "because we didn't make that much and expenses were pretty high.

"But there were a lot of nice things about it. You'd walk down the street and people might say, 'there's one of the Spaniels,' or 'there's Willie C. of the Spaniels.' Wherever you might go. You might be at a football game or you might be in a store. It's a good feeling; the ladies were really after you. They just want to be with you even if you didn't want to have anything to do with them. Just glad to be in your company or just be around or to ride in your car, or whatever.

However, according to Pookie, one Texas trip turned a little sour for Willie C., who had become enamored in New York of a beautiful young woman named Jerry.

"He was just crazy about the girl. Every time he'd get off the show they'd be out in the parking lot kissing and smooching and carrying on. She was a pretty girl. And we was in Texas one time with four or five groups and he got to talking about Jerry. And I guess 10 people must have pulled her picture out, and they said, 'You talking about this girl here? That bitch? Yeah, man, everybody done had Jerry.' Willie C. was crushed for about a month. Because he was in love.

"That was our first trip out," Pookie continued, "and we didn't know anything about no groupies. We thought the girls were in love with us. Willie C. didn't know they'd be sittin' at the door waitin' on the next group too. That's why I pray to God every night. I thank him, I thank him that people weren't into AIDS then. We'd have been in big trouble."

But Gerald, who claims, albeit a tad tongue-in-cheek, to be "scared of women to this day" said he never was the kind of person to carouse. On the other hand, Ernest likened the adulation of female fans to a sailor "with a girl in every port." He said: "We were young and if they were young and inviting, you wouldn't turn them down."

Willie's best memory was knowing they were going to

the Apollo.

"We were in Virginia working our way to New York to our proving ground. And when we got to the Apollo, and Sammy (Davis Jr.) who was there with his father and uncle (the Will Mastin Trio), talked to us and encouraged us. And Mr. Schiffman, who owned the Apollo at the time, came around. It made us feel important."

Aside from the unique camaraderie among the Spaniels, in which strong, meaningful friendships – such as Pookie and Willie C. – were the rule, one of the group's most cherished memories had to do with the great Red Skelton, with whom they were appearing at the ritzy and famous Chez Paree in Chicago in 1954, while basking in the success of "Goodnight Sweetheart." Each member of the group – Opal, Willie C., Gerald, Ernest and Pookie – recognized their good fortune and recall it with pride and pleasure.

Pookie's recollections mirrors that of the others:

"Red Skelton was the headliner, and we were singing a song at that time that Gerald was leading called 'Heart and Soul.' We didn't get to do but one other song, so Red Skelton sat and talked with us for about two hours. He told us the ups and downs of the business and how easy it is to be discouraged, but not to get discouraged.

"He told us how to carry on and how to try and make a living out of the business. But I guess we really didn't understand what he was trying to tell us because we really didn't do a good job of what we should have been doing."

Pookie said Skelton gave them the pep talk that night after the group already had blown it on stage, because after singing "Goodnight Sweetheart," they had a chance to come back and do an encore.

And "Heart and Soul" was not the one to do.

"I don't really believe they (the white audience) wanted to hear a bass lead at that time. I think they wanted to hear a typical Ink Spots' song. If we would have come out singing the Ink Spots or something of that type, we may have been more successful. Because the people that came to see us didn't know anything about the Spaniels. And the people that we knew didn't go to the Chez Paree."

Of course, the prevailing racial attitude was never far

from any of their minds. An incident that brought it back out front happened in Texas while on tour with big-voice superstar Roy Hamilton, who walked into the theater with a white woman. Hamilton's mega-hits – Ebb Tide," "You'll Never Walk Alone," "If I Loved You" and "Hurt" – had him riding high, and he showed it.

"Man, oh, man," recalled Opal, "we're down here in Texas and he comes in here with this white woman?

"I'm sure she wasn't his manager. He was the No. 1 star in the country, but we were all on the show together. We wondered what might happen to us. Back then, blacks were making avenues into athletics and sports and just didn't mess with the white man's woman."

Beyond the success or failure of the tours and the appearances and records they made, bubbling not far beneath the surface was the treatment they were receiving at the hands of Vee-Jay Records in general, and Vivian Carter in particular. After a while, this was to be the straw that broke the Spaniels' back.

And in the back of Willie C.'s mind and Opal's mind – the first two to leave the group voluntarily – was they knew they were getting screwed.

They didn't like it and they weren't going to take it much longer. But there were other reasons, as well.

Notes of personal disharmony also were beginning to be heard within the group. The boyhood buddies were finding that life on the road brought greater insights into each other's character and behavior.

And this spawned the first defection. The defector was Opal – who had been the last to become a Spaniel.

Years later, they would learn – collectively and individually – that togetherness conquers all. Especially when you can sing up a storm like the one and only Spaniels.

FIVE
Rip-Offs

"If we had gotten the money that was due us between the years of 1953 and the time they (Opal, Willie C. and Ernest) quit, and if we'd been given the guidance that we needed, we'd be millionaires. And I'm being very conservative. In those days, if you had $100,000 or $200,000, you had a lot of money." – Pookie Hudson.

The woods are full of stories about black performers of the original rhythm-and-blues years of the 1950s being cheated by their managers, recording company executives and various advisers and promoters. Indeed, it was rare when a vocal group realized any royalties from their records. Most were paid just enough to cover expenses – and sometimes not even that.

And the Spaniels were no exception. The ripoffs perpetrated on this legendary group were equally legendary. Any money they received for their hard-earned work over the years was strictly coincidental.

Gary native Henry Farag, president of Canterbury Productions of Merrillville, Ind., and his younger brother Omar, have been putting on "Let the Good Times Roll" shows at the Holiday Star Theater, a few miles outside Chicago, since 1980. With Pookie listening, Farag offers an interesting perspective on how he, like a surprisingly large number of whites, got the black R&B bug as a youngster, and his interest never waned. His recollections may help explain why such rip-offs were perpetrated on the Spaniels and other talented artists of R&B's golden era.

"I remember I was 11 years old, listening to the radio and first heard the Spaniels come over the air, hearing, to me, a sound that was strange and unusual; a group sound, to me a haunting sound. A lead that was real distinctive to me. I couldn't tell you why at that time. It just seemed very unique to me. I'd never heard anything like it.

"It made me almost fearful. And it's a hard thing to explain. Up until that time, I was used to hearing Lava soap commercials on the radio. I would always listen to the radio. That was the thing, just like every kid put their ear to the radio.

"Songs like 'The Green Door' comes to mind, and 'Stranger in Paradise.' People like the Four Aces and Perry Como and things like that. And all of a sudden I hear this sound that was almost intimidating. It *was* intimidating, but at the same time, it was very pleasurable to listen to.

"The first station that I heard was WWCA (in Chicago) and Vivian Carter. And all I heard was this loud, aggressive, bombastic, but cheerful-sounding voice that was talking about how great this sound was – whether it was the Spaniels, Dells or the El Dorados. She might play the same song, three, four times in a row.

"And that was the first station I ever really listened to on a regular basis. I wouldn't know before that what a call letter of a radio station was. That, to me, was the beginning of the end. All of a sudden everything jelled. It was strange, yet it made sense.

"But it was scary. And yet I don't know why it was scary. The only thing I can say is that it was something unknown to me, and just the unknown was fearful."

Yes, scary and fearful. The fear factor on the part of the music establishment. Could the fear of the power of this "strange," as Farag describes it, distinctly black music have played a role in making sure the young performers who invented the sound failed to profit from it?

Whatever the reason, the Spaniels suffered immeasurable, irreparable damage to their psyches, their pocketbooks and their careers. And they never did recover.

They never even came close.

Most of the adulation that accrued to the Spaniels was a direct result of "Goodnight Sweetheart, Goodnight." As second tenor Willie C. Jackson said: "We really thought we were on our way, with nice money coming; a nice record to get us better bookings and we felt real good.

"We were lied to about the record, and what happened to our royalties and our monies and everything else, and about the other people singing it. The McGuire Sisters recorded it, but Pookie wrote it, and owned the song.

"Vee-Jay Records claimed (in 1975) that we were sued for the name. When they (Vee Jay) put the name on the label, they didn't put the second 'Goodnight' on the copyright. And this was the excuse Vee-Jay used that we were sued.

"We were told the lady (Betty Giapetta) who bought all of Vee-Jay's original tapes was going to give us $50,000 apiece," said Willie C. "But the new lawyer we had, and mostly everyone else on our side, said 'no.' They said if she's going to give us $50,000, we can get more.

"So we went back into court and said we'd fight for the whole thing and ended up with nothing. At the time (in 1975), all the people who ever sung with the Spaniels were there. We found Vivian Carter cut a deal on the song with the McGuire Sisters and didn't tell us. This was a big hurt. She was our legal guardian and handled our business because our parents didn't back us like they should," Willie C. said.

"She had power of attorney over all our money and all our rights. Our parents didn't want to have anything to do with that. They were old-fashioned and figured we'd be out smoking dope and drinking. They'd always heard the bad side of entertainers and they preferred we go out and get a job and work or sing spirituals. And we wanted to pursue this so Vivian got the right to sign for us and use the money as she saw fit. That's why we never received any royalties or anything."

"Giapetta ripped-off the Spaniels' songs for a CD," said Farag, who occasionally recorded the reunited second group in recent years on his small Canterbury label. "She never kept records or paid anyone after buying Vee-Jay Records and Spaniels' masters at a bankruptcy sale. Pookie never had control of the masters. He didn't know about the sale, was not represented at it and lost all rights at the time.

"In the process of the trial," Farag said, "Gene Goodman, the publisher, said 'Goodnight Sweetheart' was the biggest title – the main title in his catalog (the Art Music of the World) – and he had thousands. He got all the titles from Vee-Jay and other companies."

Said Pookie: "During the trial, he (Goodman) said that he came down here in 1954 and gave Vee-Jay $250,000 for having it published – which I never saw any of. In fact, that was the first time I ever heard of it.

"Anyway, what the judge said was, the lawyer representing us also represented the man who sold the masters to Betty Giapetta. He said this sounded like 'double-dealing,' like 'why would you represent the one who sold them, and now you're trying to take them back?'

"And Giapetta made a statement just before the judge went through this thing that 'I got a million dollars set aside to pay royalties.' But his judgment was she didn't have to pay nothing. She could use our names, use our voices, our likeness, our records and stuff and she didn't have to pay us a dime. The only thing he gave us the right to do was re-record. The judge referred to us as the 'alleged artists.'

"The first dollar or royalty I ever got was because of Henry Farag and Ron Lehrer, around 1976-77. But we had started before I met them. Jerry Butler and a lawyer named Atkinson contacted us, Dee Clark and Jimmy Reed's widow – all Vee-Jay artists. They said we're going to put this case against this lady (Giapetta) and try to get these masters."

Added Farag: "I was a private detective then and had a good friend (Lehrer) – a West Point graduate and a successful lawyer – who was absolutely passionate about what we call 'doo-wop' now. Principally the Spaniels and the Skyliners – a white group. We used to trade records.

"One day we saw something in the paper about the group being together and went to see them work. Then we started talking to Pookie, who told us about this situation. I told Ron later, 'Let's see if we can get some money out of this Goodman guy for back royalties to Pookie.'

"So we went through the court things that he (Pookie)

had and came up with the strategy that we would just try to threaten Goodman with a lawsuit. And he sent off a few letters and it worked and Pookie got some money – $15,000 – and at least started to get him on a schedule of payment, too. But at the same time, we just missed a great opportunity, mainly because we were both broke.

"I got Calvin Carter (former Spaniels road manager, one-time group member and brother of Vivian Carter) to come in the office," Farag continued, "and he was ready to sign-off on 'Goodnight Sweetheart,' without admitting that he didn't write it.

"I'll never forget it. He had his pipe and he was sitting there bullshiting. He wanted $3,000 and we didn't have it. God, if we'd only had it. That would have been 50 percent of his for eternity back in the pot. He died soon after. Then a couple of years ago (1989) Vivian died."

"Plus, Goodman told Bracken, 'Don't!'" Pookie added, referring to Jimmy Bracken, Vivian's business partner husband.

"But Calvin was strapped at the time and we had the documents written up, but we just didn't have the money," said Farag. He said Vee-Jay later received $250,000 from Goodman for ownership of the 'Goodnight Sweetheart, Goodnight' title. In 1991 Chrysler Corp. leased the song from Goodman and began using it on Dodge car TV commercials.

However, the prime mover in getting Pookie some money for his songwriting was the late Marcia Vance in New York. A lifelong R&B fan and one-time associate editor and feature writer of *Bim Bam Boom* magazine who also had a share in a magazine called *Yesterday's Memories*, she worked unceasingly to help the Spaniels and other groups receive back royalties for some of their recordings.

"Marcia worked for some music publishing companies that handled royalty money," Pookie said. "She had the knowledge of where to go when the money wasn't coming through the performers. She told Henry and Ron, which got them involved. They contacted Gene Goodman at his company. As a result, I get paid back royalties twice a year for 'Goodnight Sweetheart' – depending on how much it's used in performances, movies, commercials and all that."

Pookie said he initially received about $9,000 of the $15,000 in back royalties Farag and Lehrer received from Goodman for "Goodnight Sweetheart, Goodnight." Since then, his semi-annual payments have ranged from about $2,000 to $8,000 a crack – a drop in the bucket compared to what he should be getting from the millions and millions his song earned and keeps earning.

* * * *

"In a way, I thought the McGuire Sisters version of 'Goodnight Sweetheart' would help," Willie C. Jackson said, "but I also thought it was cutting into our play. It didn't seem to help or hurt because they mostly sang to the whites, catered to them, and ours was going both ways. I thought maybe it would pick up on the other end. It really came down to our record had been out there a long time.

"Some of the whites had never heard or paid attention to it. Then when they (the McGuires) brought it out, whites started singing what they thought was a McGuire Sisters' song," he concluded.

"It was disappointing," said top tenor Ernest Warren, "when they told us we were sued for half the record and had to change the name. We didn't get any money. And then the McGuire Sisters began to claim they wrote the song and they didn't. We wrote it and put it together.

"And that was disappointing because everybody was singing it at that time. If I'm not mistaken, about seven different people recorded 'Goodnight Sweetheart' other than ourselves: the McGuire Sisters, I think the Ray Charles Singers and Gale Storm and someone else with a good name. Some band recorded it and that took it out of our hands."

And what about Vivian's motivation?

"I would say greed," Willie C. answered, "because money was being made and every time we would inquire about money it was always that we incurred expenses over what we made from the record. We always owed and never received anything. She would give us $200 to $300 apiece and that was supposed to satisfy us. And as we got older, we began to realize she was making some money, and it takes some money to live.

"Everybody but me got mad. I was the last one to get mad. Our wives and family needed money and we had to give excuses because excuses were given to us. And we really had no kind of financial settlements at all. We were living from performance to performance."

"Well, I think that we, really, made that . . . we solidified her (Vivian's) record company," added Ernest. "We were the first hits that they had on Vee-Jay Records. And really put them into the business. And all we ever got were advances that they always put against receipts. It never did come to a point where we got any money."

"Plus, at that particular time, our music got big, you know," said Pookie. "But we happened to be in that vice between the white and black thing. We weren't given the white exposure, all our music was played on black radio stations. The white establishment was playing King Cole, you know, but they weren't playing any rhythm and blues.

"Most white people thought this was devil music and they didn't want their children to hear it. But their children was sneakin' and buyin' the records and things. So Randy Wood (of the famed Randy's Record Shop radio show out of Nashville) comes up with the idea that we go get some white boys and white girls and we let them cover our music. We'll let them do the songs. And sure enough, when the white boys and them did it, it was successful.

"That's how the McGuire Sisters and Pat Boone and Ricky Nelson and them did what they did," Pookie went on. "They all had something to do with it. They let them cover this black music and they came out and figured the white people would accept it.

"And they did, you know. The same music we was singin', the white people accepted because some white people was singin'.

"But what could we do? We weren't really part of the establishment and those people who we depended on to take care of this kind of business for us weren't doin' it, so we were at a loss. Especially since all we did was sing. We weren't knowledgable about the money or the finances on the business end. All we knew was to get in our car and they say to us, 'Ya'll sing for so and so and so and so . . ."

The white Wood used black-sounding white DJs, such as Hoss Allen on "Randy's Record Shop." His show reached 28 states out of WLAC, and was mainly a marketing tool for his mail-order record business. In 1950, he launched Dot Records and included the aforementioned Gale Storm among his artists.

Other noted "cover" artists included Georgia Gibbs, Jo Stafford and the Diamonds, who ripped-off popular black R&B tunes by the likes of Faye Adams, LaVern Baker, and the Gladiolas. Employed by big record companies with national distribution, they would simply wait for a hit black R&B record on a small, regional label and then record it. As a result, many whites would hear a tune such as "Tweedly Dee" by Georgia Gibbs, and not realize it had been recorded in far superior fashion by LaVern Baker.

And the story behind Alan Freed not playing Spaniels' records on his popular disk jockey radio show in New York?

"Basically, Alan Freed, in return for playing 'Goodnight Sweetheart' by the Spaniels on New York radio, and to book us on his live shows, wanted his name as writer on it," Pookie said. "The company refused to do that. So consequently, he never played our records – none of our records – and he never had us back on his concert shows.

"Alan Freed's name appears on some Moonglow records, and Chuck Berry's, but he didn't write these songs. It was his type of payola at that particular time."

And how was that permitted?

"Well, I mean some people would say, hey, look man, here's the biggest man in New York and you get the record played, you get the record sold and all he want is to put his name . . . if you're not realizing really how lucrative the writing end of a song is that's recorded into a big hit . . . if you don't understand that, you do it because you might say, 'Hell, that ain't nothin', I'll write another song," Pookie continued.

"But remember now, Freed was big in New York. Not here in the Midwest. Not nationally. No. He was only one disk jockey. He only played things in New York.

"Look at the Flamingos. Look what he did with them. Only reason Chuck Berry is in the position he's in now, is because them white groups came out of England and shit and loved his music. It wasn't because of Alan Freed. The Moonglows just totally dissolved. So there's no way in the world you can prove to me that by letting him put his name on our songs that it would have been best for us.

"Freed just did it for the money," Pookie went on. "For whatever the royalties were. It might have been three writers on a song, so he'd be down as number four. Might have been two, and he'd be number three. If it wasn't but one, he'd be number two, and he'd get half the money."

"But that was done to ya'll anyway – by Calvin Carter," said baritone Opal Courtney Jr. "On 'Goodnight Sweetheart.'"

"And we didn't even have no three-two split," said Pookie.

Pookie has long bristled at the story that he sold the rights to "Goodnight Sweetheart" for $50.

"I don't know why people think that. I ain't sold the rights to 'Goodnight Sweetheart' for nothin'. I sold 'Peace of Mind' to Jimmy Bracken for $50. I had a date in court for my first wife. The judge told me I had to give her $80 a week because we was getting a separation. She said she was having another baby and I wasn't working nowhere at the time.

"So I caught the South Shore across from the court in Gary and went to Vee-Jay Records (in Chicago) and told 'em I needed a place to stay. I couldn't go back to Gary because they were fixin' to put my butt in jail. They oohed and aahed and oohed and I said, 'Well, look, 'Peace of Mind,' you know. Give me $50, Jimmy.' And they hurried up and did that.

"They gave me $50 and I went and got a room down at this hotel and got me a labor job. And basically, that's all there was to it.

"Same thing with Gerald (Gregory, the bass singer)," Pookie continued. "Vee-Jay gave him the shaft. Gerald went to court on non-support and needed $300 to get out of debt or was going to be locked up. They sat at the trial and watched 'em march Gerald to jail. They wouldn't come up with the $300."

Said Gerald: "My old lady went to Vee-Jay and said, 'You give me the $300 and I'll go down to the judge and give it to him myself and give it back to you.' But she couldn't get it from nobody. Vivian, Jimmy, not nobody."

"Well, you didn't have it. You wasn't making no money," Pookie said. "But Vivian and them was there. They could've given up the $300 to get Gerald out of that situation. And that caused a lot of problems for the group, too, being on Gerald like that. That might have helped us break up and shit, too. They fucked around and put him in jail and looked around for some other dude (Lester Williams) to sing bass. Gerald came back after six months in jail, but he missed a lot of tunes and things we did.

"I don't know, but his mind might have been on that and he might have been pissed at the company. If it had been me, I'd have been pissed at the company."

"Oh man. I was mad at the whole world," said Gerald.

"By the same token, they'd rather take my song and give me $50," Pookie said, "instead of just saying, 'Hey, man, here's $50. Go get you a room.' They were for what they could get from us, so that's what they did. We were guided the wrong way, and that was how they could take from us the little bit that we had, and not give what was due us."

"What, the recording company? asked Billy Shelton, incredulously. "That's killing the goose who laid the golden egg . . ."

"If we knew then what we know now, we'd get the lawyers," Pookie went on. "We'd be our own managers, our own booking agents. All those things we would take care of ourselves instead of letting the company do it. Because when they became involved they start getting percentages and things.

"And they were not only getting percentages, they were double-contracting us. The'd come to us and tell us we were making $1,500 a week; but I ran across a contract once that said we were making $6,500 for the same job. Plus, they would take 10 percent of the $1,500!

"You see, that's the first thing you have to do: find somebody that's on your side and see that you get our just due."

Of more than passing interest in all this is those most responsible for ripping-off the original Spaniels were not white, but black.

"We didn't have no white problem," said Pookie. "Only problem we had with them was the whites down South."

"Hey, you could put your faith in someone that you think is really in your corner, and he'll rip you off for that dollar," said Opal. "Because I never will forget they got Milo Merritt, a good friend of my mother and father. And come to tell it, Pookie just told me he said, 'Man, Milo Merritt ripped us off worse than the white man ripped us off.'

"Now he supposed to be representing us. And I don't know what happened because right after we got Milo Merritt, I left the group."

"What happened was they bought him off," Pookie said.

"They bought him off. So there you go," Opal sighed.

"The lawyer sold us down the drain," said Ernest. "He told us he couldn't help us. It seemed to me, if I can recall, when our mothers took us to the lawyer and sat down . . . the way he put it that he couldn't help us. Because of some situation with our contract."

"Money makes a lot of people do strange things," said Willie C. "Makes 'em go against family."

"When we went to the meeting, the first person sitting there was Vivian and Jimmy (Bracken)," Pookie said. "And they didn't even wait for us to come through the door. And you know they had to have their shit together. And the meeting didn't take but five minutes. 'Well, that's the way it was, ya'll,' they told us."

"It was our youth and inexperience and our parents not having the knowledge," added Willie C.

"Well, we were really too young to understand the business," said Ernest. "As schoolboys, we didn't have the know-how or the business knowledge to keep up. But the most disappointing experience of those times," he said, "Is we didn't get the backing from the manager that we should, and we didn't get the money from the records that we should have gotten from the hits that we had. Hardly anything. The only thing I can remember we got was a brand new station wagon. And then you know, well, three or four brand-new cars. But as far as receiving royalties or anything like that, uh-uh. They always had some excuse.

"Even though the numbers went up on the charts, too. At that time, if you had a record in the Top 10, it was a hit, you know. And we had two or three in the Top 10, but it didn't matter. We got nothing."

"During those days, we were so green," Gerald interjected. "We were just happy to be out there singing and going through an experience that was new to us in life. And we just happened to be unfortunate enough to have the wrong manager. I'm grateful to the manager (Vivian) giving us a chance to get out there and start a new life, but the people she had working for her were greedy.

"Everybody wanted money in their pockets; so they were taking the money from the artists and we would wind up owing money instead of getting what we were actually due. But I can't have no hard feelings because that's only going to hurt me. Have to think positively."

Said Farag: "Here's a case where it really revolved around greed, not black and white. "Vivian had an emotional love for this music – first and foremost – but basically got corrupted by her own hits. From my knowledge of it, she was influenced by two people. And that was Jimmy Bracken, who was pretty much a street gambler, and Ewart Abner, the A&R man who knew the ins and outs of how to bypass the artists.

"But that was a hard thing to do because in the early '50s all artists – black and white – were looked upon as basically slaves. This was an experimental medium, with radio jet-fueling record sales, and there were a lot of chances for anybody who had any kind of business sense to be able to say to any artist: 'Your voice is going to be heard around the world,' and without saying it, but saying it,' and that should be good enough for you.'

"And it was," Farag went on. "Because the whole culture at that time was on the streetcorner and very similar to gangs, in the sense that each group was a mini-gang with their own turf, and they looked forward to being a hero on their turf. And if they could be by virtue of radio, that was good enough. And a half-smart businessman knew that and knew the history of acts that went back into the late '40s.

The tradition started in the blues where various record companies would go into the cotton fields and other places and record blues singers and sell these things and never consider paying the artists. So there's already a tradition, a precedent and it was easy to follow."

Added Pookie: "Vivian was a victim too. She happened to be where the money was, and she was in a position where they couldn't buy her off because she was married to the man, so they flooded her, showered her, with all the stuff. She had millions of dollars. She was able to do things that black people couldn't do. The rest of it she just seemed blind to."

"I am a little forgiving of Vivian," said Farag, "only because when I know that a person truly loves the music, I know they started from an honorable place. She was not like Abner who came in as strictly business and wouldn't know a hit if it hit him in the face. But he knew distribution, publishing rights, things like that.

"And I am also a little forgiving of Alan Freed for that reason because I look at the good and bad. Yes, Alan Freed was definitely a thief and put his name on stuff that he had no business doing and took payoffs, which by the way at that time was not illegal. It was a new industry. But he also changed people's hearts and minds by exposing it, and that's what did him in.

"I always made a distinction between calculated and where you start from. To me Dick Clark should never be on the airwaves ever again. He was the most calculating phony of 'em all," Farag snarled.

"Even with Freed's history, tainted though it is, he had more influence," Farag continued. "And even with Vivian's tainted as it is, she had more influence and did more to progress this music than Dick Clark, who basically was a cover. He was a Chordettes in a single person. He was a cover of everything that came before. He whitewashed, homogenized it, and set himself up as a 'clean as silk' image playing to parents of teens because he had no guts; and he admitted it. That's why he never let kids on "American

Bandstand" without a suit and tie.

"I have a hard-on for Dick Clark," admitted Farag. "It was well-known all over the country what Alan Freed did – his good and bad. But Dick Clark was far more insidious. He had Swan Records. He had an interest in Cameo Parkway. He had publishing, record plants, record distribution, song royalties and artists – all the while having a TV show. And he was far more blatant and greedy in putting these conflicts together and at the same time claiming for himself this 'clean Gene' image, 'I love you kids,' and 'I love you parents.'

"To me, that was extremely dishonest – and to me, far worse than a guy like Alan Freed," said Farag, "who I should probably hate more for trying to get his name on one of those Spaniels records. But I don't – I absolutely don't. The only reason you saw these acts on television with Dick Clark is because it was already there. And then it got bigger in '55, '56, '57. And by the time Dick Clark came on the scene, it was already too big to avoid."

Farag said he "absolutely hated" the McGuire Sisters' syrupy covers of the Spaniels 'Goodnight Sweetheart' and the Moonglows 'Sincerely.' "All I know is that this sound was tinny compared to what I heard on 'Livin' with Vivian' on WWCA in Chicago. It was like night and day."

And just how did Pookie manage to write so many of those good songs, as he says, "in my head"?

"I don't really know," he said. "I guess it's just a gift. But we had to have songs – they told us we just have to have songs. So we would get together, and just did it for our own sakes. We didn't go out to be songwriters. For some reason or other that we didn't know, they liked what we were coming up with, and they recorded it.

"But the powers in music were down on us because our stuff was different. It wasn't the same thing that was going on. We were really ushering in a new era. Somebody knew it but they weren't telling us. That's why a lot of the songs we wrote probably sold a lot more than we could imagine. They just didn't let us know they sold them."

"I had it against them other greedy dudes – Vivian's brother (Calvin), and Abner (Ewart), said Gerald. She was working with the wrong people."

"Ewart Abner ran the company," noted Pookie. "He ran Vee-Jay."

"Abner . . . he was the manager for her," said Willie C. "he got hung up. She fired him. He hid it at that time for 18 years or somewhere along there, but he had stolen a quarter of a million dollars from the company and went to Motown. She found out about it. It was a tragedy. He made a lot of money for her – and for himself too."

"I talked to Vivian before she got sick because I just wondered about it," said Billy. "A guy named Carl Wise, he's my witness. That's when she was working here (in Gary) on Fifth. And I just asked, 'What happened? You were like the female Berry Gordy. You were the first . . . you had groups like the Beatles and the Four Seasons. What happened to you?

"'You started with the Spaniels and the group actually set Vee-Jay in the position to become powerful later.' But she told me this – and Carl Wise is around to verify it.

She said: "'Things were growing so fast' and what she 'should have done . . .' she made a mistake.' She said she 'should have had one thing herself.' She said she 'gave Abner the control' and she said 'Abner was a gambler. He was a compulsive gambler and he'd gotten up to his neck in debt with the Mafia out in Vegas running up astronomical gambling bills.' But what she didn't know, was he was reaching into the till.'

"And then she said if she 'had been on her job, then he wouldn't have been able to do it.' But when they found out it was too late. He'd stolen so much money."

Said Willie C.: "I feel one thing that really helped hurt us too was the long-term contract when we first started. I believe it was six years. The Staple Singers – Pop Staples – said he was the only one at that time that refused to do that. He said he was going six months at a time. Our contract was six years and now you're hung up; you're with the wrong people. So you couldn't negotiate if you hit it big."

Noting that over the years, the Spaniels' version of "Goodnight Sweetheart" was used in movies such as "American Grafitti," "Three Men and a Baby" and "Diner," and a country-like version of "W.W. & The Dixie Dancekings," Pookie was asked how much money in total, the group would have made with a fair shake.

"We all sitting here, we'd at least all had a million dollars," he said. "Even if they gave us that, we could have been able to do the things that the giants and them do with a million dollars.

"And we were never given guidance. We were only guided the wrong way, and that was how they could take from us the little bit that we had, and not give what was due us."

A classic example was Vee-Jay's denying the original Spaniels what may have been their greatest financial remuneration by failing to compensate the group for use of "Let's Make Up" on the flip side of "The Ballad of Davy Crockett" hit on the RCA Victor label in 1954. The latter was recorded by the popular Voices of Walter Schumann.

"That record probably made more than 'Goodnight Sweetheart,'" said Pookie, "and we didn't get any of it."

By the same token, the Spaniels were asked by Vee-Jay to back up Gary's Priscilla Bowman on a "Rockin' Good Way," and Pro McClain on "Boot Em Up." But once again, they received no money for their efforts.

Said Opal: "It's that way today, too. Because you can go into a black neighborhood and the percentile of educated young kids as to the same white kids in the same age group is all together different because of the environment."

Aside from the monumental rip-offs, how do the Spaniels feel about having been excluded, at this writing, from the Rock and Roll Hall of Fame? Or even if they're inducted later, the fact that it took so long to be recognized in this very public manner for their signal contributions to the pop culture they helped create?

"As forerunners of the music, I believe we should have been taken in. Because rock 'n' roll is nothin' but rhythm and blues sung by white boys," Pookie said. "They didn't want to call it rhythm and blues so they called it rock 'n' roll. To me it was just a color thing.

"The last four years, Henry Farag has written letters requesting that they put the Spaniels in the Hall, but they fell on deaf ears."

"I really believe that the group got shafted, because they deserve to be in other (besides the R&B Foundation) halls of fame as well," said Billy.

"If they go back far enough, as Pookie said, "they'll find it all stems from rhythm and blues – the black groups. About 1955, that's where rock 'n' roll came out, and we notice in all the books it starts in '55 or '56. They never go back to '54 or '53 for some reason."

"One of the big problems," noted Pookie, "is the people on the selection boards – like the Doo Wop Hall of Fame in Boston. They had 175 doing the choosing. Ken Held, a disk jockey in Florida who's really a lover of the music and really goes back, and has his information about as correct as you can get it, was tellin' me the boards are made up 90 percent of people under 30. 'So they don't know anything about ya'll.

"And they dealin' with what they call a 'Doo-Wop Hall of Fame.' They don't know nothin' about no 'doo-wop.' Because of their names and things, they follow the music in their area and they were picked as experts. So as experts, we weren't chosen. It's simple as that."

* * * *

And how do some Spaniels' wives feel about the game that was whipped on their talented husbands when they were at their peak?

"We (young black artists) just didn't know," said Mamie Hudson, Pookie's wife at this writing. "We thought making $50 a week was a lot. They loved it (singing) so much they probably would have done it for nothing. Being popular, being stars, having ladies fall all over them. They felt this is what they were supposed to be getting.

"I was let down when I heard the Spaniels stopped recording in the early '60s. I didn't really gravitate to the white imitators (Beatles, Elvis, Rolling Stones, etc.).

"Pookie only recently began fighting the system and the internal problems with the first group and the turmoil with the later members. The originals had families and military obligations which led to breakups. Problems also came from lack of strong family support and understanding of what they were trying to do. Their families felt they were just young boys who should be out trying to work for a living.

"They also needed professional management people who were dedicated to them – not just taking profits and putting on shows.

"These days, in addition to our happiness, my main interest in life is to help Pookie out in his business so they don't get ripped-off again," Mamie concluded.

"The Spaniels were very popular but didn't get the recognition they deserved," said Zola Jackson, wife of Willie C. "Being young, they really didn't know. They should have spoken up for themselves. They should have gotten a lawyer to help them out. Sometimes you can't trust your own people."

In those days, Pookie, Willie C. and their wives sometimes didn't have enough food. They sometimes had to go to Vivian's house to eat. That's how bad things were.

"They sang beautiful once their records came out. But you need constant money. Singing is good but you can't live with no money coming in," Zola said.

Before she got pregnant, Zola said she always had a job. But while pregnant, she had a lot of complications. She told Willie C. he can't be on the road while his wife was sick. Vivian was cheating them out of their money and she had no money coming in.

As a result, Willie C. packed it in with the Spaniels in 1956, not to rejoin the group until 1991.

SIX
Opal, Gerald

"Professionalism comes with time and age. You don't become a professional overnight. You can be a star, but it takes time to be a professional" – Opal Courtney Jr.

Despite their hometown roots and boyish growing-up-togetherness, the Spaniels – like their unique singing voices – were disparate personalities. Fortunately, these differences enhanced their sound as well as the quality of their stage presence, which always was, and still is, second to none.

For example, the well-spoken Opal – the baby of the group – who sang baritone as well as top tenor, was, perhaps, the most middle-class member. The last one to join the Spaniels, he later would become the first to leave, owing to a strong sense of disapproval of some of the personal behavior he saw on the road.

In school, Opal always considered himself a nerd-type and, as a younger kid, did not run in the same circles as his future co-vocalizers. "I did a whole lot of studying because this was demanded by my family. All they talked about was college, college, college," he said. And he agreed. Yet, he never did make it to college.

Opal's eagerness to go on the Apollo tour with two weeks left in school in June 1954, precipitated a decisive falling-out with his mother and dad. One that he'd come to regret.

"I told my mother, 'Mom, I want to go to the Apollo Theater with the Spaniels. And the old man was sitting over there and he said, 'Well, there's only one man in my house, and all my boys are going to finish school. So if you're going to go to the Apollo Theater, you've got to leave.'

"I was 17 years old, still in high school, and so I moved over on Harrison Street with Pookie – right across the street from Gary Roosevelt. But even though the others had graduated, and I was in school alone, I was the same person. I've never been tied up with being a celebrity. We were just singing and we had a record out.

"And I've always been a team player. Being a background singer, you need assistance from your fellow background singers. This is something we've always enjoyed – close harmony so that we can hear each other. Plus, it adds to the group. And it's the way I live."

In addition to scholastic interests, Opal inherited a strong background in athletics from his dad, Opal "Shag" Courtney – an original Harlem Globetrotter.

"He always wanted one of his sons to be a ballplayer. Abe Saperstein (who ran the Trotters) would regularly play four blacks and a white. Abe used to play, along with my father, Inman Jackson and the rest."

While Opal was at Roosevelt High, the basketball team won the Indiana state championship five consecutive years. He played on the varsity as a freshman "along with the whole freshman team," he said.

"We were that good. I played with Dick 'Skull' Barnett, who later played at Tennessee State and with the New York Knicks. As a matter of fact, in high school we went to the state finals and we played against Oscar Robertson and them, and they beat our socks off," he chuckled.

"I had about 16 basketball scholarship offers and probably would have gone to a smaller school. I heard from Howard, Tennessee State, Knoxville College – all black colleges. It was a very big letdown to everybody because they thought I was going to play college ball."

But Opal wanted to sing with the Spaniels – for better or worse. And he enjoyed it while it lasted, although he swears the group rarely encountered special treatment as stars.

"The Spaniels came on first most of the time when I was there," he said. "They used to tell us if you're first you have to start it. If you have a bad opening act it's going to be a bad show. So the onus was on us, and we did our jobs – North or South. But it did get tiresome down South running across the tracks if you wanted something to eat.

"And you know, I ran into the same discrimination in the service when I joined up after I left the group and finished school. I was right back down South again – Biloxi, Miss. It was just like (what) we had when we were on tour. The segregated bathrooms, the white this, black that, white this, black that. You got a water fountain with separate 'colored' and 'white' and water still coming out of the same hole, hooking the same pipe, using the same drain."

When the group needed someone to fill in for Opal after he split, Calvin Carter, Vivian's brother, was chosen in a stop-gap move. Vee-Jay's artist-and-repertoire man, Calvin also was road manager on the successful, eventful Roy Hamilton tour set up by the Gale Agency.

"I remember we were someplace, and the guys were kidding around. Somebody said: 'Hey, Carter, come on and sing.' And Calvin said: If you asked me what I do for a living, I'd say, I'm a road manager. Well, I didn't ask you to be a road manager, so why ask me to sing?'"

"And Calvin couldn't sing. Yeah, you've seen the pictures of Calvin with the group, but that's all part of the Vee-Jay thing. And the demise of the Spaniels. His inadequacies as a singer were overshadowed in the five-man group. They just needed a fifth at that time."

After Opal left the Spaniels on Oct. 31, 1954, he returned to high school and finished in February 1955.

He got his diploma with the June 1955 graduating class and enlisted in the Air Force on July 4.

"I joined to see the world and I saw Texas and Mississippi," he laughed. "I stayed in the Air Force until October 1958.

"During those years, I was hearing things like 'Peace of Mind' and 'I Lost You .' Oh, the Spaniels had a fabulous sound. As a matter of fact, I went to their show; they were in Texas. But I never went to see them. I never went to say hello. They didn't know I was there.

"It was in the Fort Worth-Dallas area. Pookie, Gerald,

Donald, Carl and Dimp. And they sounded so good. They were good. I just looked at them and thought, 'Hey, that could have been you.' And the people around me didn't know. I never told anybody I was singing with the Spaniels. I'm not a hound for recognition. I just like to be in the background. But every time I'd hear them, I wished I still belonged.

"After I got out of the service, I never wanted to go to college. Maybe it was the letdown of not singing anymore or just the regimented life that I lived when I was in my mother and father's home. Because I booked it. I had to get my studies because it was demanded of us. So I just didn't want to study anymore.

"When I did get out of the service, I went with the Dells. I was with them two-and-a-half years. We made 'If It Ain't One Thing It's Another.' I got with them when they were in limbo after being with Dinah Washington as Dinah's Gents. But Chuck (Barksdale) and Johnny (Carter) left because of a low, lull in the career. Johnny used to be with the Flamingos, you know.

"It was Marvin, Mickey, Vernon and myself. You have reorganizations – the same thing like with the Spaniels when I left and Willie C. left. You know, you change groups, you change personnel.

"But as things would have it, the money wasn't there, and I'm traveling from Gary to Harvey, Ill., to practice three or four times a week. I got to catch the South Shore to 115th Street, over to Martin Luther King Dr. and then catch the Harvey bus to go out and practice. My priorities had begun to change," he noted.

"Even when I was singing I was fascinated with hair," Opal said. "When I left the Dells, I was still doing men's processing. So I went to Philly and I learned how to hairweave. Then I came back here and I was working in a shop in Gary and a friend of mine called from Norfolk, Va., and invited me down. So I went to Norfolk and was doing hair and doing real good there. Then I got homesick and came back and got into the same field here.

"But they had this heavy street gang. They call it the 'Family' here, and some people call it the 'Blackstone

Rangers' in Chicago. And I never will forget. I was doing hair and they came into my shop and said 'We're going to sell dope out of this shop.'

"So I closed it up on Nov. 18, 1968, and the next day I was on my job at Gillespie Ford. I never opened the doors again. I was threatened for my life and I wasn't going to involve myself in narcotics nor was I going to let someone use my place to sell narcotics out of. They patterned themselves behind the 'Godfather' and all that stuff. And they were treacherous.

"I sold cars for a long time, then went into management. I managed in the used car area and then I managed new car areas. Then I went into the leasing office where I've been for about eight or nine years now.

"When I first got back to Gary, I rarely came in contact with any of the Spaniels. When I would go down to the bank on Fifth Avenue I'd see Gerald standing out with the boys on the corner. And he'd be doing the same thing – drinking and singing with the fellas. Hopefully, he's stopped, but he would do that tomorrow. I saw Willie C. maybe one or two times. And I didn't see Ernest until we all met here in my house before the Smithsonian honor in New York (February 1991). Billy moved over to Illinois. It was a different circle alltogether.

Opal makes no bones about his relationship problems with Gerald in the salad days of the original Spaniels. As a matter of fact, the last one came right before he decided to split from the group and go back to high school.

"We'd had a confrontation over his Dr. Jekyll and Mr. Hyde style. When Gerald is drinking he's a different person. He's demanding, he's abusive, he does not have respect for any females that's around him – even his lady. And that has come out even since we've been back together now (1991)."

Yet he would never denigrate the bass singer's talent. No way. Because Opal, like everyone else who has ever heard him, knows, in a word, that the happy-go-lucky Gerald Gregory was awesome.

* * * *

"My deep voice is just natural; it's a gift from God," says

Gerald. "I always studied other bass singers, learning and borrowing from them, (and) my grandparents. In addition to idolizing the Ravens' great Jimmy Ricks, I got my 'Heart and Soul' from the spiritual group, the Golden Gates.

"The thing that surprised me was the 'Do do do do doooo . . ." for 'Goodnight Sweetheart.' I didn't realize at first how popular it was. It was just a natural thing for us to do, being together. And Pookie, of course – my lead singer – has always been our inspiration; that's how we wrote the songs. He usually would start it and we'd fill it; we'd fill out one verse and Pookie would take care of it from there. He always was brilliant in writing music," Gerald said.

"I thought I was pretty good writing at one time but I don't do it any more. I guess because I don't have the release, by me not learning how to play any music. But it was too much in the mind so I kind of let it go, which I shouldn't have done.

"It's a funny thing, but that 'Goodnight Sweetheart' opening seems to crack people up. I get a laugh out of 'em every time I do it. I say, 'What they laughin' about?'"

Like each and every one of the Spaniels, Gerald never really realized just how popular the group was – especially among its base constituency of black fans from coast-to-coast. A testimonial perhaps, to managers who chose to keep them in the dark for their own purposes.

"I was too wrapped up in the experience we were getting of traveling," Gerald said. "It's just the new life that we were living. But not really the magnitude of what could be accomplished.

"It's something I take for granted. As long as the people like us, that's the thing. But as far as the ego of it, no. The ego is simply them telling me, 'You are beautiful.' It's the same thing with women and other hangers-on.

"I couldn't say that part was good, because I look back over my past and I've gotten into a little of everything. It's trying. It never got to a point where it got detrimental. But still, overindulgence is bad, in any shape or form. But as far as girls are concerned it's nice, having the fame and whatever that goes long with it. But I'm still happy that I never been the type of fellow that I would let it affect me.

"I'm just that type of fellow. I'm very quiet.

"But as far as feeling different because we were famous – Oh yes. I must say I get a joy out of singing for somebody and they like it. By them coming back after the show, that's how I get my joy; by them telling me how much they enjoyed the show."

Perhaps Gerald's most popular bass lead turns with the Spaniels were 'Bounce,' the rollicking flip side of 'Baby, It's You', and 'Housecleaning', which backed up 'The Bells Ring Out.'

As a matter of fact, famed New York disk jockey Bobby Jay – himself a bass singer with several R&B groups in the '60s and '70s – calls Gerald "Mr. Bounce" and credits the Spaniels' bass man with his desire to sing.

According to Gerald, the story of "Bounce" closely parallels his own behavior at the time.

"Well, I hate to say it, but in school, probably the last year, the group got closer and we were riding in these cars.

"I got me a little blue car. And I had my first taste of joy juice – wine, grapes. And we would ride around and sing. And the words to 'Bounce,' you know . . . "I been drinkin' moonshine and now I want to bounce. My head's going 'round, up and down and I don't weigh an ounce . . .' So that's really how 'Bounce' came to be.

"As for Bobby Jay's special introduction of me that way at Radio City – that makes me feel very good.

"Yeah, in fact, I don't even think I knew how to sing in the old days. Really. I didn't particularly care for any songs that I did, because I thought at the time, naturally, I was into it. But as I look, as I listen from time to time, you know, it never did really move me that much. But still I'm happy that . . . maybe it's because I was sincere."

Gerald credits the idea for the saucily suggestive "Housecleaning," on which he is an all-purpose cleaner avaliable to women, "to a friend of mine. So it's not too much I can say about what was on their mind. But I might've added a few words to it," he said with a wink.

Gerald said the high points of his Spaniels career in the old days had to do with the traveling around the country.

"I have learned so much in knowing and meeting new

people, I think its one of the fastest ways you can learn. Like you say, just seeing a picture is better than a thousand words. Seeing for yourself instead of reading. Our experiences on the road was life it self. I just had to put it to life. From learning the things I have."

One of the learning experiences had to do with an appearance on TV's "American Bandstand" in Philadelphia, with Dick Clark in 1958.

"The only thing I really remember about that is bad because our manager at the time – Jimmy Bracken – thought one of the fellas said something derogatory toward him. He said Donald (Porter) called him 'a little pipsqueak.'

"I had just got Donald in the group not too long before, so Bracken was going to get back at Donald by saying he could not appear on the show. He sent word on the phone and that kind of messed up the spirit of the show. But we went on anyway.

"We also played Las Vegas two or three times in the '50s, but never on the Strip. We'd appear in one of those big auditoriums on one of those big shows with seven or eight stars like Roy Hamilton, Illinois Jacquet, Della Reese, Drifters, (and) a new group like the Nutmegs.

"And let's not forget that time we met up with Red Skelton at that nice club (Chez Paree) in Chicago.

"That was beautiful. He sat down and talked quite a while. He wished us luck and everything and gave us a briefing about life itself.

"I'll always remember Red. He was a beautiful fellow. He was complimentary toward us. Sure enough."

Since the Spaniels were warned about the customs of the Deep South, prior to their initial tour, Gerald wasn't surprised at what awaited them in many places. Not usually.

"What did surprise me is after we got down to the Deep South, we would sometime see another race of people catering to us. We've been taught that this is not the way it's supposed to be; any kind of mingling. We were scared, I mean, that this would happen. Because I've been taught one way and here this is happening another way.

"Like one city I remember especially – Atlanta – when we first went down there. The whites were around us. They were coming to the show the first time we were there, and the next time they were sitting around the stage. And the next time we went there . . . even the teen-agers.

"We were living in this motel and all night long they'd play all down in the foyer downstairs, you know. I said 'What's going on? This is Georgia.' These type of things surprised me. You have to be careful, too, because they're looking . . . even today."

Gerald was known for his personal demons – especially drinking and drugs. And he readily admits they cost him dearly.

"Most sincerely, I went through my worst part in life already. And that was because I wasn't singing. And the worst part I got over once I started back (to) any kind of singing. I never had a problem as far as demons were concerned, as we say, as long as I was singing. It's when I wasn't singing. But it's no problem saying 'no' to anything.

"But, yes, I did a little bit of everything and I know how the demons come out. You end up having them all. It was just another way of going to sleep, let's say. That's the reason the last thing that disappointed me so much was when I got hoarse. I said, 'Uh, oh. No more. Because I'm dead. If I lose that, I'm dead. Life is no more worth living.' That's the way I feel about it. I know this is what I was meant to do."

And, of course, the regrets remain.

"Regrets is No. 1, the people we were working for and working with, we couldn't get together. Everything could have been so beautiful today. For instance, like Motown. These people that own everything now. It's a shame that we couldn't get together like we should have. And other than that, I regret that the group, the Spaniels itself – that we didn't stick together through all of this."

And the low point of the glory days?

"I can't think of a low point when we were singing. My work on stage was the only way I could get it out. On stage.

"Otherwise, if I hadn't been singing, I would have been in trouble. The low points in my life come from not singing; it happened off and on; familywise, not growing up with my children.

"Those green suits we wore sometimes remind me of

once in Washington, D.C., when I'm fixin' to go on stage and these two tall white fellas come up and they say, 'Is your name Gerald Gregory?' And I say, 'Yes,' and they say 'I think you better come with us.' I say 'Look what is it?'

"It was about the service; the armed service. I was supposed to have been in.

"I said, 'Let me make this last show and I'll go right with you.' Man, they lifted me up and took me all through the audience and I was embarrassed. But I eventually got it straight, though. I was lucky enough to have talked to the major already because I figured it was about that time. By me being on the road, I just didn't take care of business as far as the armed service.

"But I went and talked to the service again, there in Baltimore. A young fellow talked to me and luckily he knew the group very well and I spent a half hour talking about my experience as a Spaniel. He said, 'I don't know what to do with you; to take you in or let you go.' I said, 'Man, I got a show this evening.' But that didn't work."

Despite tours with other vocal groups when not actively performing with the Spaniels, Gerald has never found it difficult to remember his part on any song.

"Really, I get mine from our leader, Pookie. Once I hear him, I'm inspired. Now I know why the bass is called a drummer. Once they hear me, then they'll come in , and keep it going from there.

"Now I've sung with quite a few groups. I've always idolized the old group Sonny Til and the Orioles. And I've been with one of the original sets of Ink Spots before. What I'm saying is, when you sing with other groups, then you have to go into remembering, exactly. But in knowing most of their tunes, it wasn't that hard. But certain songs I didn't know so naturally, that's when it becomes work.

And how did Gerald feel in the '50s and '60s when white performers were making hay with black music?

"Well, when a group like Sha Na Na comes along, they get a lot of recognition because of 'Goodnight Sweetheart.' That was our song and they used it as their theme. And we didn't get hired that much.

"I liked the McGuire Sisters' 'Goodnight Sweetheart.' I

liked it. That didn't bother me that much, you know.

"But then here comes this group called the Beatles. Aw man, they didn't even have to breathe, you know? That made me feel kind of funny, too.

"We didn't get the money. My name should have been on 'Goodnight Sweetheart' and two or three others. But my mind wasn't on this because I didn't realize what writers' royalties was all about. I was a part writer of 'Baby, It's You,' too. But I was green, you know."

Among Gerald's favorite Spaniels' bass leads were "So Deep Within," which he'd like to record again, and "Jessie Mae."

"That's a song (the latter) that Pookie originally was recording and gave up on. He said he just didn't like it. It was back in the studio when it happened. I never would have suggested me because words seemed wobbly to me on the playback. I never really did get the words out the way I wanted to. But originally, Pookie started recording it at the studio. I just took it over because they asked me to when he wouldn't do it."

Like many black R&B records in those days, neither were heard a lot. "No, the stations weren't opening up the way they are now," he said. "Sure enough. I figure a lot of those songs could make it today."

And who does the great Gerald Gregory, bass man supreme of the mighty Spaniels, consider the best groups of yesterday and today?

"Of today's groups, I like the O'Jays. It's three of 'em and they make quite a sound just for three people.

"But as far as one-on-one, the Spaniels go up against anybody. Sure enough.

"But really, my groups that l like go back a little farther. I particularly like the Dominos and the Clovers. And the El Dorados, who were on Vee-Jay, too. But if I had to pick one of the groups of our so-called era, it would be the Flamingos. They sing some beautiful songs. They go back pretty far, you know. I'll never forget 'em. They'll always be in my heart, those particular groups."

Is it true that the Spaniels' "False Love" was the first record to use 'doo-wop?'

"I don't know. Maybe it was 'Let's Make Up.': I got a taste of . . . Come on, let's make up, I got a taste of the blues . . . Doo-wop, do doo-wop, do doo-wop, do doo, I got a taste of the blues . . .' That was a way long time ago."

You can say that again. But the greatness of so many original Spaniels classics will never die – aided and abetted by Opal Courtney Jr. and Gerald Gregory.

SEVEN
Ernest, Willie C., Billy

"As the years went on, I thought we had a certain amount of professionalism where we could be considered stars. Especially when we went to the Apollo Theater and we headlined the show there.

"You know you didn't just headline the show at the Apollo at that time without some notoriety. – Ernest Warren.

Ernest Warren, top tenor of the Spaniels when it all started in 1952, is the only member not back for the present-day reincarnation of the original group.

"I think it would have been a conflict of interest," he said. "I don't think that I could possibly on one hand try to encourage a person to accept the Lord and then on the other hand, have him dancing and cavorting and thinking sexually. So I just couldn't do the two.

"But it made me feel good that they wanted me. Now I will say this: When I was with them in New York for the Smithsonian Institution award (Feb. 21, 1991) we did kind of 'tune-up' a little bit to see if we still had it, and we do.

"But it's a choice that I made, and it was my choice. My wife didn't have anything to do with it. It was just my choice.

"And I notice they didn't lose their voices. It's because of the type of song, the type of singing. It's really not hollering, it's singing. And you have a chance to relax and go back at it. And that has a lot to do with it.

"The types of songs today, people try to stretch their range to impress people, but I don't think that was what we had to do. We could stay in our natural ranges and just

page 72

relax and sing. And part of it too, was the love of just singing."

* * * *

Like all of the original Spaniels, Ernest knew at an early
agethat his voice was something special. And, like so many
other black youngsters who could sing, he got his start in
church. But singing professionally was a different story.

"My folks really didn't want me singing outside of the
church choir and the school glee club. I'm the son of a holiness preacher and he didn't like it. Neither did my mother.
But I was kind of sneaking around singing anyway."

Of course, Ernest knew Pookie, who lived about a half-
block away, and shared some of his classes. And he also
knew of his prodigious talent as a silky voiced balladeer.

"When I used to see Pookie cut through my yard on his
way to school, I knew I was late. When I heard him sing in
a church quartet, I liked what they were doing and tried to
join them. And then at school, I was successful at it."

Later, after he and Pookie and others hooked up in what
would evolve into the Spaniels, the chemistry was instanta-
neous.

"We practiced everywhere we could. Actually, they wer-
en't rehearsals, it just that we loved to sing together. You
know how guys are when they stand around on the street
corner and start singing," he said.

"When we thought that we had something to offer was
when we really went into formal rehearsals. We sang on the
street corner, we sang in the back of the car, over to each
other's house and out on the park. Wherever we could get
together. It was hard to stop.

"Pookie wrote 'Baby, It's You.' He brought the song to
us, and as was our custom when we first started, we just
started singing and putting harmony together and going
over different ideas and rehearsing until we got it down to
its final condition. And that's really how we did it.

"It was something that was just natural with us. We had a
natural harmony. Our voices blended well, and it seems
like we had a camaraderie that lent it self to us just being
able to pick up where one dropped off as far as the song
was concerned.

"But oh, yes, we did practice a lot."

Ernest said he wasn't "really surprised that the group became so popular so soon because, as I said, we sang before
we went professional. We sang on talent shows and our
class functions. And we were really good. I'll just have to
say it like that."

And yet, in a trait that is common among the Spaniels, he
didn't really consider himself a celebrity or a star. On the
other hand, playing the world-famous Apollo Theater – and
headlining the show after a couple of records, meant they
were definitely doing something right.

"The Apollo was a highlight, I would say. To be recognized. Well, to tell the truth, we had to audition in New
York to even go in there. And we'd done our audition for
this talent agent and he said we didn't sound like a bunch of
dogs. As a matter of fact, he thought we were great.

"Of course, one of our tunes the agent liked was 'The
Bells Ring Out,' which I think was the most beautiful. It
was soft and melodious and just a pleasure to sing. To sing
those numbers that we had basically put the music to ourselves – that was what was gratifying.

"And it really was a highlight in those days to be able to
go to the Apollo and to headline the show over top groups
like the Five Satins and the Hearts."

Ernest recalled that part of the fun "was to go to a new
place and a different place, but there were other things involved in that too. I was young and unmarried and I didn't
turn many of them (girls) down."

Back in those days, healthy young American males faced
the military draft, and many who had high-profile careers in
sports and entertainment were called into the Army or
Navy at the peak of their careers. Ernest was no exception.

"Uh-uh, I didn't quit. I'd never done that. I left the group
because I had to go to the service. I was drafted in March of
'56 for almost two years. When I came back I had a little
hard time because the fellas that they had in the group –
they didn't really want me back.

"Some of the fellas that were there, like Donald (Porter),
because I didn't have the voice of the fella that was singing
with them. I had a hard time getting a place back in the

group.

"I wanted to come back," he emphasized. "That was my desire. As a matter of fact, when I was in the service I sang with a group overseas. I never did stop singing. I actually went TDY (on temporary duty) in the service singing at the enlisted men's clubs with a group. So when I came back, I was looking for my place, but it was kind of hard to get.

"And they knew in the service that I was a Spaniel. Oh, yes. I was somewhat of a celebrity in service. I didn't have to soldier too much. And it made me feel pretty good to know that the Spaniels were still working and still sticking with it," he said.

"I've often compared the two groups," Ernest continued. "As a matter of fact, there's been several combinations of Spaniels, but that group that was singing while I was in the service – they were good.

"But when I got back, they didn't accept me at first. This other fellow was singing with them and they had, I suppose, build a rapport among themselves – sort of a different kind of group. And I didn't at that time fit into their plans until one of the fellas (Carl Rainge) quit. Then I was able to come back in that way, in 1957. I stayed until 1962."

Ernest proudly pointed out that he was a Spaniel for many of the group's best recordings, including 'Stormy Weather.' "Yes, I was with them for that. All of those, 'Here is Why I Love You,' which I think was the most beautiful record we made other than 'The Bells Ring Out.'"

And why would a young man with a great opportunity for fame and fortune voluntarily leave the Spaniels when he did?

"That was one of my lifelong desires. My father was a minister and I idolized him and idolized the type of life that he lived before us, and for his children. And my mother was an extremely religious person, so I guess it was always inbred in me.

"My wife used to tell me that when I was singing that the first time I got drunk that would be the first thing I'd start talking about – becoming a preacher – which I did in 1976."

*   *   *   *

As it developed, Willie C. parted from the group only a month or so after Ernest – in April 1956.

This left the Spaniels with just two originals – Pookie and Gerald. And Pookie was soon to follow suit.

But while Willie C. was a Spaniel, he did some great things with this, the best of all the original black rhythm and blues vocal groups.

Willie C. said the Spaniels made "quite a few records" during his three years with them – from 1953-56.

"When I left, we had a lot of sides on the shelf. I would say about 24. Quite a few were released after I left. At that time, when we'd go for a (recording) session, we'd have to do a least 10 or 15 songs. They weren't releasing albums. Mostly just single 78s and 45s. So as albums appeared, you were able to put more songs out at one time."

He said they would record the same song in a couple of different versions – with a little different melody.

Of his signature record "Play it Cool," which has been described by some as the original "rap" record, Willie C. had this to say:

"We hadn't practiced that song; we hadn't wrote it or anything. It just happened. We were just taking a little break and the guys up in the studio – like the piano player – just started playing a spiritual and I started clowning around like I was preaching. And Ernest just made up the words. When we finished, they said 'that was good; we recorded it.' Now I had to turn around and learn the words."

"Play it Cool" truly was a one-of-a-kind tune. Recorded as the flip side of "Let's Make Up" in March 1954 and released as Vee-Jay 116, it was to develop a huge following in black America. Later, it would become a cult favorite.

But even though "Play it Cool," was the Spaniels' record which provided his nickname and the only one on which he sang lead, the soft-spoken Willie C. claimed it was not his favorite. He saved that distinction for, what else, "Goodnight Sweetheart, Goodnight."

"At first I didn't like it, but after it began to be played, really began to like it," he said.

In the long run, Willie C. came to truly regret his decision to leave the Spaniels. He said the first time was in

1957, when the group came back to Gary to appear at the Palace Theater.

"It really did something to me. I felt I should have been up there with them. People were always on me about not being back with the Spaniels. When I first went to work, guys were teasing me when I walked down the road on the way to the job, 'Hey, Willie C. of the Spaniels, man, what you doing out here? I just paid six or seven dollars to see you last night.'

"People still said I was a Spaniel. Everybody knew I was working there in the steel mill and I had to put up with it whenever the group would be in town. They rode me like that for years. It eventually died down, but I had many dreams and nightmares about it."

When he heard the first records that came out after he left, "it was a miserable feeling, I'll tell you," Willie C. said. "I knew it should be me, but that didn't stop me from watchin' 'em. Sometimes I'd go see 'em sing and it just hurt me so bad. That even stopped me from going to see some of their performances and I said, well, I'm just hurtin' myself when I keep going back.

"I tried to say that I was glad for 'em, but I still felt it should have been me; that I was a part of it. I felt that they were ready to make some money. They had been around for a while now, had learned the ropes and changing of managers. I thought they were ready to go and it really got to me."

Willie C. hastened to add that he had absolutely no animosity for his fellow singers who remained, or the new replacements.

"No, it was all on me. It was on my part. They continued to have problems but I was always saying, well, maybe I'll get my chance again. I always did want to sing, but I never did tell Pookie. But he never asked me, either.

"He'd come to town, we'd go places and do things but the conversation never came up about me; that I wanted to sing again or was thinking about singing again. I wanted to, but I was waiting for him to say it. I would have come back if he'd asked, but he never knew it.

"If I had to do it all over again, I wouldn't have quit,"

Willie C. readily admitted. "I would have stayed with it. With the experience and knowledge I have, it wouldn't be no problem. But I was younger then and I was thinking more so of myself and my wife than I was the group.

"It was hard to leave behind. It was a nice era because I was a part of the Spaniels and anytime anyone mentioned the Spaniels, I felt I should have been there.

"But I gave it up. If I was like a baseball player that got too old to play, I wouldn't feel so bad. But I quit at my peak. I guess since I got involved in Masonry and the church, I guess I kept Pookie and everybody thinking that is what I wanted to do."

Willie C. did what he felt he had to do. He had his reasons – the most important of which were his wife, Zola, and his family.

Willie met Zola at a roller skating rink in Gary in the summer of 1953, when she was in town from St. Louis to visit her aunt. He was already with the Spaniels and on his way to fame, but not fortune.

"His singing didn't bother me," she said. "I just figured they were whoopin' and hollerin'.

"Willie was dating a friend of my cousin and I was dating a preacher's son he was visiting. And then some girl wrote me a letter. She had the nerve to tell me to 'leave Willie C. alone.' She said they were engaged. She had a little ring which may have been a class ring.

"Willie C. had a few other girls and I had to set them straight," Zola recalled. "One girl tried to trip me at night while we were skating. I waited for her outside and they had to pull me off of her."

At the time they got married in 1956, Willie C. was rooming with Pookie and his mother. "Willie's mother was a church woman and didn't think he would ever leave her," Zola said.

After the marriage – in a double ceremony with Pookie and his first wife, Alice Morton – the two couples shared a house on 25th Street and Pennsylvania Avenue for about two years. Each had their own bedroom and shared the rest of the house.

Less than a year later, the unthinkable would happen.

Willie C. and Pookie would both be ex-Spaniels. But neither would be the first to go.

"Opal had left before I did," said Willie C. "He went back to school and then joined the service. Ernest went to the service and he came back. Gerald went to the service and he came back. They were drafted when they were still with the group, but I was drafted after I'd quit. They all came back and kept on going."

Ernest left the group twice – first for the military and then for his religious work. According to Willie C., "he said God called him to preach.

"See these guys – Dimp, Donald and Parma Lee (Carl Rainge), they were an understudy group when we were first starting out, when we made our first record. They had a little group and they used to come to our rehearsals and listen to us sing. And they had been singing together a long time, and their voices really blended together well.

"So when the opportunity arose, they came into our group one by one. The Spaniels' sound then began to change a little bit, with that high pitch that Rainge had. He had that true tenor, he had a real high voice and they just had that sound that we didn't have before then.

"When we first started we sang doo-wop, and they came in and they began to sing melodies and a nice-sounding harmony."

But time heals all (or most) wounds. So Pookie rejoined the group after only a few months.

But Willie C. would wait 35 long years.

"We talked about Willie going back to the Spaniels, but decided he should stay with his job because he'll have a pension check after he retires (in early 1992), said Zola.

Zola Jackson, herself, retired early on disability from U.S. Steel in 1987 after 26 years.

* * * *

"I just had to sing," said Billy Shelton, who, with his son, Teddy, were the last to join the reborn Spaniels of the 1990s. Added Billy, a slightly older schoolmate of Pookie, Gerald, Willie C., Ernest and Opal, who declined to join the original group in 1952:

"I was destined to be a singer because I loved it. Have

you ever done anything that you said, 'That's for me?' Well, that's how singing came into my life.

"I grew up at the time of the Ink Spots, the Mills Brothers – groups like that. Way back. As a matter of fact, when Pookie and I started, that's what we were basically doing – the ballad-type songs. So I love it.

"I feel this way: I think that happiness is when you can get paid and make a living doing something you'd be doing free anyway. That's the way it is with singing. I'd be singing in the bathtub, walking up and down the street singing at every opportunity.

"Now you take the Spaniels," Billy continued. "In a professional way, when they first started, they sang from feeling. I followed their career and they certainly had to rank among the top groups of their day. Later on, when Parma Lee (Rainge) and Donald Porter and Dimp (Cochran) came into the group, it added. It kind of was a revolution. It made the group more high-tech than just soulful, and I had to recognize that. It made them technically even better.

"Songs like 'Stormy Weather' and things like that. Some group even named themselves after that record (Henry Farag's group on Canterbury). The Spaniels became more of an exciting group. Dimp was one of the best choreographers in the business. All the guys were stars when they came into the group. And I think Dimp did the dancing and it just made 'em red hot – a group to be reckoned with, you know. When the Spaniels first started they weren't like that," Billy emphasized.

And his favorite Spaniels record?

"Peace of Mind," he answered, unhesitatingly.

"Gary is a quartet town and 'Peace of Mind' is kind of a spiritual. It goes back to the spiritual groups of old – the Golden Gates, Soul Stirrers, Pilgrim Travelers (with Lou Rawls), Swan Silvertones, Five Blind Boys and Spirit of Memphis, who later recorded 'Peace of Mind' with different words – calling it 'He Washed My Sins Away.'"

R&B was evolving from spirituals when the Spaniels were formed, preceded by the Three Bees (Billy, Pookie and Calvin Fossett) and, on occasion, Four Bees (with William Dooley or Joe Jackson, father of the Jackson Five).

"People mainly wanted to steal Calvin's clear, bell tenor," Billy said. "Pookie and I were the wallpaper.

"I was inspired by Paul Robeson, especially on 'Old Man River.'"

Billy said he got started with a gospel group because the bass singer was a drunk and was always about 45 minutes late. So Billy would get there early and sing until the man, named Beckwith, showed up.

The Blackwood Brothers, who sang with Elvis near the end, featured the deepest bass he ever heard – J.D. Sumner. "He could hit low G and tutored Richard Sterbin of the Oak Ridge Boys."

After moving to Gary in 1948 from Chicago's Oakwood Boulevard – from which an impressive number of musical stars hailed – and hooking up with Calvin and Pookie, Billy already had discovered that "music is my life. That's all there was to it.

"We grew up together and that's when principles were established. We learned then that we were to be brothers. In other words, whatever one had, the other would have. We shared with each other. It was more than just singing.

"In those days, Pookie liked the smooth, Ink Spots-style of music and I was a fiend for that type of music – everything smooth and no strain. In the '40s, that was the standard of music. That's the time when a singer had to be articulate. He almost had to sound white in his delivery. And with the coming of rhythm and blues, it became more of a natural sound.

"Back then, I had very little respect for groups like the Clovers because I had to compare 'em with the Ink Spots and I'd say, 'Well, that nice but . . .' Now it took me all these years to see that it was necessary and it was coming. It's like going back to the grass roots.

"So Pookie, having the ideas that he had, and me and Calvin, we like the real close harmony. I think that was the nucleus for the Spaniels who later formed. These guys used to come and listen to us; come to rehearsals. We all sang in the Boys Glee Club together and Mixed Chorus, so it was a camaraderie developed there.

"I don't mind saying that I was very stupid at that time –

and I think that probably Calvin made a bad move because we had something; we could have actually been the original Spaniels. Calvin came from the other side of the tracks. His family had pretty good money and wanted to send him to college.

"At the time, Pookie was about to graduate and he didn't want to end up workin in the mill," Billy went on. "Out of the three of us, Pookie had the foresight. I didn't. At that time, I knew I loved to sing out but I didn't think we had a chance to make it. I really didn't.

"So Calvin went to the Navy and that kind of busted us up, and I moved back to Chicago to get a job. And it left Pookie by himself. Well, the guys who were coming around listening to our rehearsals – Willie C. and Gerald and all of them – they liked Pookie. As a matter of fact, they liked our group. So they told Pookie, 'Look, we'll sing with you,' because Calvin and I graduated one year before Pookie – in '52 – so that left Pookie with the other guys at the school. That's how the Spaniels got formed.

"Later on, Pookie came to me and asked me to come to the group," Billy recounted. "I'd say this was 1954. Now I was in college then and all the time I'm thinking I can't cut the mustard (with the group). These guys have been out there on the road. This was really the reason. I used the college thing as an excuse. But I turned Pookie down then, and that was another mistake I made. So this is like a chance for me to really get back in.

"I was very surprised that they would come to me last year (1991). Gerald and I have been very close and it's a funny thing. I'm really a bass singer. I've got a good range. Teddy's the same way. He can sing all the parts and so can I, but at home being a bass singer, it's really wierd that I really respected Gerald as being that guy.

"Gerald was the guy that pushed 'em. Willie C. is the guy that kept the group together. Each guy had a function. And so, Gerald, for years he bore the burden of the group, pushing 'em. I think Gerald mentioned to the guys, 'What about Billy Shelton?' because they were only one guy short. So they thought about me and they called me up and I told them: 'This is an opportunity for me. I'm glad I can walk into a group that is not only established but legendary.'

"And I feel I should be part of the group because of the history. I knew the guys and they all had respect for me just like I had respect for them. At that time, Parma Lee and Donald Porter were in the group – they were the Spaniels, so I was the low guy on the totem pole and I had to learn the baritone. Dimp has had throat problems and hasn't been able to sing. He hasn't even been able to go to work. For some reason he didn't come back with the group because there were talking about the group going into the Hall of Fame at the time.

"That (second) group didn't go into the Hall of Fame, but it was so much good publicity off of it that they had a little tour lined up and needed one other guy.

"So I seized that opportunity," Billy emphasized, "and I thanked them for considering me because they didn't have to. It was a lot of guys who would give their right arm to walk in there. And through fate the way the Lord would work it, because Donald Porter, who lives in Boston, would have to fly in here any time we had a gig. So we had to turn down lesser paying gigs for that. He was just too far from the rest of the group and that's the trouble that he was going through.

"Later on, another article came out in the newspaper and these guys got the letters in the mail that they were going to be in the Rhythm and Blues Hall of Fame but they only wanted the originals. And the original group consisted of guys that we have now, although the other group had done so much to keep the group afloat. And when they went down there and got their awards, somebody came up with the idea of getting back together."

Were Porter, Rainge and Cochran upset about the origni-al background singers being recognized instead of them, since they made most of the Spaniels' records?

"I haven't talked to any of them, but Pookie told me that Donald (Porter) called him from Boston to congratulate him," Billy said. "But I imagine they probably felt the same way that the original group felt when they (second group) were out there on the road. You know, life works like that. I think you get what's coming to you sooner or later.

"So that was the group – the Donald Porter, Parma Lee and Dimp arrangement of the group – which actually made more records and they stayed out there longer. They were the high-tech group and the group people normally think of. But that's the way it is."

Billy went on to say that the late 1980s and 1991 reincarnation of the group "was having a lot of internal problems in the last year. The distance thing with Donald was one. Then it was a personality thing. These guys were 'up' all the time. I mean, nerves. The group had stopped rehearsing for years, because they had gotten so much experience on the road that they really didn't need to rehearse. They could go out just from the experience and do a good show.

"But that was one of my criticisms," Billy emphasized. "I believe in hard rehearsing; that you're only as good as your last rehearsal. And I think that how good a group is can be figured by how many rehearsals you've had. That's what makes you. So they didn't rehearse. They were always good, but not what they should have been.

"The original group, that's all they know to do is rehearse because that's how it all started. We sang whenever we got a chance – in the toilet, walking down the hallways. So it's like going back home to the grass roots.

"So I think those guys (the second group) are probably happy for us. Whatever happens – if there's an opening or something – then they're all ready. They can just walk in because they've been there. I think it's like sweet-sour. But being an entertainer, I know they want to be up there on the stage performing instead of watching the show."

And how did Billy feel over all the years when he wasn't actually a Spaniel in name, and the group was making so many big records?

"I felt like I should be with them and I was proud. I felt each person deserved what he got because they all really toed the mark. I didn't have to suffer with them in the bad times. I was always starting up a new group. That was just my life. And by the time the group would get good then they'd break up or the guys would get the big head.

"But I've been so busy because I've always been singing one way or another, you know. But at the same time, I kind of wish I could have been with the guys."

Teddy Shelton, Billy's son and music director-guitar player of the present-day Spaniels, said he was "about 4-years-old as far as I can remember – around 1965," when he first heard this kind of music.

"To be honest about it, I really didn't think much of the '50s groups," he noted. "On a lot of the recordings I would hear, the singers would be flat or the instruments would be untuned and it bothered me. While in the '60s, they kind of got it more together. I don't know if it was the technology or what. It really didn't move me at the time. I was used to listening to high-tech singers groups like the Hi-Los and the Four Freshmen. I really didn't learn to appreciate it until I got older and I realized it was the simplicity that made it so great.

"Now, I think if the old stuff, done exactly like it was and maybe cleaned-up a little, will sell today. Everybody's tired of what's going on now. There's just so much stuff. The mixing, you know, and the scratching and all of that. There's just something about the simplicity of original R&B that really says something."

How does young Teddy feel being a part of the tradition of a group like the Spaniels?

"It's an honor for me," he said. "It really is. I met Pookie probably about '83 or '84, but I felt I knew him all the time because my Dad would talk about him all the time. So he was like an uncle to me before I even met him. And I really felt honored the day he called and asked me if I'd be part of it. That really did something for me. It kind of inspired me to work hard and get things together for what I have to do from my position in the group.

"I feel what I do with the Spaniels is quite important. Singers always have gotten over bigger than musicians. But if the music's not correct, then singers can look awfully bad. You have some bands that start at the wrong key, the wrong tempo and it's just a catastrophe. So what I do is important," Teddy stressed.

"He not only keeps the band in check and talks to them, he's also a singer," said Bily. "So that gives us a backup voice in case anything should happen. We've got a fail-safe operation here where we can always go on and perform no matter what.

"I'm very proud that the guys considered him to be part of the group. Pookie is the one who asked him directly to join. I thought that Pookie would have him in the group but more or less as a free-lance musician. But Pookie thought enough of him to let him be a Spaniel.

"And that's really great. I'm just happy because out of all my kids – and we don't see everything eye-to-eye all the time – we're together.

"We work together and we're performing together," Billy said. "I can start singing a song he's never heard before, and he just falls right in and starts playing it and it's ready to record.

"We feel we can, just like Pookie and I through the years. So I'm very happy and I'm really excited about our strategy for the future."

EIGHT
Pookie

"I think Pookie is one of the great ballad singers of all time. If the Spaniels had gone in the direction, say, of the Platters and done more ballads – instead of limiting themselves to rhythm and blues – I think the group would have been way on top." – Billy Shelton.

Of all the lead singers of the 1950s – the golden age of original black rhythm and blues – none could hold a candle to the phenomenal James (Pookie) Hudson. And this takes in a lot of territory and a lot of outstanding R&B performers. To wit:
- Sonny Til (Orioles);
- Clyde McPhatter (Dominoes, Drifters);
- Bobby Lester (Moonglows);
- Willie Winfield (Harptones);
- Rudy West (Five Keys);
- Tony Williams (Platters);
- Hank Ballard (Midnighters);
- Frankie Lymon (Teenagers);
- Dean Barlow (Crickets);
- Buddy Bailey (Clovers);
- Pirkle Lee Moses Jr. (El Dorados);
- Herbie Cox (Cleftones);
- J.R. Bailey (Cadillacs);
- Dallas Taylor (Danderliers), and many more great ones.

But there was only one Pookie.

Listen carefully to the Spaniels' stuff from the period and you'll hear his precise phrasing, his unique way of pronouncing words such as "baby," "cry," "love" and even "I'll" and "you." You'll hear him soar to the high notes and cruise to the lows. You'll feel the warmth and emotion oozing through on slow songs such as "Let's Make Up," "I.O.U.," "You Gave Me Peace of Mind" and "Here is Why I Love You." And you'll feel the rhythm reverberating from faster songs such as "Please Don't Tease," "Do-Wah," "Everybody's Laughing" and the astounding "Stormy Weather."

As is usually the case with the great ones in the entertainment industry, Pookie's star might have shone even brighter had not fate occasionally stepped in. One such instance was Vee-Jay's failure to permit the Spaniels to record "The Twist," which became a mega-hit for Chubby Checker.

The reason? It was deemed too suggestive.

"We were in Washington, D.C. at the time," Pookie recalled, "and a gospel group called the Nightingales called us down to their hotel room and sang "The Twist" and a couple of other tunes for us. Then they said, 'Look man, ya'll can put your name on this; ya'll can sing it, ya'll can have it. We can't sing it because we're a gospel group.'

"So we took it back and we did it word-for-word like they did it, but our company said it was too suggestive. I'm not too sure that we didn't record this song. We may have recorded it and Vee-Jay Records has it some place. If it was, it was never released by us."

In retrospect, Pookie says "The Twist" would have been "much bigger for us that 'Goodnight Sweetheart' because it was upbeat and it became a dance. But when it was given to us, it wasn't given as a dance.

"It was basically a suggestive song.

"Hank Ballard and the Midnighters did it first," Pookie continued. "Hank had put his name on it as writer, but it basically was a suggestive situation and didn't go too big. The song didn't go big until Chubby Checker took it and made a dance song out of it."

The mere thought of Pookie's velvet voice leading the Spaniels on "The Twist" is enough to give you goose bumps. And who knows? With "Goodnight Sweetheart" and "The Twist" in their kick, the Gary, Ind. teen-agers-

turned mellow adult professionals might well be sitting
pretty – and rich – today.

* * * *

Professional near misses notwithstanding, Pookie's life
and career were full of ups and downs, like water seeking
its level. But it was the kind of stuff befitting a great talent
who never quite reached the summit, yet still became a musical legend.

Among Pookie's personal traits over the years was a penchant for falling in-and-out of love. And he lists this as one
of the key reasons he was able to write so many songs –
some 200 in all – many of which the Spaniels recorded.

"I always go to my head to write," he said. "And since I
was always in-and-out of love and getting ditched – I got
ditched a lot – I always found some reason to cry. And so
in crying, I found a way to write a song.

"I wrote a song called 'Once a Star, Always a Star.' I never thought that you'd ever be out of the business. I didn't
think there would be any ups and downs. I didn't know that
they could snuff you out as fast as they could put you in."

Pookie considers "You Gave Me Peace of Mind" his personal favorite. I wrote it as a gospel tune and the company
had me change a couple of words to make it contemporary.
In fact, Joe Hinton and the Spirits of Memphis did a rendi-
tion of it. They did it the way I wrote it. The company basically wanted to make a love song out of it.

"I wrote this on my lunch hour when I worked at a place
in East Chicago, Ind. called General American, making
boxcars. I worked at night and I used to watch the stars and
things and I wrote this particular song the way I felt it."

And of all Pookie's pleadingly emotional leads, none was
more visceral, more touching than "Peace of Mind" – a romantic R&B classic to this day.

Yet, despite his seemingly natural predilection toward
composing love songs and the God-given, silky smooth
voice which enabled him to connect emotionally with his
fans – especially females – Pookie continued to be unlucky
in love.

"Basically, man, I was really shy and retired so I really
didn't pay that much attention to women. I paid attention,

but I was always one of those fellas that would say if some certain person turned me down I'm going to be embarrassed. So rather than not be embarrassed, I would say nothing. Like I say, until I got high, then I'd talk to 'em. But a lot of them just came to you on their own, which made it easier to deal with.

"I've never been what you call a 'talker' – never been one who saw some woman and I'm gonna walk over there and I'm gonna talk to her. I've never been like that.

"With James (Dimple) Cochran, now that was his type of thing. He'd see a woman he wanted, he'd go over and talk to her. I don't care if she had her husband on her arm. He'd go talk to to her, one way or the other.

"I had my encounters. I had my share and a few other's shares. I guess I could call myself a womanizer.

"I didn't turn 'em down, if they offered it, and there were a few that did."

But he did turn down LaVern Baker, he was reminded, speaking of the fabled R&B songstress of "Tweedley Dee" fame.

"But LaVern was just not my type. LaVern was real boyish, real mannish. She was really, a 'take charge' woman. She wanted to call the shots on everything, you know. Let's put it that way. I didn't know how to take LaVern. Of course, this was at a time when I was 18, 19. I didn't know about no women. She was a real pushy lady."

And she was much older than him as well.

"Yeah, and like I told you, she got mad at me and told me, 'You gon' go out there and fuck them young girls and they ain't going to give you nothin' but diseases, and you gon' mess with me, who's gonna' give you everything,' you know. She never really moved me. We were good friends, but she never really moved me that way."

But how about that scene you described in the hotel room? When she was there and you . . .

"Like I said, she was layin' up there naked and askin' me questions, you know, about how come I didn't want to be bothered with her. And I really couldn't tell her. I didn't think about it that way at that time."

Did he have anything to say to her at the Smithsonian's

Rhythm and Blues Foundation Awards in New York (Feb. 21, 1991)?

"It almost took her an hour to recognize who I was," Pookie replied. "When I told her my name, it took her a few minutes. All she said was, 'how you doin?', and then got to talkin' about her piles from all the sittin' down. She couldn't sit down."

How about other well-known ladies he was involved with?

"Well, there was that girl from the Staple Singers. I can't think of her name. That's a damn shame."

"Mavis Taylor?" said Calvin Fossett, an original member of pre-Spaniels' 'Three Bees,' who was sitting in on the interview in Pookie's living room.

"Who? Naw, not Mavis," Pookie said. "Her sister."

"Not Carolyn. You call her name, and I'll tell you. Let's see it was Mavis, her daddy Purvis, and what's that other girl's name? Not Carolyn, the other one. She did most of the singing with 'em. She's the oldest sister. Carolyn took her place. I got some letters some place with my Mom. She used to write me from all across the country. I was starving to death at the time (Pookie said her name was Cleotha).

"I moved back over to Chicago about '63, '64, and stayed at the Pershing Hotel before they tore it down. The Staple Singers' mama used to call me up and I used to go down there and do a little odd work for her and stuff in their house about four, five, six blocks from the Pershing.

"They knew what was going on. It was just before Vee-Jay went under.

"I used to go down to Vee-Jay and try to get some money out of them and I was tryin' to get some recordings by myself. I didn't know they was getting ready to go out of business because they had moved back to town. See, they were in California. Then they moved back down on Michigan Avenue after they had problems in California. That's when they was getting ready to go under.

"I never really dealt with the entertainers, never really. Most of those were taken anyway, you know, like that girl that sings "Tell Mama." The big girl. She's doing a lot of blues now. She's really having a comeback now .

"She's out in California now. Light skinned girl. What's her name? She's been on TV but basically, she's doing' a lot of gigs. She had a thing called "The Bells.""

"I can't think of her name now. She was goin' with Harvey (Fuqua) of the Moonglows.

"Wait.. It was Etta James.

"Yeah. But most of them girls, you understand, had boy-friends that were already in the singin' thing. Like I remember one time one of the Platters and one of the Flamingos and one of the boys in the Clovers were fightin' over the girl in the Platters. Zola Taylor, yeah. That was right down here at the Palace Theater, in Gary.

"So I'm sayin' that most of those girls that made names, had, you know, their men in the business – artists, you know – so you didn't do much messin' with 'em. So basically, the ones we messed with weren't really oriented as far as music is concerned."

Did he ever recall passing up offers of female companionship prior to a show – like an athlete in training?

"No. If it was offered, I didn't pass it up."

Chimed in Billy Shelton: "With his style of singing, you couldn't tell if he was tired or not. What difference would it make anyway?"

"And them gals stayed backstage," Pookie laughed. You found out that the ones that did, they were there for every show – not only yours. But I didn't know how to say 'thank you' and 'no thank you.' Nowadays if they approach you, flash the ring on your finger. They back off a lot. There was a few times in the last four, five years a few (who) would come around, but I'm not dealing with it like I was dealing with it then. And with all this AIDS today, I wouldn't dare."

Were many white girls coming around back in those days?

"There were a few. I've never been turned on to white girls. I've never really cared for 'em, so it's not much that I would do."

What about that time in Mexico you mentioned?

"You're talking about Juarez in 1957, '58. We were singing over in El Paso, so to pass the day, we went to Juarez. When you got over the border, you had these people who would take you out to different shows. They had the x-rated movies, and they'd run you through. And they had a place where they had this mule, a donkey. And somehow they would do something to him to make him have an erection that damned near touched the ground, and then they had this woman who would crawl on top of him and take most of the mule's penis. And she would do her act on the thing.

"Then they would take you from there to this bar, where at that time you could buy a fifth of gin or a fifth of most alcohol for a dollar. But in the back they had the prostitutes, and you could get a woman for a dollar. They had a nurse there who would take your penis and she'd feel it and she'd powder it down to make sure you had no diseases. Then you'd go in a room.

"I went into the room with one of these Mexican prostitutes I had and when I tried to enter her I was so big she started calling for the police. What happened, they said once they finish they use that alum to tighten it up. She was just too tight. She yelled 'Policia, Policia,' and about four of her pimps came in and they threw me out into the bar. They asked me if I was trying to ruin their girls. And I had to sit out and drink while the rest of 'em was in the back.

"But this was unusual on the road – even for us. We happened to be there and it happened to be an available situation so we tried it. This was the second Spaniels group. Everybody took part.

Was this the kind of thing most of the groups of that time would get into?

"Yeah, sure," he said. "If they had the chance.

"Used to be a time when I was younger, we'd go to the Howard Theater in Washington and I had 'em lined up out the door. I had about 10 or 15 out the door. And they would sit there until I would finish with each one and I'd take 'em in as they came, all night long. Every once in a while I'd sneak out during the show, because most of the tiem we would close the show and we'd have about an hour-and-a-half before we went on. But basically it was after the show.

"There were a lot of girls out of Howard University who used to come down. You know, we was young and dumb and drinkin' and carryin' on and really not realizing what we were doing. We were just into that sex thing at that par-ticualr time. Everybody who could find a girl took part."

You recall any other well-known female singers you made it with?

"Not off hand; I can't think of their names. But there was one young girl in the Hearts. I had an experience with her in Atlanta. I had talked to her and talked to her during this little tour we had and she finally consented to go to bed with me. And when I did I ended up splittin' her and they had to take her to the hospital.

"She was a virgin and they had to pull her vagina inside out and sew it back up. So no need to tell that she never came my way again.

"This kind of thing lasted throughout that period and I thank God it did. Because if it had happened now, with all this AIDS goin' around, we'd have been in trouble. I kept the clap at that time and I was just fortunate none of it ever turned into anything but that and I thank God for that.

"A lot of times I'm sorry I went through things I did when I did instead of really solidifying my position in life and trying to raise a family correctly. You know, trying to really be the light that the Lord asks us to be in His name because I definitely was not that light. And I was not really representing my people as I should have.

"I was only adding to the fallacy that white people feel that blacks are only lazy and all they want to do is lay and drink and they have no ambition. And truly I showed in my way even though I was singing, that my ambition was very small. And I love the Lord that He has let us live this long. Maybe we can't rectify that particular area, but maybe we can change things around and live the life we'd like to live in Christ's name."

Would he (Pookie) do things differently?

"Well, I don't know man," Pookie replied, "the way things are going today, I don't think I'd want to be too fast to do anything. The way the disease is going, you don't know who got it now. I'm truly fortunate.

"I didn't wear no drawers till I was 35. I figured it would slow me down when I was gettin' in bed with a woman. I've been married four times, got six children in marriage and about 94 out of marriage.

"That's a fact. I started counting. I'll take you to 'em. Every one that I know was presented to me, in one way or the other. At least, they acknowledged the fact.

"Never had a problem of being asked for support or money. Only time I had that was with my first wife, which I had to leave Gary because I ain't had no money then. All the other women I had children by have never asked me for a dime. And most of 'em went out and got married and the fellas took the kids on their own.

"I've had people come up to me, like in Philadelphia, a girl and her husband came clean across the street and said they named the baby Pookie, you know. The man standin' here, I'm sweatin' and I don't know why anyone would do this. And he was in awe of the Spaniels, you know."

"If I hadn't been with the Spaniels I'd still be married to the first wife. I think most of 'em just got tired of bein' alone, or whatever. And I don't know if it's because of being an entertainer, but I think just personally, I have a different outlook on life than a lot of people.

"If the situation had been different. If I'd been smart and she'd been smart, we would have waited. But that's hindsight. It's hard to even say that we'd still be married or not.

"Most women I have been with are realists. They see things as they are and I see things as they should be, or how I would like to see them, and I work toward that goal.

"But I had problems with one lady, one of those wives. You know, numbers was a thing with me. That was when they first started the lottery over in Illinois. And I played 'em and one time I hit for $5,000, you know, and I thought I couldn't lose. And damned if I didn't spend the $5,000 in the bank playin' the numbers. So that in turn left a bad taste in her mouth. A lot of times what I'd do, instead of tellin' her, I'd go get some money out of the bank and go play the numbers. I figured once I hit this number again, I'm gon' give her the money and she gon' be happy."

Does Pookie feel he would have fallen into a street life if he hadn't become a singer?

"I think I would have gotten a job. I was not cut out to be a crook. When I was a kid I used to try to steal and every time I stole I got caught. I've just been fortunate with the drugs never to get in a situation, you know. I thank God for that. If they didn't catch me then, they ain't gon' catch me now because I ain't gon' do nothin.'

"Luckily, we (the group) never were caught down South with drugs or alcohol, or we'd have really been in trouble. But one time, riding buses on a tour after we sang in Tyler, Texas, we were going to the next city and got down the road and the State Police pulled us over and nobody knew why.

"They got on the bus and went straight to this dude in the band. He had some reefer on him he had picked up on some woman the night before, and left some reefer with her, and she told the police. He was tryin' to throw it out the window when they got on the bus. So what they did, they didn't take (just) him, they took the whole busload of us back to Tyler. They paraded us through the jail.

"This was '57, '58. It was us, Buddy Johnson's band, or Erskine Hawkins' band, maybe LaVern Baker, a couple more acts. They put us in jail and they were hollerin' out: 'Yeah, we got a whole busload of them singin' niggers here.' After awhile some dude, Charlie somebody who was the man who was headin' the tour, got us out but couldn't get the dude out.

"I understand that dude got 12 years for smokin' reefer."

* * * *

Pookie was married the first time at 20 (she was 15) and they had a baby, in 1955 – the first of two children. "She was a child and I was a child and our marriage deteriorated. We had no idea of responsibility. The marriage failed and she moved back with her mama and them and I was staying in this apartment by myself," he explained.

His second marriage, came in 1967, when he was 33 and his wife was 20. That one produced two kids. His third marriage came April 1, 1980, at age 46, to a 26-year-old woman, and resulted in two more children.

Pookie's fourth union was Feb. 16, 1991, when he was 48. His fifth wife is Lillian, who was 39 when they wed on Jan. 22, 1993. At this writing , they make their home in the Washington-area with 2-year-old daughter, Jazmine, whom they also call Casey.

"My biggest regret is that me and the other members of the group were unable to provide for our families. I see other people today, in some instances, have done less with their lives than we've done but have profitted more. The've been able to get their mother's homes and things and we were never in that ballpark and never able to do those things."

One of the catalysts for Pookie's domestic problems was his admitted triple penchant for drinking, sex and drugs. In effect, he became a slave to each in its own addictive way.

"I was heavy into the wine, any kind of wine. Basically, it was whatever the fad was. One time it was apple wine, then there was port, then there was Wild Irish Rose when it first came out, and Thunderbird. All the wine and things. I had this false feeling of security that if I took a drink and I was high enough, then I would be able to perform better. I guess I was an alcoholic. I'd go to bed with it, I'd wake up with it. And I was a womanizer.

"I'd chase the women. I don't know, I loved women and I used what little fame I had to do those that I wanted, those that I could get. It meant a whole lot of children, which I'm sometimes sorry I brought into the world because most of 'em I didn't have a chance to even know or even help raise.

"As a youngster I liked to play basketball so I didn't drink or smoke or nothin.' I got into the drinking thing, truthfully, with Gerald, because Gerald drank. You know, he'd have a little wine or something and we'd go to rehearsal and buy a pint of dark port and we all take to drinking dark port and all five of us (Courtney didn't drink at all), we'd get a little high and it got to the point the high started feeling good to me, so I'd go out and buy me some more.

"I liked it so well I just had to have some every day. You know, one thing led to another and I was able to communicate better, I thought, especially with the girls. I was able to talk. Basically, I was shy, and I'd stay away from the girls. But I got to drinkin,' and I was able to get in their face and talk. I guess I used it as a crutch. And became a big crutch and I got to the point I depended on it.

"We always had our drinks backstage before we went on.

In a place like the Apollo, you do six, seven shows a night and you end up drinking six, seven fifths. You'd be drunk before you could think about it and it would be too late to worry about it.

"Basically, it didn't affect my performance much because if I got to the point I was too drunk they'd just stand around me and hold me up and let me sing. Bring me on and bring me off. And sometimes someone in the audience would say, 'Man, you drunk as a skunk.'

"It got where they would accuse me of being drunk when I wasn't drunk because they had seen me drunk so many times they just took it for granted. See, I've always had a problem – my eyes have always been like this, in a squint. When I first started singing with Billy and them – Billy and Calvin – they used to call me 'Sleepy.' So I always had the look like I was high, which I wasn't. So most times, you couldn't tell whether I was or not.

"I got a reputation of being able to drink, so I got to the point where I would try to prove that I could drink. Buddy Johnson had a dude playing drums named "Foots." When Foots would go to the restaurant, he'd order a breakfast like he was at the supermarket. He'd get a loaf of bread, a pound of bacon, a dozen eggs and 20 pancakes and eat all that mess up, and then we'd go out and drink. He would line his stomach, and I'd be ready to drink. While he'd be eating, I'd be drinking. And the idea was, that Pookie drank the most.

"Usually, I'd end up winning. 'Yeah, Pookie drank the most,' they said, and I tried to live up to that, that I could drink that much – not realizing that I was hurting myself, not helping myself. And alienating a lot of promoters because they didn't want nobody all drunk-up and that's what I was doing. I was hurting the group as much as I was hurting myself."

* * * *

And then Pookie launched into an incredible tale of what it was like to be a black R&B star who'd been screwed in the bad old days by the very people who were supposed to look out for him.

"For me, drugs came in down the line. I came into the drug thing – heroin, cocaine, reefer – about 1970. Well, I'd gotten married again and lost another job and things was really falling apart. I ran into some people in Philadelphia, some friends, don't know if I should call 'em friends or not, who were into drugs.

"A couple of 'em dead now. They knew I was in bad shape, didn't have no money and wasn't doing nothing. So they gave me a piece of the drugs and I took it back to Washington and started selling.

"I was selling heroin and I met some people who gave me some cocaine and I was selling cocaine.

"But in the process, I was watching everybody else messing with it, although I never messed with drugs; that's one thing I had never messed with until I was about 40 years old," he said.

"It got so big I started watching other people snorting cocaine and others snorting heroin. I said the shit couldn't be that bad, so I started and the next thing I knew I was hooked snortin'.

"I was always snortin'.

"So for about 2 1/2 years, I snorted heroin. And that came because we were gettin' it wholesale, you know. I didn't have to buy it, so it was readily available.

"I never shot it. But I mean, it's just as bad. When you're hooked, you're hooked, it don't make no difference.

The next thing I know I was in it big-time. I was sellin' it fast and furious – me and a couple of other people.

"The money was fantastic. Every weekend we had $8,000, $9,000 on the take. It got so good and I was dealing so fast, I made so much money. It got that good.

"Basically, we was sellin' to the dudes that was distributing. We'd make up packages and sell to them, and they in turn would go out and sell to the youths.

"I wasn't on the street selling. But in the meantime, watchin' everybody else snortin' and carryin' on, I figured I could do it too. That's really how I got hooked.

"And I knew it.

"One day, I was selling in Washington and some girl called me to bring her some stuff. She said she wanted some heroin. And I got stuck up in this place where a man put a shotgun in my face. When I got to her house I walked

in the door and these two dudes broke-in behind me. She
set it up. And they was talking about killing me if I didn't
give 'em these drugs and what money I had. I politely gave
'em the drugs and the money and they went about their
business. When I went home I quit – cold turkey.

"When he put that shotgun in my face, I said I can't deal
with this no more. When I got home, I told my wife, 'Look
here, I'm closing this door, leave me alone, I ain't talking to
nobody, don't bother me.' I stayed there for three days, I vo-
mitted, messed on myself, pissed on myself and saw some
blood stains. But when I came out of there I was clean, like
a brand-new man, and I had no more desire. And haven't
bothered with it since. And that was like 1973," he boasted.

"Before we get off the drug thing, I didn't want to tell
you around my wife, but two years ago (1989) I got hooked
into cocaine – I mean smokin' the cocaine, OK? This was
'89. I came up here (to Gary) because my mother's husband
had passed and she put my name on her bank book because
she had some money, which I'm givin' back. And I ended
up one month spending $10,000 of her money smokin' co-
caine, which I cut off, you know, once the money's spent.

"She was in the hospital and I took advantage of her. I
ain't gon' lie. She knows about it because I went straight to
her when it was over and stuff, which I replaced that money
plus some more. Right here in Gary. The fella I was gettin'
it from is in jail now.

"Hey, man, I don't know about now, but at that time, I
think everybody in town was sellin' cocaine. You could go
from one house to another and get cocaine in this town.

"I stopped because I didn't have the money," Pookie admitted. "Cocaine is a mind drug, it's not basically a body
drug. You don't really go into no . . . I mean maybe a day
you have discomforts. But smoking cocaine, you always
think about the high that you got – which is one hell of a
high, I'm not gon' lie – but it's always there; you always
think about that high from that cocaine. And that's the ad-
dictiveness of cocaine.

"And I tried crack. I did crack in Washington. I got the
best – from the people who brought it, on the boat from Ja-
maica, who pride themselves on the best stuff. But, naw, it

ain't too swift. But what happens is, it's who you buy it from, and good crack is the crack that you don't get addicted to, because it's only pure cooked cocaine. You got people who put it in different oils or put it in PCP and that's when you start having problems. So when you don't know who you're buying from is when you have trouble.

"Yeah, I was doin' freebase. And as far as what happened to Richard Pryor, hey, you know how that goes: It can't happen to me. And when you gettin' high, you don't give a damn who it happens to, you understand? You lose all your desire, man. And people be talkin' about all they did when they smoked cocaine. And they full of shit. All you thinkin' about is another puff of that cocaine, you ain't thinkin' about no pussy.

"I wasn't singing at that time. I could have. It wouldn't have been no problem singin'." He shrugged.

"In the group, our first drug encounter was with Gerald. He had gotten into the drug scene and tried to keep it from us. First he was smokin' reefer and he was doin' that pretty heavy. But he was doin' that during school. But as we got on the road, I remember one time we was headin' back this way from New York and our license plate was hangin' and they stopped us in New Jersey.

"They took the car and took us all down to this state police station. And for some reason or other – I'll never know – they searched everybody but the fella who was with us as a valet. We called him Doo-Doo. His name was William Downs. They let him go to the bathroom. When they couldn't find nothin', they let us go. Then I saw Doo-Doo sweatin' and I didn't know why.

"When he got in the car and Gerald asked him, 'Where's my stuff?' he said 'Man, I flushed the stuff down the toilet.' Gerald said, 'Man, you flushed my pile of reefer down the toilet?' See, we didn't know this man got this reefer.

"Doo-Doo said, 'Yeah, I ain't going to jail. If they end up searchin' me, what was I supposed to do with the reefer? I had to flush it down the toilet.'

"That was when we really realized that Gerald was into it as heavy as he was. Then through stories and other people, I found out that Gerald was shootin' heroin. Gerald was shootin' for a long time. I've seen Gerald shoot and walk around with a needle in his arm, and never take it out.

"(It was) back in the '60s. But he never did a whole lot of drugs around us – once he realized that we knew. But I have been in places where he was shootin' and it was natural for him to do.

"I don't think anyone else (members of the group) saw him but me. I was in his room and he just fired up, you know. And I guess he trusted me because I was always that type of person to say 'to each his own. If that's what you want to do, that's what you want to do.' And so he never had qualms doing it in front of me.

"But it was mostly heroin and reefer. In them particular days, cocaine wasn't really popular. It was such an expensive drug, more expensive than heroin. So most people stuck to heroin at that time that I knew.

"Finally, I think the habit got rid of Gerald. I think what happened was Gerald came back to Gary and he got on those long depressed times and he really didn't have no money and stuff, and then the stuff started gettin' bad. In other words, the stuff he was shootin' wasn't doin' him no good and basically he just kicked it. I mean he didn't have no choice but to kick it because he couldn't afford the good stuff and all he could get was the bad stuff and the bad stuff wasn't doin' him no good. So he started drinking the wine.

"To my knowledge, he hasn't been doing any drugs since then. But the drinking was going on with him – and me – throughout that period.

"Oh yeah, I was a big drinker. I got started during rehearsals. Sometimes we'd buy a pint of wine, you know. So we just stayed that way, I mean those who drink.

"Like I said, Courtney never drank as far as I know. Ernest, myself, Willie C. and Gerald, we'd take a drink . . . We'd drink this pint and we was feelin' good, so one pint led to another pint and at that time you (could) buy a pint of wine for about 40 cents. And it got so it was makin' us feel good and I was more outward after drinkin' because I was an introvert and drinkin' brought me out.

"So I drank basically so I could converse and be able to talk to people," Pookie continued. "But it never affected my singing. Everybody would tell me the same thing: I never missed a beat and never missed a note. But you could tell by looking at me that I was drunk.

"You see, we were successful in having records and things but not as far as makin' money. I mean we was doin' worse than most people who had a job, and basically, entertainers do much better than people who have jobs. In a way, maybe, deep inside, this might have contributed to my drinkin'. I don't know.

"But my thing was, I started a thing which gave me a reputation as being a drinker: That I could out-drink anybody in the entertainment business, and I went about tryin' to prove that at times.

"This was known throughout the business and a lot of fans knew too. And I got 'em now, you know, they'll say, 'Man, are you still drinkin'? Are you still gettin' drunk? I know you was so drunk, man, but you sang.'

"With me, personally it was alcohol which I went to bed with and got up with. Wine, whisky, whatever was available, I'd drink. And it was kinda' hard to shed the image for a long time. I finally got it basically to the point that most people know that I don't do no whole lot of drinkin' now. In fact, very seldom do I drink.

"We had problems with drinking in the second group. The same person who promoted the show the last time we were in Los Angeles – the one who gave our last show in Radio City Music Hall – was Tony DiLauro. He said at that particular show, Gerald was so drunk and they (Donald Porter, Carl Rainge and James Cochran) were so drunk that he didn't want to use us any more because it was not conducive to his shows.

"And he never did until we went to California and to Radio City (June 8, 1991) when we came back with the original group, with better attitudes, non-drinkers to the point where – like I say, Courtney don't drink, Billy don't drink, his son don't drink and once in a while I might take a shot and once in while Willie C. might take a shot. But Gerald is our problem continuously to the point that he still drinks. It effects his singing and it becomes a problem."

* * * *

In 1956, after Pookie left the group in the wake of the departures of Opal, Willie C. and Ernest for military service, he was asked to come back when the second group was floundering.

"Gerald and them came to me and said, 'Man, look here, Carl (Rainge) is hoarse and we need somebody to sing the lead.' They were working on a song Otis Blackwell wrote, 'Please Don't Tease.' At the same session we did 'You Gave Me Peace of Mind," which I wrote.

"From that time on, I was back with the Spaniels, and since then I've never been without the Spaniels."

Speaking of the great "Peace of Mind," of all the drama and heartache of Pookie Hudson's life with the Spaniels, perhaps none was more typical than the time he felt the need to sell this, one of his finest songs, for a pittance.

"And it was the only song I ever sold," he said. "'Peace of Mind.' I'd like to get that straight.

"I never sold 'Goodnight Sweetheart'.

"It was real cold in Chicago – I guess about zero – and I was walkin' past this bar goin' back to the hotel and they had this talent show. At that time, the grand prize was $10, and that was a piece of money. I had rented a room – they called 'em suites – at the hotel for $22.50 for the week, which is unheard of now.

"So I go in there and at the time, 'You Send Me' by Sam (Cooke) was out. So I sang 'You Send Me' figurin' to win the $10. And people came out of the audience to perform. And I lost."

And who did the great Pookie Hudson admire as the best of his peers? Who did he consider really outstanding R&B singers and groups in the Spaniels' heyday?

"Well, when we came along, of course, there was Sonny Til, and there was B.B. King, because they're the ones who really started the really soul-crying. He, and of course, Clyde (McPhatter). I liked the Clovers – Buddy (Bailey) and the Clovers.

"I was crazy about the Dominoes. I happened to see them on a couple of shows. I just liked their stage presence. That's when they had Clyde and they had Jackie (Wilson), you know, singing lead. I always thought they were fantastic. I thought they were top of the crop.

"There was a lot. You just can't name 'em all, and you hate to leave anybody out because there were some, like Rudy. You know, Rudy West of the Five Keys, who was great."

And the Five Satins?

"They were after us. They were way after us. And they basically did that one record thing, you know, 'In the Still of the Night.' But you know, there were the Flamingos; they had Nate (Nelson). And the Dells, with Marvin Junior. Then the groups as a whole, like Perk (Perkle Lee Moses Jr.) with the El Dorados. I liked Perk's voice. And Jerry (Butler) when he first started. He came right in behind us."

How would those groups – or the Spaniels of 1954 – do if they were around today and at their peak, given what's around today?

"We'd do great," Pookie emphasized. "If the music was acceptable and the people accepted it like they did then, I think it would be four times as great. We'd have big audiences and we'd do it all and make a lot of money.

"See, in those days, we would have what they call 'Battle of the Groups' shows. You'd have four, five groups on a show and everybody would be singin' their tunes and things. Sure enough, some of 'em you went to and all the groups sound alike, you know. But then you put the Flamingos, the Spaniels, Clovers, Five Keys, and say even Clyde and them on the show, you got five different, distinct groups. They were singin' five different types of music even though they were all classified rhythm and blues."

And today's rap?

"I truly, personally don't call that music. They say it's music but I say it's just somebody talking to a beat. Music to me . . . you have to be able to sing it, play it and be able to convey it without being explicit and downright nasty and you got to have imagination to be able to apply imagination. You have to have people listen and for them to be able to imagine what they want from it.

"In other words, they ain't got to get exactly what you're saying to form their own opinions. And it doesn't have to be, 'I got to take you to bed and snatch your clothes off and you got to suck my dick,' and all that. I don't think that's necessary. You can say what you have to say without going through that and I personally don't like it.

"By the same token, people are making a living out of it so what can I say? But some people don't like to think. Some people just like for you to tell them what they want to hear and they go along with it and don't have to think or imagine or put anything together. It's told to them like they want it."

Did Pookie ever think of going out as a single as other lead singers did?

"No, not at that time (the mid-'50s). We were a group and we felt like brothers and I felt if I did something like that I would have betrayed them. The company asked me to do so but I refused and told 'em I'd rather stay with the group so they never approached me with it again."

During the Spaniels' hey-day, in the the mid-to-late '50s, when they were constantly touring, they made one appearance in Hawaii.

"It was a big show in Honolulu," said Pookie, "but all we did was three or four songs and we were out of there. Las Vegas was a little different, but that was when they had 'blacks across the tracks.' You really didn't go into the white neighborhood. We played what blacks considered a casino in their area. They had dancing and stuff. We stayed in somebody's house instead of a hotel, but that was before blacks really started going there and spending money.

"My best memories of the group is the camaraderie between me and Willie C. We were real tight – more than anybody in the group. He stayed at my house, I stayed at his house; we ran together.

"And I fondly remember Gerald in the real early days. He was a little more conservative that we were at that time. He worked in a pool room and used to stay sharp all the time; always wore a suit – I don't care if it was real hot out – 90 degrees. Wore a suit, tie, white shirt, kept his face powdered. He didn't run with us.

"And I remember our shot on Dick Clark's *American Bandstand* in 1957. We did a song called 'Crazee Baby' which was just released. I just thought that we were ready to do a TV show. At that particular time it was new and it was being seen across the country, and we were just happy to do it. It didn't have no impact. We just didn't think like that, which was part of our downfall. We did not take those kind of things seriously."

Career-wise, what would you do different if you could do it again?

"Only way I could do it differently is if I could know then what I know now. The whole thing. Signing up, being in control of our situation. Having a decent lawyer.

"At that time, they didn;t have music lawyers and music law is almost a new law. Somebody you trust that would speak up for you, stand up for you. We all could have shared. Everybody could have been happy. Everybody could have made money. It just appalls me that someone feels they got to have it all and those who were responsible for making it didn't have none. I never could understand that.

"But we were great in our day," Pookie concluded.

* * * *

Pookie's fourth wife, Mamie, a 48-year-old (in 1991) Chicago native, came to Gary in January 1962 – the day of her high school graduation. Her mother was living in Gary.

She had always listened to the Spaniels and other R&B and would go to the shows at the Regal in Chicago.

She had lots of records. She admitted to being in "fantasy love" with Pookie; she loved his voice, and his distinctive sound. And when she couldn't find his records, she'd buy records by Walter Jackson, who sounded like Pookie.

Years later, in 1975, Pookie moved back to Gary from Washington and got married again in 1976. He and that wife moved back to Washington.

Meanwhile, Mamie moved to California early in 1986 for about a year to be with her ill mother, who died on Feb. 26.

In March of that year, she moved to Vallejo, Calif.

Coincidentally, Pookie was living in Los Angeles at the time, but she didn't see him.

Tiring of the Golden State, where she'd always worked as a nurse, Mamie returned to Gary in November 1987. She got involved in politics when a friend (Thomas Crump), who ran the nursing home where she worked, later ran for Calument Township assessor. She spent part of her time working in his campaign in the ladies' support group.

Mamie never saw Pookie after she got back in 1987 until he returned from his Virginia dairy job in 1990 when his father-in-law died. Her late husband, Lanny Heflin, owned Heflin's Blue Room Lounge and the Spaniels would always sing there when Pookie was in town.

She met Pookie there one night – introduced by Frank Ballard, 3rd District Councilman – during a political fundraiser. Ballard had flown in Pookie from Washington.

Mamie and Pookie became friends big-time – spending the night together.

They met often at the lounge after that, getting to know each other better. Mamie recounted one occasion when the Spaniels were supposed to sing there, but only Pookie and Gerald showed up. "So I got three ladies from the audience to sing background and they did a great show," she smiled.

Pookie proposed to Mamie on Aug. 4, 1990, in the car on the way to her boss' (Crump) birthday party. She laughed it off – telling him she didn't take him seriously. She had always had these feelings for him but no words ever passed between them until then. "But he wooed me with flowers he'd send to my job every day for two weeks."

The day she told her younger brother – a big Spaniels fan – she was going to marry Pookie, he said: "Oh, this is only infatuation."

They were married on Feb. 16, 1991 – five days before the R&B Foundation Awards – and went to New York, Philadelphia and Atlantic City on their honeymoon. The other Spaniels were with them on tour the whole time.

Sid Booker, who owns a three-floor lounge in Philadelphia and is a big supporter of Pookie and group – put on a big party in the couple's honor. Pookie had been the first act when the lounge opened in October 1990 and unlike many business types the Spaniels dealt with in their career, Booker demonstrated how grateful he was.

NINE
Split-up

"Ernest was drafted, Willie C. had his dispute and thought some money was being taken and stuff, so he quit. And after that I quit, so Gerald carried the group on. He already had Dimp, so like he said, he picked up Donald and Carl." – Pookie Hudson.

Like any close-knit, small group of guys, the Spaniels had their internal frictions. No matter how good things were going – or even how bad – their individual personalities and traits occasionally would become worrisome. Added to the fact that they were now realizing they weren't adequately compensated for their work, well, you have all the elements for a split.

The first serious crack in their collective armor appeared in the fall of 1954, during the nationwide tour that followed the second Apollo gig. The Spaniels were accompanied by Roy Hamilton, Big Maybelle, the Drifters, Faye Adams and Erskine Hawkins' big band. The last stop was in Rochester, N.Y. where they appeared on a Halloween night show with saxophone great Illinois Jacquet.

Opal Courtney Jr., who'd developed ongoing differences with Gerald Gregory, made a fateful decision to split from the group. And his memories of those days and his reason for deciding to leave after only two years, remain vivid:

"During this time, young person that I was, I had become disillusioned. The money wasn't there. You get pressured from home and there's inside pressure because – I don't know if it's arrogance or what – but I've always felt like I could do anything I want to do if I put my mind to it. And that rubs people the wrong way," Opal said.

"So being like I was, we had great internal friction. So when the friction became so that I . . . it just came to a head in Rochester.

"Something happened being out on the road," Opal continued. "I had to grow up real fast. Being 16, out on the road, handling money, handling situations a grown-up should have taken care of. We only had Pookie looking out for us."

Opal pointed out that Calvin Carter, Vivian's brother, was with them, as was Count Morris Wilkerson, the piano player. They both were adults. But the group needed more.

"You place a whole lot of faith in someone you think would know," said Opal. "Pookie and Gerald were the oldest. But Carter, he was the leader. He was the arm of Vee-Jay, supposed to be the overseer, the caretaker, whatever you want to call him. He took care of us, alright.

"We stayed at the Theresa Hotel in Harlem on our first Apollo gig – in two rooms with three people each. Calvin always had a separate room. From there, we'd play the five-city, five-theater circuit. We would do four or five shows a day to packed, all-black audiences.

"And we had money problems. We were out on the road without funds. Had we known it then, we could have farmed ourselves out for gigs at a reduced price. But we didn't concern ourselves with such things, or that separate contracts were being used."

Another problem, according to Opal, was the fast life of a young entertainer – especially when you're traveling.

"We'd come in contact with all types of people," he said. "They want to be around you because you are an entertainer, and many of them would like to be entertainers; they want to be around you for self-gain."

He said it was the "self-gain" type of people that one or two of the guys in the bunch would associate themselves with.

"Back then, it was narcotics – things like that. It was reefer and I think it was heroin. They put it in their arms; actually shot up.

"Let's deal with our bass singer" (Gerald Gregory)," Opal

went on. "This was back in the early '50s and he'd come in contact with these people and it came into play. I suspected this, because of the environment and the people he was with, but I never actually saw it. But he would have a personality change; he would go into a Dr. Jekyll and Mr. Hyde thing. I was the youngest but I've always been a real good judge of character. If you're around me every day, I can tell the differences, and I saw it.

"Quite a few of the group drank, too," he said, "but it was the narcotics part that scared me, because we were stopped so many times when we were on the road by cops – blacks, entertainers in a station wagon. If one goes, we all go. And that led up to why I actually left the group."

Opal strongly emphasized that he doesn't know of any other Spaniels shooting heroin.

"Ernest and I were pretty tight," he said. "Willie C. has always been like a rock. Pookie has always been low key; if he does something you'd never know it. Back then, I can't recall anyone going on stage messed up. Everyone always did their jobs.

"But the crowd, that would always be around. I would not associate with them. A few people came backstage, but the hookups most of the time were females. There were a lot of females; lots of introductions and things like that. You saw a few fellas, but not many. To this day, if it was a matter of life and death I might say no. But it was just how I suspected things; my suspicions."

Opal's status as the group's youngest member also was a factor.

"I questioned some of the actions toward me because I was so very outspoken as a youngster. But even though I was young, I met a lot of people and I had a lot of confidence in myself. I confronted, quite a few times, that individual (Gerald) directly about drugs and he said, 'You don't know it. What do you know about it? So you leave it alone.'

"But it got to the point where it was a head-on conflict with Gerald and I. And as of today, in 1991, there still is a conflict with Gerald. A barrier has been built up – not by me – but by him, I think. As far as me as an entertainer, as far as me as a singer, Gerald said: 'This is a hobby, and it's not dedication.'

"Sure enough, everybody is not as dedicated, to have stayed (as Gerald did). That's a long time – from 1954 until now; that's 37 years. But your lifestyles change and I saw that when I left – in Rochester, N.Y., at Halloween time, 1954."

Opal recalled that their differences over Gerald's behavior and associates had become so pronounced that they almost developed into physical confrontations on several occasions.

"We had to almost go to blows, and I think I weighed 98 pounds soaking wet in those days," he laughed, "and I wasn't big as a . . . but I had a big mouth and I was arrogant. I've always believed that if I want to work for you I can associate with you, but I don't have to spend my life with you.

"As an entertainer, you cannot be out on a corner with the boys like Gerald does," he continued. "All of that. You have to be just a step above. You have to be able to hold something in reserve if they have a question about as far as, 'Hey, let's go and see them sing.' But you can't hang out on the corner with the boys and expect the boys to come and pay to see you."

Ironically, Opal said he wasn't dissatisfied with the group's pay situation because he didn't know enough about it and wasn't with the Spaniels long enough at the time to recognize it.

"When I got with them, we went to the Apollo, and right after that they put us on the Roy Hamilton show and we were on the road all summer. And then we went to New York and the money ran out. But still, as a youngster, you don't believe that someone who is supposed to be in your corner is actually not in your corner. You're just that naive."

Opal said he didn't realize what had been going on about getting shortchanged on money until after he left the group.

"We stayed at the Coleman Hotel in the black part of Newark after being invited to entertain there. They had two adjoining rooms for us. It was right before I quit. Screamin' Jay Hawkins was there, too. And we were going back-and-forth to New York for the Apollo.

"Calvin was staying at his suite in the Theresa Hotel in New York. Our food ran out but the people in the hotel were very gracious. We were just waiting for the company to send us some money so we could get back home. Finally, we got some handouts from Father Devine's mission down the street. It was horrible."

The combination of suspected drugs within the group, drinking, and the constant, unwelcome attention (from his viewpoint) of hangers-on, finally convinced Opal to split.

"Nobody knew I was going to quit," he said. "We played a gig in Rochester and got back to Gary on Oct. 31, 1954. It was a Wednesday. We'd had – me and Gerald – we'd had our little argument, and being from a close family, I came home and talked to my mother about it. And if you've ever seen your mother cry, about something that you could control . . . Well, it's a hurting thing to see.

"I went out to Roosevelt High School that night, hair conked to the bone. I had no intention of leaving the group, but I went out to see a movie. They showed movies at school on Wednesday night. Mr. (Warren) Anderson, the principal, said, 'Hi, Courtney. How you doing? How's the group?' that kind of small talk. 'When are you coming back to school?' I said, well I'll be back tomorrow. He said 'Come on in the office,' and he grabbed my hand and I enrolled in school at 10:30 that night and I never regretted it."

More irony: This was the night before Milo Merritt became the Spaniels' lawyer and helped grease the skids for their slide down the financial drain.

And did Pookie or anybody else try to talk him out of leaving?

"Not really," he replied. "Someone might have said, 'Hey, now don't do it.' But I'm sure they knew why I left. It was the confrontation between Gerald and I. I just couldn't take any more of him. On the road being with him for a period of time; if water gets up to your nose . . . And then when I came home and my mother and I talked about it and I saw her cry . . ."

In retrospect, Opal feels that if Gerald had been a different kind of person, he might have stayed with the Spaniels.

But the conflict was too big and it's still there, he said, as of this writing (1991).

* * * *

In 1955, Willie C. got married. Except for the younger Opal, he was the last member of the group to do so. And to a large extent, his marital status triggered his departure from the Spaniels.

According to Pookie, Willie C. at the time "had this little problem. He'd gotten married and he thought the money was being taken; that we (me and Gerald) weren't being honest about the money. This wasn't true between me and Gerald. We were being taken through the record company.

"Vee-Jay sent us to California in April 1956 on a tour with the El Dorados by car," Pookie continued. "We had to drive all the way from Gary and they paid us $100 apiece. Out of that, we had to pay our hotel bills and we had to eat and stuff. We was out there two, three weeks and ran out of food."

"I'll never forget when we got stuck out in California," Willie C. said. "That's when I made my decision to leave the group. We were waiting for our pay to come through. And I got hungry. We were really hung up out there. No way to get home, no money. That was a horrible experience. They lied to us about sending us money, so I just made up my mind. I said I'm tired of this. I got a wife home, no money to feed her and no money to feed myself. No food, and I remember I had one orange – eat part now or save it for later. You could just hear those hunger pangs . . . errr.

"And no royalties. If you had royalties coming in, you might could survive. Our payday, we were supposed to get paid for the last gig. At that time we were with Gale Booking Agency. They would send the money to Vivian (Carter) and she would send it on to us, but this time we didn't get the money. It looks like if you're making money for somebody they should try to keep you happy. This is what I could never understand.

"So I decided that when I get home I'm going to get me a job. And I did," Willie C. went on. "I told Pookie first. Then when we got home, I told them I was finished and I told Vivian Carter. She was very angry. She told me that I broke the contract and I'd never sing anywhere else again on no labels. She said I was lucky that she didn't sue me. We were under a six-year contract – with three more years to go. She threatened me in a lot of different ways, but it didn't matter. What could she sue me for? I didn't have nothing. She already had all my money.

"The group was doing well, but I guess at the time it was more that it was a little pride, too. I had been saying I wanted to take care of my family and I was unable to do it. And I wanted to do this real bad," admitted Willie C. "And now, we had been out there for a little while, we found out that it takes money to live and you have to have it. I just said that I got to do something."

"Willie C. recalled that Pookie talked to him about the future. "He said, 'Well, hang on there a little while longer.' He said, 'Things are going to get better.' He said, 'Later on in life, your kids will grow up and say 'My daddy used to be a Spaniel . . . He could be one now but be quit. What do you value about that?'"

Willie C. said: "Well, right now, I got to get a job. Thinking the way maybe a young person would think. I felt the pressure was on me; I brought it on myself. My wife, she never said anything about me quitting. She wanted me to keep on.

"Then I said I was going to be gone for six months. Then they got Donald (Porter), because Dimp (Cochran) had already been in. I wanted to go back in the group but I never did – for years. I regretted it a million times over."

*   *   *   *

According to Gerald, the original Spaniels didn't stick together mainly due to domestic difficulties.

"We actually split up a number of times," he said. "For instance, the first time we broke up my lead singer (Pookie) and Willie C., whose house we're in now, had a double-wedding. Then the two couples began to share a house.

"It's a shame that the wives at the time didn't want their husbands on the road singing. I guess they were afraid they might, you know, lose 'em one way or another and they wanted them at home. They wanted a regular job for 'em and they (Pookie and Willie C.) loved 'em enough to give up singing.

"It took me quite a while to forgive the fellas for doing it – for leaving me by myself like that," he continued. "It really hurt me, and that's when I got Carl, Dimp and Donald – Carl Rainge, James Cochran and Donald Porter. And that started the new group."

After Ernest left in March 1956 – and before the second group was formed – Pookie asked Billy Shelton to join. And Billy, who later wished he'd never left Pookie when they were part of the Three Bees, regrettably declined the invitation.

The group went with four singers after that. Ernest was replaced by Dimp Cochran. They recorded sporadically until Willie C. left in April 1956 – followed shortly thereafter by Pookie.

"The way things were going," said Pookie, "It wasn't going to improve if they had stayed. It would have been the same thing. Courtney went on to the service, and was replaced by Calvin Carter, Vivian's brother, for two months or so. But he had no real talent. His voice was lost int he background."

Thus, the original Spaniels were no more – not to be reunited until 1991. But the Spaniels were not dead. Not by a long shot. The second group was born.

And it was pure dynamite.

TEN
Second Group

"I think that all the years' experience that we (the second Spaniels) had together, they (the original, reunited Spaniels) have a long way to go to come up to what we did. For example, we broke-in singing all their songs. They haven't been singing for a long time so they not only have to reacquaint themselves with their songs, they have to learn how to sing our song." – Donald (Duck) Porter.

The debonair looks and demeanor of Donald Porter belies the nickname "Duck," hung on him by his fellow Spaniels during the group's glory years in the mid-to-late 1950s.

Porter , whose soaring second tenor lifted the Spaniels unequaled background harmony on hits such as "You're Gonna Cry," "Stormy Weather" and "You Gave Me Peace of Mind," began his serious singing career in Gary at age 15 with another future Spaniel, James (Dimples) Cochran.

"It was just the two of us at first," Porter recalled. "Both of us are from Chicago and we each moved to Gary. The next thing I know he was living on the street across from me and we met each other and realized we had Chicago in common.

"Dimp sang spirituals with a Chicago group and also had performed in Gary many times. There was a spiritual group in Gary called Jordan's Five Trumpets that immediately drafted him as the lead singer. I subsequently became his best friend and started to go around with the group, and he actually taught me the basics of how to sing. That's how I learned spirituals.

"About that time, Dimp and I formed a group called

page 117

the Medallions, and we sang around Gary doing Clovers' songs, Flamingos' songs and Drifters' songs. We would also do a lot of Sam Cooke records because Dimp grew up right in the neighborhood with Sam. And the Flamingos were also from that neighborhood in Chicago.

"I didn't know Pookie or the other guys – except for Gerald Gregory," Porter said. "They were older than me. I knew of them. I liked their sound and they compared favorably with the other popular groups – the Moonglows, Clovers and others."

In late '55, the original Spaniels broke up. Porter was recruited into the group by Dimp in June 1956, at 18, after graduation from Gary Roosevelt High. Cochran and Carl Rainge had earlier been recruited by Gerald after Pookie left, and they needed another voice.

"Gerald was actually looking for a guy who used to sing with the Five Echos to step in and sing," said Porter, "but Dimp told him, 'I've got a guy that can sing right now. We've been singing together for a couple of years and I trained him. He can come in and sing a part.'

"Then Gerald asked me if I'd be interested and I said yes. So we started performing as the Spaniels. Carl was singing lead and Dimp and I were singing background with Gerald on bass.

"We stayed at the Coleman Hotel in Newark while touring on one-nighters down in Virginia and further south into Alabama for a few months. It wasn't too successful and sometime people would say that except for Gerald, 'Ya'll ain't the Spaniels.' Had it not been for Gerald sometime, we might've got jumped. They had pictures out with Pookie and when they looked at all of us, they didn't see the Spaniels. They said, 'Well, where are the Spaniels?'

"So we went home and we all suggested that we get Pookie. He was working at the General American boxcar plant in Gary, where they make railroad cars. So we picked him up from work one day. When he got in the car, he said he had a song, 'You Gave Me Peace of Mind.' He sang that for us and it became the first one we recorded together, with 'Please Don't Tease' on the other side.

"'Peace of Mind' was a big hit among black people,"

Porter said. "It almost became No. 1 in all the major cities on the black charts. After that, we made 'I.O.U.,' 'Everyone's Laughing,' 'I Lost You,' 'You're Gonna Cry,' 'Crazee Baby,' 'I Need Your Kisses,' 'Here is Why I Love You,' Gerald's 'Heart and Soul,' 'Stormy Weather . . .'

"Of all those, 'Everyone's Laughing' was the biggest on the charts. There was a brief period when Lester Williams was singing bass in place of Gerald when Gerald had his non-support problem. They came and got him – arrested him in Greencastle, Ind. during a show, while we were on a big coast-to-coast tour out of New York with the Drifters.

"Lester fit in alright, but there was only one Gerald. So when he came back everything was fine.

"We went on Dick Clark's 'American Bandstand' in '57 and sang 'Stormy Weather' and 'I Lost You,' and in '58 behind 'Crazee Baby, which was just released. We did local TV in places where we were appearing on tour – like Washington, Baltimore, Philadelphia. We were on local TV quite a few times in towns where we played."

Porter and the rest of the Spaniels broke up in 1959 and in the interim, he got married and joined the church in Boston, where he has lived ever since. But needless to say, the end is nowhere in sight for the second coming of the legendary Spaniels. In 1973, they got together again and began touring.

Said Porter: "I contacted Pookie, Gerald, Dimp and Carl and we worked quite frequently – at discos, and we would do R&B revival-type shows for mainly white audiences, and at colleges. We didn't cut any records except for the ones at Canterbury with Henry Farag, when he tried to update some of our old stuff.

"I know we didn't get a real shot during this period. The main reason I found was that the record industry had a different outlook and a different caliber of music. They had no appreciation for us and what we sang. I had gotten a tape together and I was running around trying to get us a recording contract, and they really wouldn't give me the time of day.

"We continued to perform sporadically in the '80s. We all had jobs and I became a security guard in Boston."

Aside from having the opportunity to sing for a living, Porter considers touring with the group the best thing about his years with the Spaniels.

"I got to see the whole country during our travels on tours over the whole United States," he said. "And we did what was called 'The Biggest Show of 1956' on a tour. The biggest thrill for me was to visit every major city. The tours were predominantly black, but we did have one or two white artists.

"And I was in on the transition from rhythm and blues to rock 'n roll," he continued. "It was on the first tour when they began to try to call us rock 'n roll artists. They had artists on the tour like Bobby Charles and Cathy Carr who made 'Ivory Tower,' and the Everly Brothers, with 'Bye, Bye Love.' So what we experienced when we went down South is that black and white artists could not perform on the same show.

"Another instance I'll never forget was at this particular place in Alabama. They had a white audience on one side and a black audience on the other side and we were playing to the wall. We almost had a riot because when the curtain came up and we got out on the stage we turned toward the blacks. They had to call out the state troopers because the white audience started throwing eggs.

"And, of course, we always had to use the black – the colored – facilities in the black part of town. You know, for lodging. We had to go to the back of places to get served, to eat; things like that. This kind of thing never happened up North."

Porter's second iteration of Spaniels was not included in February 1991 when the group received Lifetime Achievement Awards from the Smithsonian Institution's Rhythm and Blues Foundation. He said this didn't matter much to him, but you could tell it really did:

"Well, in reality it didn't bother me because I thought the original group should be honored. I came in on the foundation they had established. So they deserved to be acknowledged for having made the original records. On the other hand, I think the honor should have been extended to us because we performed more than they performed and we're the group that went all over the country. We sang for more people and there should have been an acknowledgement for that. Both of us should have been accepted."

Did he feel Pookie should have asked him and Rainge and Cochran – the prolific second Spaniels – to be the reborn group after the Smithsonian Awards?

"Yes, I do. To be frank about it, they, uh, when we came into the group, we brought the expertise of knowing what we were doing. We added a different . . . I would think we improved the quality. So Gerald and Pookie didn't teach us anything. Also the choregraphy. James Cochran, Carl and I came in and put together all those songs. There were many times when we actually showed Gerald how we wanted the bass. They (the first group) more or less sang at random. Nobody had a distinct part. And some of it came out real good.

"But when we came in with specific, designated . . . you're first tenor, and I'm second tenor and I'm baritone. These are the distinct parts that you sing. And it worked very well for us."

Thus, Porter obviously feels his version of the Spaniels was superior to the original.

"Yeah, it's not hard to prove," he said. "That's just a matter of practice. I think part of it is by virtue of us coming from that operative, spiritual background, and that James Cochran and I had a group before that and were able to perform and sing other group's songs, note-for-note. We brought this experience and know-how to the Spaniels, which at that time they did not have."

Why then, he was again asked, did he think Pookie opted to go back to the original group for the most recent comeback? Could it be due to reported friction between your (second) Spaniels and Pookie over how he wanted to do songs and how you wanted to work?

"Well, Pookie has always been the kind of guy that kind of goes slow. Gerald is not inhibited. He leans toward creative stuff. I think Gerald . . . I know Gerald would have preferred that it be us. Plus, even, well, what can I say. Pookie, just . . . he wasn't quite straight with us.

"First of all, we didn't know what he was going to do.

Second of all, I'm the one who instigated the whole thing with the Rhythm and Blues Foundation. I'm the one who was in contact with 'em. I'm the one who did the initiating and the organizing. Pookie could come into contact with my contacts and begin to deal with them as the lead singer.

"I think for it to be acknowledged properly, he should have insisted that we be involved. When you go out and buy the Spaniels . . . well you don't buy a record so much anymore, you buy an album. And the songs on there – half of which if not most – are the songs we made," Porter insisted.

Are there strained feelings because of this?

"Here's what I'm saying. I haven't talked to Pookie since the induction (by the Smithsonian) and he did it on the QT. And here I am sending you (the author) pictures, and I'm working on things, and here all of a sudden he does this without me even knowing about it. I can acknowledge that fact with the rest of the guys. I even had a program under which I wanted us to get all the group back together anyway and take all the credit. So as far as I'm concerned the whole idea is still working for the group."

Would he entertain a proposal to get your three guys back together with Pookie and Gerald even now?

"Well, in other words, as a result of the way he (Pookie) did what he did, and left us out and called the shots and didn't even tell us, it'd be hard. What I want to do is . . . I mean I can understand they want to . . . Pookie might want to primarily go around and perform all over the place. My whole goal in the first place was when I got the group back together, my purpose was to try and find some way to get some money from our royalties. All these records we made. I had discovered that most of these people thought that we were dead. So one of my purposes was to prove that the Spaniels were still alive and kicking.

"And it goes way back," Porter said. "Vivian Carter, all of them. They gave us a raw deal. That was primarily because of Ewald Abner – the president. He's the one that helped Berry Gordy build Motown. He went to Motown after Vee-Jay and the last I heard of him he was Stevie Wonder's manager. But the point is, he's the one who literally sold out all the Vee-Jay artists. It ended up he was the one responsible for Benny Goodman's brother owning part of 'Goodnight Sweetheart.' . . . It was the whole nine yards.

"But the point is, we haven't gotten any kind of remuneration, royalty-wise yet," Porter continued. "I figure we're due a fortune. I mean enough for us to be millionaires. You figure that over the years, from the late 1950s till now, they've been selling our albums. Every year, there's a different version of our music coming out; a different combination.

"The official reason for our situation was because of what a black label did. It was a black label. And this is true of all the artists that were on Vee-Jay – the Dells, El Dorados – all the Vee-Jay artists."

And these days?

"I've been trying to put together a video to help educate today's kids about our music. I've been in touch with my friends the Dells and the El Dorados and the Flamingos and I'm going to start the video off telling about the origination of doo-wop. We're going to come and shoot. I was hoping to get Pookie but if I don't, I've got some footage on Pookie. But I'm pretty sure I'll get Gerald, and I'm going to catch up with Carl and Dimp.

"I have a scene opening up with Gary, Ind. and the steel mills. And then I move it to Chicago with the Flamingos, the Dells, the El Dorados and us. We'd be singing the songs with these groups. We'll try to put together a professional video and market it."

* * * *

What, specifically, does Pookie recall about reforming with three new members with minds of their own after the breakup of the original Spaniels – the group that gave America and the world the languid, unforgettable "Goodnight Sweetheart, Goodnight"?

"Willie C. left, Ernest left, Courtney left and I myself stopped singin' around the first part of '56. I stayed out a year. We already had Dimp with us because he took Ernest's place. So Gerald picked up Donald, who was a good friend of Dimp, and Carl Rainge, who also was a good friend of Dimp and Donald, and they became the Spaniels.

They did all the tours and all the shows the rest of '56. But they never recorded.

"They sang the rest of the year. They sang as the Spaniels. They carried the name well. They caught me at the right time because me and my marriage had gone down the drain. So I was ready to sing again at that particular time.

"Around the first of '57, my wife and I was breakin' up, in fact we broke up. She went home to her mother and I was by myself and they happened to come down to my apartment and asked me if I would do the lead for them to record because I think Carl was singin' lead but he was hoarse or something.

"So I agreed and we did 'Please Don't Tease.' I always thought 'You Gave Me Peace of Mind' was the first song, but it wasn't. Because I had written 'Peace of Mind' workin' at the General American Budd plant making boxcars, and I didn't bring that tune as the first one. Let's see, 'Please Don't Tease,' . . . I don't know if it was 'I.O.U.'

". . . Oh, I know what happened. They came back and got me and before the recording session they had two or three gigs, that's what it was, and I came back in the group singin'. And between then and the time to record and the gigs, they had learned 'Peace of Mind,' which I started singin' for them in the station wagon comin' from Peoria, Ill., if I'm not mistaken. I sang it for 'em and they began to put the background to it. So they worked on it and they finished it up after we got back from Gary.

"And we ended up recordin' 'Peace of Mind' and 'Please Don't Tease,' which Otis Blackwell wrote. The second group was technically better than the first group, which sang through feeling and what was inside. The second group sang through basic knowledge of music. They knew the notes, they knew how to reach the pinnacle of the songs and things and it was more than a feelin' with them; it was more in bein' right musically. And that's how they worked."

Said Opal:

"The original recording of 'Peace of Mind' comes from the new Spaniels with Dimp, Donald and Carl. Really, that's what it comes from because they brought a different sound; they brought a professional sound to the Spaniels.

More technical. Not saying that they did not sing with much feeling; we sang with what we knew how to do."

"I guess you could say the singin' was better; maybe not as soulful. But the singin' was better," Pookie agreed.

Pookie was asked his reaction to Porter's contention that the second, hit-making Spaniels have not received enough individual recognition, inasmuch as they weren't acknowledged by the Rhythm and Blues Foundation as was the first group.

"If the people (at the Smithsonian) had dug into the history of the Spaniels, then there would be no other way but for the Porter group to be in it. Because two groups made the Spaniels, although the first group was fortunate to have the song 'Goodnight Sweetheart,' which basically is what we are known by. But as far as the singin' goes, the second group were the singers."

*   *   *   *

How about the bad feelings that developed as time went on?

"Well, for a while, it went great," Pookie said. "We was basically getting the same shaft, you know, as far as the company was concerned, but we were workin' more, and we jelled as a group. But the thing was, we didn't look to the future. We were workin' it day-by-day.

"Like I told you, I wrote a song called 'Once a Star, Always a Star.' I didn't think that there would ever be any ups and downs. I never thought you'd ever be out the business. I didn't know that they could snuff you out just as fast as they could put you in.

"It got to the point that, even with these fellas, the money started gettin' smaller and smaller and the work started gettin' shorter and shorter, so we just ended up breakin' up in 1959 and '60 in Washington, D.C."

Any jealousies involved in this?

"Not really, not as far as the group was concerned. No. If it was, it never showed. Oh, we had our differences. One of our problems was, Donald had gotten into this religion and, uh, him and Gerald used to sit around and watch the clouds and they'd make faces and pictures . . . and Ted Armstrong (the evangelist) was kind of strong at that time and they were readin' his thing. And Donald went into this Saturday sabbath day thing. So his thing was from Friday night at 6 o'clock til Saturday at 6 o'clock, he didn't do no singin.' So if we had a gig on Saturday and we'd go to the show and he ain't there, the man look at me and he said we supposed to have five. And he ain't want to hear no shit about no religion. So we ended up getting fined and stuff and people got a little turned-off by it. Then I think Carl left first, then Dimp left, then Donald left."

Did it occur to you to ask Willie C. and Opal to rejoin the group at that time?

"I had no idea they were interested," said Pookie. "They all had their jobs and they all were successful at what they were doin', you know. They had their homes and families and things. It never dawned on me they wanted to sing. I never asked them and they never asked me. Because I put the group back together a couple of times, which I could have done with them. We have might have been a hundred percent further along now if I had."

Billy Shelton, and original member of the Spaniels' precursors, The Three Bees and the baritone of the reborn aggregation of the '90s, was asked to join the group in 1956 to replace Gerald on bass "because Gerald was on drugs, drinking too much and scared the hell out of Pookie when it was his turn to drive," he said. "But, I'd just started college and didn't really feel I could cut the mustard then. I'd just been singing around Gary.

"They needed a cohesive force to hold them together," Billy added. "They were kids. I'd been president of the Boys Glee Club and was like the daddy of the group – the first sergeant."

Said the great Gerald Gregory:

"The second group helped me to a point where I knew that I had to produce. It came naturally, thank God. We did some of our best numbers with them, after Pookie came back. With the exception of our beginning on 'Goodnight Sweetheart,' our best songs were made with this particular group of Spaniels.

So why does he think they're not part of the revitalization as the Spaniels try to recapture past glories?

"What it is," he said, "is that Carl (Rainge) has always had a strong ego and by him being top tenor, the fellas have always followed him. He's the leader of the background and we always had a democratic group – the majority rules. So, that gave him a lot of power. They took my strength away because they would outvote me. They played politics on me all the time so they made me kind of meek with a cautious attitude. And they were actually running things to a point.

"But Pookie wouldn't say anything," Gerald went on. "Pookie just was cool and let 'em go ahead on, you know. So by them being this way, Pookie didn't feel that close to 'em.

"So when it got to the point after we were back together (in the '70s and '80s) for a while, Pookie been doing our promoting mostly himself. And they got so they would question him and didn't like the way he was doing things. I didn't think that was right because Pookie was the only one who was doing anything."

"What they had," Pookie said, "was a different way of wanting to do business. So I'm saying, 'Look, if you don't like it then you do it,' you know what I mean? It was causing tension. That's why they're not here today."

It's always sad when great vocal groups break up. And the public doesn't like to see it happen. Unfortunately, the legendary Spaniels, whose "Goodnight Sweetheart, Goodnight" in 1954 introduced black music to millions of white Americans, were no exception.

Added Gerald: "And it's also too bad that our greatest entertainers seem to be dying. You know, like Jackie, Sam, Marvin . . . Oh, man. That hurts. Sincerely. A lot of my friends couldn't take the fall. Those things hurt. One particular one that comes to mind is Dee Clark. And Curtis Mayfield in that freak accident.

"Like the others, I can say it was a matter of overindulgence, you know. Some great ones . . ."

ELEVEN
Through the Years

"I turned down money and a promotion on my job to stay with the Spaniels. I love the group. Love is a whole lot deeper than a dollar or a cent. We're going to be a group like we used to be. I don't have nothing but love. I don't see nothing but togetherness. I have nothing but positive feelings." – Opal Courtney Jr.

"After Dimp and Donald and Carl left, me and Gerald called around and picked up a group out of Washington," Pookie recalled. "Ernest was with us with Billy Carey and Andy Magruder on baritone, and Pete Simmons. The last thing we did was 'I Know.' It's the last recording we did for Vee-Jay. We worked about a year-and-a-half and then it broke down again and Gerald left and went and formed his own group.

How could you replace Gerald Gregory's bass?

"We didn't go out to replace his bass, we just went to get a bass. It would be next to impossible to replace him. But then he got back in the thing with us, but he wanted to do things the way he wanted to do 'em, you know, and I guess I wanted to do things the way I wanted to do 'em. And that pulled us apart."

Meanwhile, Willie C. and Opal – and Ernest after he departed for good – lived their lives out of the spotlight.

But what about the original Spaniels – Pookie and Gerald? How did they occupy themselves until 1991, when the great old guard unexpectedly got back together?

"There came a time, around '61, when I joined the Neptune label and then the Double L label with Lloyd Price. At first, I used some fellas out of Washington (Alvin Wheeler, Charles Douglas, Andrew Lawyer and Alvin Lloyd, a.k.a. Sonny West) as the Spaniels and that failed and then I began to record by myself with Lloyd Price. I did a tune called 'I Know, I Know,' with 'Jealous Heart' on the flip side. And it was successful – top 40 on the rhythm and blues charts – and I did a little solo work. But basically, I'm not a solo singer. I can sing a solo but I feel self-conscious without a group. With a group, I feel 100 percent better."

Pookie was back on "I Know, I Know" on Double L in 1964 by the Imperials (Clarence Collins, Sam Strain and Ernest Wright), who also accompanied him in 1970 on a tune called "Fairy Tales." His other significant new work during this period included "Stand in Line"/"Lonely Man" (1971), and "Money Blues"/"Come Back to These Arms" (1972), on North American, and an a cappella version of "Danny Boy" with the Spaniels (Rainge, Cochran, Porter and Lester Williams) on Canterbury in 1974.

"Let me tell you a story about 'I Know, I Know.' This was in '61. I was living in New York at the time, and Lloyd Price done sent me on a personal appearance in Pittsburgh – you know, where disk jockeys would have these little dances and play your record and the artist would come. It wasn't no money involved. They just flew me in and I didn't have but a one-way ticket and I thought the other people was supposed to send me back and they didn't.

"For some reason or other – I could never understand it – they had booked a hotel room for me for a week, and after the show they dropped me off at the hotel. I wasn't able to find Lloyd Price and Harold Logan, who at the time were partners. They had gone on vacation for some holiday, maybe Labor Day. When I called the office, nobody was there because it was closed for two weeks. Here I was sittin' in this hotel. I stayed in the hotel for a whole week and I didn't have a dime. All I did was drink water. I ain't had no money. Couldn't find 'em. I didn't know nobody in Pittsburgh and I couldn't find no money.

"I got there on a Saturday to do the thing for 'em and stayed to next Monday in the hotel room. I walked up and down the street to see if I could find somebody – anything.

Man, I didn't eat for a whole week. When they came back
that next Monday they were very apologetic.

"'Man, we're sorry, we didn't know . . .' They thought the
man was going to give me some money and he didn't and
they didn't know I was going to be there. Anyway, what
happened was they immediately sent me some money and
then they had three jobs for me – in Baltimore and in
Washington, D.C., and in a way it kind of made up for it.
But that was one time, boy, I was hungry.

"When I first went to New York, in '60, it was almost the
same thing," Pookie continued. "I lived with a girl in Philadelphia and me and her broke up so I guess to save face, me
and a fella named Gas caught the bus to New York. This
was just before Christmas. When we got there I had about
$7 left. My man kind of petered out on me that first day. He
changed his mind and went back. He musta' had some money I didn't know about.

"So I went to Grand Central Station – this was like on
the 22nd of December – and put my clothes in a locker for
25 cents a day. And I'd go down to Central Park and sleep
on benches for two weeks, up to January 7th or 8th. It was
the same situation. Lloyd and them had gone on vacation.
In the day time, I'd walk from Central Park at 59th Street to
125th, hoping I might run into somebody I knew. But I never did. So I had to walk back down through the park. At
that time, it wasn't no problem about safety. I found my
bench, and got me some newspapers. The snow would be
that high.

"I had $7 so I went to a place around 125th that you
could buy two pigs feet and something else you could get
for 85 cents. So every day I'd buy me the pigs feet. I finally
ran into a girl I knew and ended up staying with her for a
little while but she had five roomates. What I would do,
they all worked so I'd clean up the house and when they
come home, I'd be done cooked the dinner, I'd wash their
clothes. They didn't ask me to but I said well hell, I'm here,
and I ain't doin' nothin', so I try to make myself worthy of
bein' there.

"And the girl was real nice to me and that's when I got
the job counting beads at Macy's after the holiday for their

inventory. So I got enough money together and moved to the Theresa Hotel and stayed for six-seven months. That's when Lloyd and them came back, and when I started recording for them. And they'd give me a piece of money every week and things got better."

Thus, the celebrated lead singer of the celebrated Spaniels did whatever he had to do to keep body and soul together in the up-and-down 1960s, '70s and '80s.

"Here in Indiana, I worked in the steel mills – U.S. Steel," Pookie said. "I worked in East Chicago at General American making boxcars and I did that Macy's job in New York counting beads that people wear around their neck. They had a New Year's inventory and they had this great big room with nothin' but beads in it. I must have counted beads for a month. Oh, man, I had so many jobs.

In Riverdale, Md., I was a garbage collector. In Washington, I was assistant superintendent of maintenance for Paradise Mayfair – a housing complex with 5,000 people. I made sure it was cleaned up and the work was done. I taught retarded kids for a year in Washington at the Jewish Foundation for Retarded Children."

And what did he list as experience when applying for jobs?

"Entertainer," he replied. "People asked me if I had any other prior work, and I explained to 'em about steel mills and things like that. Being an entertainer helped with most of 'em, except for Macy's – which didn't take no brains to sit there and count some beads – like the assistant superintendent's job I got through some friends. Same with the retarded kids foundation. First I would drive a bus and pick 'em up and bring 'em to school and things and teach 'em how to eat and dress themselves and (go to) the bathroom.

"The last job I had, at the Shenandoah Pride Dairy, in Virginia, was through some cousins. So basically, most jobs I got was because somebody knew me and took an interest in me.

"The most I was paid on my last job, where I was making $14-an hour, plus all overtime was $28-hour. And I was making a whole lot of overtime on this milk thing. I was the last man running whatever the milk order was. I had to clean the machine, so sometimes I wouldn't finish. I'd go to work at 10 at night and run milk until 1 o'clock in the afternoon on Saturday. And it would take me two or three hours to clean the machine. So I'd be there until five, six o'clock in evening from 10 Saturday night. But that's the job I hurt myself on.

"The first time," he recalled, "I was there about a month and I was steppin' on a truck to clean it out and the driver pulled off. I fell about six feet down across the abutment which was there to stop the truck, and broke three ribs. So I was out six months.

"When I went back, they put me on a dock pulling cases off the trucks. In tryin' to pull open one of the truck doors, which had been bent, I pulled my back out of place. And then in bottling, we were packaging gallon bottles we made to be sent out to another plant, and I tried to snatch on one of these machines that went down and pulled my back again. It's bothered me ever since.

"I've tried to get disability, Social Security. But on stage, we been doin' about 20, 30 minutes, and as long as I'm standing still it really doesn't bother me. If I get to movin' or something then it gives me problems."

It was suggested that with the hoped-for success of the Spaniels' comeback, Pookie shouldn't ever have to do manual labor again.

"I hope I'll never have to go back to that stuff," he agreed, "and hope I'll be able to pay back all the money that was ever given to me to help me prolong myself until the day comes when we really start making the money that we should.

"I was on welfare when I was in Washington in '75, '76, with my family," he admitted. "I've gotten food stamps. I got food stamps here (in Gary). The job wasn't makin' no money. I worked for Lake County government here as a garage attendant and I wasn't bringin' home but $209 every two weeks, which wasn't really enough to do nothin'. On top of that, I had to pay my boss . . . I had to give him 2 percent of my pay every pay . . ."

Why would he have to pay his boss to work?

"Well, if I wanted the job. That's what everybody does.

That's the way they run the government here. If one of these people give you a job, the one that you vote for, the one you put in office, the one who's supposed to work for you, you got to pay him to get a job."

During this period, Pookie also recorded a few of the original Spaniels' tunes in syrupy, schmaltzed-up versions in an attempt by Henry Farag, on his small, Merrillville, Ind.-based Canterbury label, to cross over into the white market. The primary vehicles were "Goodnight Sweetheart" and "You Gave Me Peace of Mind."

"I did a couple of things," said Pookie. "I did one with a group out of Washington – 'Goodnight Sweetheart with strings. We tried it, but they don't touch the originals; they don't touch that first thing that came from the heart. And that's what counts.

"That and 'Peace of Mind' was a white person's (Farag's) idea of how he thought it should go and so he laid the music track and asked me would I come in and put the vocal on top of it. He's a good friend of mine and this is what he thought the song . . . in fact, the Drifters did it too. He's got two or three of those things – one a white boy did – Frankie Ford, off the same track. Three or four people have done it.

"I particularly didn't like it. In fact, I listened to it and it's not 'Peace of Mind.'"

Has he ever thought about what might have been had he gone out as a single when Vee-Jay asked him to?

"No. It never crossed my mind," he said. "I never looked back on it. It was something I didn't want to do so I didn't dwell on whether I did or not. It might have been just as disastrous as it would have been profitable.

"I'd like to say one thing. I got some dudes I got to praise. this was the Coasters. At this time, the Coasters was Billy Guy, Doug Jones, Carl, uh, Gordon, and Speedo Brooks, when he was with them. And they were doing things at the Apollo and I was doin' bad. So they respected me so much, I mean I hung out at one of them things and visted their room and carryin' on, and they let me stay around. But, uh, they never asked me like to do anything for them.

They wanted to give me money but they didn't want to offend me by giving me money. So it got to the point where

I said like, 'Hey, man, let me valet for ya'll, you know, at the Apollo. And they really didn't want that so what they'd do, they'd make up things. They'd said, like 'Hey, man, take this $10, I need a shirt' (a shirt didn't cost them but $3) and keep the change.' Or, 'Will you do me a favor and get . . .' They would do this," he recalled.

"They knew I was doin' bad but they would never allude to that. So they would go out of their way to do things to make it seem like I was earnin' money. I wasn't doin' nothin' to earn it really.

"When I finished doing things for a whole week for them, man, I think I ended up with more money than they ended up with. And they was makin' like $3,000 – some nice dollars at that time, around '60-'61 – because they had 'Yakety-Yak.'

"In fact, we did a record for Doug Jones, Speedo – me and Speedo wrote the tunes – Billy, Guy and Carl. We did a couple of tunes and called ourselves 'The Individuals.' And we can't find this record nowhere. We did it for this dude who used to do all the saxophone solos for Atlantic Records for the groups – Charles Singleton. Then he started oing some albums on his own Chase Records.

"I was singin' lead and the rest of them sang the background. I can't think of the name of the song. Me and Speedo wrote another song that I do – 'Great Googley Moo.' If I ever in my life get to a chance to repay their kindness, I would like to do it back to them, and if not to them I'd like to do it to someone, to pass it on. Because I know some people in some groups would not have done that. They'd have passed that off as, 'Hey, man, that's your problem,' and wen't about they business."

When you hit this bad period, Pookie, what was Vivian Carter doing?

"Vee-Jay had just acquired the Beatles in 1962. They had the first three records on the chart with on Vee-Jay Records."

Did you ever hear from the Vee-Jay people or from any of your original group members during those days?

"No. See, me and Gerald got back together with the second group for live gigs beginning in 1973. But in recent years, I had my problems with them. We just looked at . . . the way we looked at it, business was different. They felt that they could get $4,000, $5,000 a night and they tried to bring up the point saying that you don't think we're worth it. It's not that I don't think we're worth it, it's that I know the people not gon' give it. And I know it's something that you have to work up to. The only thing we had was those records that we had done years ago.

"They tried to compare us with the Dells. They could not compare us with the Dells because the Dells stayed there, and they have more recent records than we had. So they were able to establish themselves as far as a group today, for the simple reason that they did stay in there. And they had some bad times.

"I know that many times they wanted to quit," Pookie went on, "and they wanted to jump on Cal, but they stuck with it and they became a winner for it. And we cannot put ourselves in their category because we did not have that perseverance. We did not try to stick with it even though through the thick and thin we could have, but nobody wanted to.

Everybody came home and took care of their families – including me. And so they sacrificed the singin'."

Do you dispute Porter's contention that it was his initial contact with the Smithsonian that resulted in the Spaniels getting the R&B Foundation Award in 1991?

"The contact I got was through a white reporter out of Virginia whom I was talking to. He called me and let me know that he had talked to Suzan Jenkins and they was getting ready to have this thing. He gave me her phone number in Washington and told me to call her. I called her and in turn I told Donald about it and I think Donald sent them some material and stuff they might need at that particular time. And, no, he was not the initial person to do that.

But he did initiate your contact with Henry Farag in the early '70s, right?

"Right. He was the first one. He talked to Henry first. But Donald has a way of rubbing people wrong because of all the promoters and things I have talked to, they would tell me: 'I don't want to talk to that Donald Porter.'

"These days, Donald still has that religous calling," Poo-kie said. "But he also has a thing about not giving ground. I mean he is so sure he can demand from these people things that a lot of acts that got the records don't demand. People don't like his attitude, the way he talks. and they say, 'if I got to deal with the Spaniels I don't want to deal with Don-ald."

Are there any anti-white attitudes here?

"Well, Carl and Donald, they had that type of attitude. White people are all wrong and all they want to do is beat you and take advantage of you. It came out when we were dealing with Henry Farag. He came to me and said, 'Man, I'll help you, but I can't do nothing for your group.'"

Did this have any effect on your decision when you wanted to get the group back together around the time of the Smithsonian awards?

"I was going to get a group anyway, and that was before Willie C. and Courtney had made their decision that they wanted to sing, which pleased me very well. I was going to find two other fellows along with Gerald, and do it."

"And is it also true that you were the one who told him about my interest in the Spaniels, rather than the other way around, as he contends?" I asked.

"Oh yeah. He didn't know nothing about your Daily News column. You sent it to me and I called him and told him about it. In fact, I sent him a couple copies of the col-umn."

What did you mean when you said Donald and Carl Rainge and Dimples Cochran "take the joy out of it?"

"Well, it got to the point there was so much tension if things didn't go their way. If I did things one way and they didn't want to do it that way, there was always just like . . . you know, it just wasn't fun. It used to be a time when it was fun. It got to the point when you had to scratch every-body's back and you had to please everybody. And if you don't, they got those loud mouths and insults and whole lot of shit going on that I deem unnecessary."

Any chance of getting them back in the group, as Donald has said he'd like — acknowledging that it would be your choice?

"That would mean getting rid of the other group," Pookie explained. "No. No time soon."

Do you have any bitterness about any of this?

"I had some bitterness at one time," he said, "but I found that to be bitter only held me back. And to be revengeful only hold you back, so I try to make my peace with those that I felt had done me wrong and try to move on to another plateau. So instead of looking back, we're looking for-ward."

*   *   *   *

Gerald Gregory, on the other hand, never completely stopped singing for all of those in-between years.

"In 1960, I lost my second family and I was depressed and returned to drugs," he said. "Before that, I had only been smoking a little. I couldn't get back with my family. The drugs kept me asleep all the time and stopped me from worrying.

In Washington that year, I was away from the Spaniels and met this beautiful lady from New York who offered me six or seven bags of this stuff to introduce her to my leader, Pookie. So I went back to New York and got the girl and the drugs.

"I left the Spaniels in 1962 and went with Sonny Til and the Orioles. I was in New York when I met Sonny. He was passing by and I was living in Brooklyn at the time and he happened to see me and he said, 'Hey, man,' do you know anybody that . . .?' I said 'Yeah.' I said, 'Meet me in Phila-delphia Friday.' And that's two fellas that can make any-body's sound – Sonny and Billy Taylor. Any group. Can you imagine two fellas being able to do that? I know he'd like 'em. He heard one song and that was it. Before he died, we made an album with Sonny I'd love for you to hear.

"I was in bad shape then," Gerald said, "but thanks to Sonny and Billy, I survived. They sent me to the hospital and took care of me. But even though I enjoyed Sonny so much, still always my heart is with the Spaniels.

"Another thing I noticed when I was with these other groups. We'd sing in the hills in California, like. And very seldom did I see a brother, you know. But I kept working off and on, and for me the home base would be like St.

Louis. When we were not working, we'd stay there somewhere until the next gig came along. I was with the Ink Spots out west replacing Deke Watson for a while, who was one of the originals. I'm thankful I was able to really fit in.

"Other than that it was just odds and ends – driving a cab or whatever. You know what I mean. Just different jobs, you know. But I'm thankful that I've been with these different groups and that I've created a couple of groups to be with.

"The high point of my career was when I came back to the Spaniels. We played the Star Theater in Merrillville, Ind., and when the group was introduced, I got another round of applause all to myself. 'Hey, Gerald,' " the people shouted.

* * * *

"Gerald never really went to work," said Billy Shelton. "He never left the road. He sang with the Orioles and the Ink Spots. Pookie came back to Gary and got a job parking cars, Willie C. went to work at a steel mill, Courtney was into his hair dressing and then the used cars and Ernest worked every day and became a preacher. But Gerald kept right on doing what he did best – singing."

Said Pookie:

"I had no idea they (the original group) wanted to sing again. It just so happened . . . just to show you how things just fall into place. We were getting rid of one group, then this rhythm and blues award thing came into play. It put us all back together and we were able to talk and everything came out. We found that everybody wanted to sing. And I think it all came around the right time. We didn't go out looking for this. It was brought to us through providence."

"The audience knows when you love 'em," added Billy. "And I think everybody in this group loves the audience."

Translation: The original Spaniels are back!

TWELVE
Rehearsing

"We rehearsed more in the old days because we sang from feeling. So it was very important for us to be together and sing as much as we possibly could so we got that feeling correct. It's easy to make a mistake when you're singing from feeling. We didn't really look at mistakes as long as the feeling was there.

"And the feeling has to be real." – Gerald Gregory.

The Midwest was in the midst of a record-setting heat wave. Seated on the piano bench in the living room of Billy Shelton's home at 1340 Rutledge St. in Gary, I sipped a glass of ice water and mopped my brow. It was really hot.

The casually attired Spaniels' background singers – in their mid-to-late 50s – went through their paces in front of an open window for four hours as the steaming sunshine streamed in unopposed. Three world-class singers and first-class human beings whom, happily, I had gotten to know.

As I watched and listened to them rehearse – two sharing a couch and the third in a nearby chair – I was struck at how, oblivious to the heat and the sounds of a next-door neighbor and his son painting their house and talking, togetherness reigned.

In addition to Billy, who sings baritone, there was Opal Courtney Jr. on top tenor, and Willie C. Jackson, the second tenor. The mood was serious but nice and loose – befitting three men who really enjoy each other's company. And love working together.

page 139

Since Pookie and Gerald – the lone holdovers from the original Spaniels – are so familiar with their specialties, the rehearsals these days sometimes consist only of the background singers working to tapes of Spaniels' records. And this was one of those times.

The object of this particular session was for Opal, Willie C. and Billy to learn their parts in some of the many songs recorded by the Spaniels from 1956-60. Most had been done by Donald (Duck) Porter, Parma Lee (Carl) Rainge and James (Dimples) Cochran – the talented, highly disciplined background singers – and several rehearsed from 1961-74 when various iterations of the group performed sporadically in R&B revival shows and reunions.

The task at hand was "Heart and Soul" (1958), featuring Gerald's dynamite bass lead; "Red Sails in the Sunset" (Vee-Jay LP 1051 from 1962); "I Know, I Know" (1963); "Stormy Weather" (1958); "I Know" (1960), and "A Lovely Way to Spend an Evening" (Vee-Jay LP 1002 from 1957). Each had to be practiced and mastered.

The detail-oriented Opal was in charge of cueing through the tapes until he reached a tune they wanted to work on.

In so doing, we'd hear bits and pieces of many Spaniels' records – most of which the singers would hum along with and all of which I would gladly have listened to in their entirety.

Throughout the session, Billy kept everyone tuned-up with his pitch pipe – the kind of gadget my music teacher used with us in high school. That's how serious these guys were. And each singer would comment from time-to-time on what they were doing – right and wrong:

"Easy," someone would say. "You know, we don't all have to go up," another would say.

After 'Lovely Way': "Yeah, I like that. That's another one like 'Danny Boy.' Kind of reminds you of 'Danny Boy,'" a third would chime in.

"That's 'Three Little Words.' That's a pretty song." "You know something else? We don't all have to make those changes in the song." "That was Dimp – James Cochran – on lead." "Now the other 'I Know.'" "People Will Say We're in Love.' That's pretty too. We need more up-tempo songs, too. As long as Willie dances."

"Run that back. We'll record that right away. We don't even have to listen to that."

And before, during and after the singing, there was this kind of patter you'd expect of musicians who are happy with their work:

"You know, those guys (Porter, Rainge and Cochran) were fantastic singers," opined Billy. "All three of them were stars. To me, James Cochran out of the three, he was the best. The best all-round singer of the Spaniels.

"Marvin Gaye had nothing on this guy. Sam Cooke had nothing on him."

Now it was time to rehearse the two Spaniels' recordings of "I Know" – an up-tempo, 1960 tune that was the group's last really big hit, and a ballad, "I Know, I Know," the Spaniels recorded in 1963 which, Billy emphasized, "was written by one of the Imperials."

"It's beautiful," said Opal.

"And then Pookie used to sing the song with us: 'I Know' – a standard: 'I know, oh yes, I know, if you and I . . .,' vocalized Billy. "It was three 'I Knows.'"

"Which one you want?" asked Opal. "The second one is closest."

"That's what makes a great group, this kind of stuff," Billy continued. "And people just see you up on the stage and think you just walked up there. And groups forget about it. They forget what made them."

Once the singers were satisfied that each had his part down pat – after calmly starting and stopping a number of times – they'd tape-record it. Then they'd play and study it in hopes of making it even better.

Music on. Music off. On. Off. On. Off. Over and over again. All of which demonstrates what makes real pros the best at what they do. And these were consumate pros in action.

"OK, 'Heart and Soul,'" said Opal.

"Instead of recording it right now, let's get on track first," Billy said.

Opal turned on one of several tape recorders and Gerald's big voice boomed out ever so smoothly on the classic

Hoagy Carmichael-Frank Loesser tune as the talented singers again closed ranks. They worked and worked until they
had the background exactly as they wanted it. This meant
as close as possible to perfection of the record that hit big
in 1958 with Porter, Rainge and Cochran backing up Pookie and Gerald.

Music on. Music off.

"Yeah, that's where I go up," said Opal. "You hear it?"

"Sounds like 'She Wore Blue Velvet' for some reason in
some places," Billy laughed.

"See now, that's where we're going," Opal said. "Now
we're going to see whether or not Willie can go there.

"Listen to this."

"Yeah, that's pretty there," said Willie C.

Music on. Music off.

"OK, then we go back," Opal said. "Stay there. Hold on,
hold on. No. Right there, when we go up, stay there, Willie.
Yeah, now listen. OK, listen. Listen. 'Cause I'm going to
stay up. And if I stay up, it's got to be right below me."

They tried again, and once again stopped short.

"No, no. Look. Stay right there. See what I'm talking
about?" insisted Opal.

"Willie, the same note that you all just hit . . . oooahh . . .
just so you'll know it," said Billy.

Music on. Music off.

"Stay right there, added Opal. "Uh, uh. Stay there Willie."

"I stayed there," said Willie C.

"Ooo, ooo, like that. Heart and souuul . . ." said Billy.
"Now sing up. Let's see how it works."

"You can go up," said Opal.

Music on. Music off.

"That's the problem right here," Opal said. "Stay there."

"Yeah, right where you are," Billy added. "Now stay
right there and don't go back down lower. That's it; go up,
go up."

Music on. Music off.

"You see that? Opal asked. "Willie, that's top there.
That's top," he noted, approvingly.

"You guys are getting really good at this," Billy smiled.

"We can deal with all these changes?" asked Opal.

"OK. We're gonna change the back end of it so why not make it a little bit sweeter?" Opal noted. "Go on back down. See what I'm talking about? If we're going to leave it like that, ain't no need in you going up high. We just might as well stay down like it is. That way, Willie can go back to the melody part."

"That's right," agreed Billy. "Just leave it like it was. As you were. As you were. I think the problem is, we should try to make it as simple as possible."

Music on. Music off.

"OK, now we got it; we go up to it. Later for that," said Opal. "So rather than go up, like they (Porter, Rainge and Cochran) go up on the second time, we'll just stay here. Because they go, if you listen . . ."

Music on. Music off.

"I tell you," said Billy. "I like the going up."

"I do too," chimed in Willie C.

"But if it's going to create a . . ." Opal cautioned.

"I think we can do it," said Billy.

"I know we can," Willie C. seconded.

"I like going up," Opal went on. "It's easier for me to go up than to stay between the tenor and the . . .OK.

Music on. Music off.

"Hear, they're up now. Oooo, oooo, oooo, oooo . . ."Opal mimicked.

"We're going to do the first one down and the second one up and the third one down," Billy reminded.

"He's singing baritone now and you're (Billy) singing his piece," Opal said. "I'm going up."

"I'm going with you this time," replied Billy.

"If you can" said Opal.

Music on. Music off.

"You know, when you're singing, your throat can hit some terrific temperatures," Billy said. "So if you pour ice-cold water on there it's like even if you've got a hot stove and you pour ice-cold water it creates all that mucus. You should just drink it room temperature," Billy continued.

"Billy Williams told me that. He said whenever you drink cold water just let it out of the pipe. Let it sit up. You remember Billy Williams on 'Your Show of Shows" on TV. The Billy Williams Quartet? That was my idol. That guy was really something."

Music on. Music off.

And between songs sometimes is more important," Billy said. "Like for instance, you might find out who's throwing rehearsal off. It might be one guy who's burying the rehearsal through negative talk."

"That's where it is," encouraged Billy. "Just stick to the song. Believe in the song."

"I ain't worried. I can't . . ." said Willie C.

"I know, but see, you have to do that on your own time is what I'm talking about. It's a personal thing. We can show you in a half-hour but Willie, what I can do, I can come by sometime and we can work on it together."

Music on. Music off.

"That's it," said Opal. "That's the note."

"Yeah. One thing about Willie," smiled Billy, "he's like a pillar. Once he knows the note, he can hit it any time."

"What's next?" said Opal. "'Lovely Way to Spend an Evening' or 'People Will Say We're in Love'"?

"'Lovely Way to Spend an Evening'" said Billy. "Turn it over."

"OK, I'll flip it over to find it," Opal said.
Right on there," he smiled. "Alright, 'Lovely Way . . .' "

"Don't record it yet. Let's run it through," said Billy.

And so it went – over and over again – until they were satisfied they had it right. Willie C., Opal and Billy – working as a team to give the group its extra-special harmony. And today's Spaniels, truly are a harmonious aggregation – in ways that transcend their wonderful rhythm and blues music. The original, real thing. The genuine article.

THIRTEEN
Honesty

"I'm lucky. I feel like I'm one of the luckiest guys alive to be with these guys because they paid the price. They suffered and everything, but thank God that Gerald stayed out there when things were going bad." – Billy Shelton.

In addition to their melodious harmonizing, the musings of the three Spaniels' background singers about the past, present and future – including honest, off-the-cuff comments about other group members – helped make this day most memorable in this, the story of the Spaniels.

"Have you talked to Gerald yet? Billy asked me.

"Just that day in the basement," I replied.

"It made me feel good to see you raising hell and everything like that. Because I'm sure, you know, you're writing this book and you've got to deal with the truth. I heard that Gerald said he tried to clean up his act for you.

"But, uh, even on the stage," Billy continued, "for his benefit, if he don't want to go, we're going without him. Because we've got a lot of guys that believe they're bass singers. And for people, outside of the old connoisseurs, you know, we can make it, you know. And he knows that. And it's like Pookie said this guy told him: 'Well, you can lead a horse to the water but you can't make him drink – unless you give him some salt.' This might be his salt. If he has a fear of not being a part of the group.

"I was so happy the first day that you came in," Billy went on, "and Gerald was clean, and talking like he should be. He's too great to let anything stand in his way. Like something that overpowers your life and letting it take precedent. Now that would be wrong."

"Well, your wife was giving him hell down there," I said to Willie C. "When we were eating. Whew!

'Yeah, she stays on him,' Willie acknowledged.

"And someone should get on him," said Billy. "You owe this to the world because God gave it to you, you know."

"She stays on him every time she see him," Willie C. continued.

"Well I sure didn't know she gave him hell," Opal said.

"What makes her upset about Gerald is he don't work and all he does is just sit around," said Willie C. "When we met Gerald he'd just be singing and clowning. With alcohol around, you . . ."

After listening to a smidgen of the group's novelty 1960 hit "Bus Fare Home," I said: "If you were playing a New York gig and you could choose the songs, that would be a good song: 'Bus Fare Home.'"

"It sure would," said Billy.

"Yeah, New York. Boy! You talk about needing some bus fare home," said Opal. "I was telling him how we used to just look forward to eating a couple of hot dogs a day, Willie."

"Yeah," Willie C. agreed.

"On the corner of 125th Street and Eighth Avenue with that old hot dog stand around the corner from the Apollo," Opal sighed.

"Talkin' about lookin' busted," said Willie C.

"Aw, man, those were the days. Those were the days," said Opal.

"Hey Richard," said Willie C., "one time, did we tell you the time we went to New York and somebody got sick. I think it was Ernest. And come time to get paid, we didn't get no money. They said we broke the contract."

"Let 'em sing for a whole week," said Billy. "Ain't that something?"

"So that was an experience," Willie C. went on.

"Learn the hard way," said Billy.

"You signed a contract that said five guys, you going to have to get somebody out of the audience and put them up there as the Spaniels," Willie C. laughed.

"And then we get caught for white slavery," Opal sighed. "I didn't tell you that, did I?"

"I hope the tape's running," I said. "The tape's running?"

"Uh huh, we did. Ernest and I. What happened it was a couple of girls; a girls' singing group out of Kankakee. It was three of 'em. I still see one of 'em now and then when I got to a chapter meeting. So we were living in the Coleman Hotel (in Newark) when we were playing the Apollo Theater. That's how we got in there because the rates were cheaper. Remember that?

"I knew one of the girls and I got one of 'em and I took her back. Ernest took one back. And boy, he talked about how he went to bed with her and stuff like that? And we got up there and we got back to the Apollo Theater and we kicked off the first show right into the hands of the police. They cost us, what, $250? And I thought that was a rip-off there. I didn't want to give 'em nothing," Opal concluded.

"You tell me these stories like that," Billy said, "I mean, it makes me think of this Western Union commercial on TV with these black guys, when they've got this cop. You know, Cool Hand Luke with the glasses. When they get the money they sing: 'Cruisin . . .'"

"But they did," said Opal. "They wasn't going to let us go on the second show until we got that money to 'em."

"You could tell that was a rip-off," Willie C. said, "because Ernest usually would never spend his money."

"Ernest was talking about, 'Man, I really did her. Man I had her hollering and screaming. But when the police got there, Ernest was talking, "I didn't touch her, I didn't touch her . . ." laughed Opal.

"I ain't going to lie, because me and that girl, we had a ball. But that's New York for you."

"Could I ask you guys a personal question," said Billy. "We've got the tape on. I've been hearing everything that happened and stuff like that. Would you guys bear any of the burden? I mean I'm looking for a bunch of high school kids that got on the road and here's the girls . . .

"They were nice," Opal jumped in.

". . . the notoriety, the fame and stuff. Didn't you guys do something bad while you were out there, I mean . . ."

"Yeah, we did something bad," Willie interrupted.

"Bad like what now?" Opal asked.

"Like Dimp was telling me years ago, that everybody was blaming certain people, 'but we messed up a whole lot too . . .' Billy went on.

"We had to contribute to it," Willie blurted.

"He told me, 'We acted a fool out there so we couldn't act like we didn't,'" Billy said.

"We", there's a whole lot of things you could do differently," Opal said, "but at the time, you put them girls in front of you and you're going to be led by your joint."

"It's the fast life and you're on the train. Like I said, we didn't care about the money when we first started," Willie C. said. "It was more the glory of it and following the girls . . ."

"And see, all the people behind you knew that. They were using that to get you away from thinking about your money," Billy noted.

"We were enjoying . . . We were getting half-paid for things we enjoyed doing – which was singing," said Opal.

"Like we'd be traveling on a six-month tour or a three-month tour and Pookie's shirt gets dirty – he'd just throw it away," Willie C. said. "He didn't worry about it. He never washed a shirt. He'd buy a hundred dollars worth of comic books. That's what he liked. He'd buy a whole stack of comic books, read 'em and throw 'em out the window."

"But you know, that's when you had a great big stack like this, of yellow pieces of paper, which was a contract. That's what a contract is on. Yellow sheets. You had a stack like that and you could thumb through and say, 'well, this is what we're going to do.' I want it to be like that now."

"It's going to be," said Billy.

"I want it to be. I enjoy it more, now. Like I say, this is second for me and I enjoy rehearsing. You know that?" Opal said.

Said Billy: "Yeah, I know that. Willie C. does too. That's why I love these guys. And Pookie and Gerald do too. The only thing about it is, by Pookie taking care of the the business, you know he's getting phone calls and he's got to make meetings and stuff like that, so we want to know,

look, if you can make it by, we'll get it together and something like that.

"And Gerald the same way. Usually, Gerald doesn't have
a car so by the time . . . we have stolen moments that we
can get together. By the same time somebody has to drive
over and pick him up and stuff like that. And we could've
been through, almost, with the rehearsal, so we just go on.
And it's just great. Man, I really love a bunch of guys who
want to improve and want to see what the potential is, and
these guys never quit doing that.

"We try to rehearse every day. And everybody is loaded
with business and things like that, but we're going to get together – especially with this thing going to London and the
Apollo and stuff like that," Billy said.

Eagerly agreeing, Opal said he practices his background
harmonies by listening and singing along to Spaniels' tapes
whenever he drives his van.

"With new material, Pookie and them will probably have
to be here more consistently," Willie C. added. "With this
old stuff, they know it, been doing it for 39 years and they
don't really have a need for them (as many rehearsals) right
now."

*   *   *   *

Opal enthusiastically described his return to the Spaniels
in 1991 after 37 years:

"Pookie called me on the phone and said 'Cobo' – that's
what he always called me. He said 'Cobo, we might be going to New York. They're going to give us some money.'
But down through the years, he's called me and said we
might be getting some money, so I took that with a grain of
salt. So it finally came. The letter came to my mother's
house from the Institute (Smithsonian). And I have all of
the letters; I have everything. So we all met here (in his
house in Gary) and we decided what we were going to do.
We decided we would go as a group. We would all be
dressed alike. As you noticed, we all had on tuxes; we
bought the tuxes, the same tuxes.

"And at that time, a newspaperman came here to the
house and he asked if we ever hit a note before or since?
And I said, 'Man, we hadn't sung together since 1954.' And

we sang a song right here and you know the wine I've got downstairs? We drank four or five bottles or wine and we had a real nice time.

"Then I think it was in New York for the Award, Pookie said, 'Hey, how about it? You guys want to sing? My concern was about Carl, Donald and Dimp. 'What do they have to do with us going to New York?' Pookie said 'nothing,' because the R&B Foundation wanted the original group.

I have heard nothing from them," Opal continued. "I saw Carl one day and I spoke to him and he said 'Hello.' No accolades, no nothing. Just 'Hello, how you doing?' And I'm concerned, but I'm not concerned. I'm concerned primarily because they, well, let's just put it this way: They were the Spaniels moreso than we were the Spaniels. They had a lot of good records and they had a hell of a sound and I love the sound today. And whether we're emulating them in our own right; that's what we're doing.

"We made 'Baby, It's You' and 'Goodnight, Sweetheart,' but they're the ones who made 'Stormy Weather,' 'Peace of Mind,' 'IOU,' 'I Lost You,' 'Danny Boy' and the rest. These are the songs that they put together. I have a problem with it now, because Gerald brought it to me: 'Hey man, don't you know that they're really good?' This is a problem that me and Gerald have. Gerald still says that. He would always bring up Dimp and Donald; Dimp and Donald, because he didn't want Willie C. and I. He wanted Billy Shelton to get a couple of more guys – I guess guys he could control. Always Dimp, Donald and Carl.

"I said if they were so great, why is it that the reputation they got is so tarnished? And why is it they are not with the Spaniels today? They are known as troublemakers, militants and alcoholics," Opal went on.

"This little kid, this little white guy that gave the recent show in California said, 'Do you realize that if they had been with the Spaniels I would not have booked the Spaniels. The only reason I am booking the Spaniels out here now is that it's the original group. He said, 'How is Gerald?' I said 'Gerald is fine.' Everything is not black or white. Why should you berate the white man because he has something that you need – money. And the biggest fans of ours are white.

"Times have changed and business has a lot to do with it. Even though we are not directly included . . . we are included. We're responsible in getting gigs and things. We are all aware of what's going on. We are also adult males. And what I might see in a shortcoming of someone that's trying to deal with us on an appearance, say, with monies, Willie C. might see something and have an altogether different feeling toward this individual and say, 'Hey, we better back up a little bit and let's check this dude out a little bit more.'"

"Willie might know somebody that can check him out. He (Billy) might know somebody. And it's not all glory. Everything's not glory. Like the gentleman that put on our show in Washington, D.C. – Lawrence. As you know, when ya'll left me – they left me out there to the wolves. I had to ride back with him and he was talking. And he said, 'You know, a lot of people out here that would love to book ya'll, and things like that, but be aware. Be aware.' That's all he said. 'Because the things that ya'll went through a long time ago, these people are now sophisticated enough that they're going to come at you a different way, but still try to do the same thing.'

"He said, 'Don't jump into anything. Don't jump into recordings. He said ya'll be aware of what ya'll going to do. I don't know whether or not it was for Lawrence to benefit Lawrence through his conversations with me, but we did become close. But that's the truth. I ain't no fool about money. Oh, no. I'm not a fool about business."

Added Billy: "The group, basically, is not going to be had. Because everybody in the group is capable or running a good, tight business. Now the mistakes, I think, is so much fun that's why I like being in a group. Let the pitfalls that we have experienced in the past, let our competition run into that now. In other words, if we have a show with a young group, let these guys be victims. If we meet them on stage, we've got the advantage."

"Like in New York at Radio City last month," Opal said.

"You were there. You remember this group, 'Yesterday, Today.'"? Billy continued. "Now they actually stole the show for a moment there when they did 'Gloria.' They had the place in the palm of their hands."

"They sure did," Opal agreed.

"And people were like going for the underdogs, too. Here's a group we never hear of them before and man, they got up and here's the big Spaniels have to come behind them now, and they done kicked the Spaniels. You know, it's that type of thing; the audience likes to do that. And you couldn't take anything away from them. They just happened to hit. Everything was just right and they did a beautiful job. But, they made a mistake that I wouldn't have made. They came back.

"No. 1, they shouldn't have come back because we were on a time schedule. We had to all get out of there. They guy explained to us no matter what happens, you sing and get off. No matter how much the audience liked you, because we're not in competition with each other and he's trying to sandwich this program here. It's experience. And these guys said 'Hey! Hey, we got the audience. Man, we can take this show. Let's go back.'"

"And that wasn't as bad. But the sound that they picked they weren't familiar . . . It's like one of the songs that we're working on. It's pretty good, but not quite, and they picked that song instead of something that they knew. And they had to stop and start again. That's another thing you never do. The audience doesn't know. I wasn't aware that somebody had messed up. And then: 'Wait a minute. Stop fellas. Excuse us. We've got to start over.'"

"And came back on the same key," noted Opal.

"They told everybody that they're a bunch of amateurs. We got lucky once and now we messed up. And then, from then on, they delivered . . . what did you say Courtney?"

"Remember what I told you? It's on the tape. I said, 'Well, hey, we got 'em now.' And Willie remembers this," Opal concluded. "I wish he had the tape. You could hear it."

"That's my forte," Billy went on. "In running into competition and coming out ahead. In 1959, the group that I had in the Army won the All-Army entertainment thing which was on the Ed Sullivan Show, and we had to compete against every Army post in the world. And we came out first place. The last thing we did was in Chicago in 1984. We won the Chicago Talent Search, which was sponsored by the Chicago Park District, over 1,513 different . . .not people but acts. And we came out No. 1 in that. So that's what it is. We might have to learn a jazz tune. You sing for your audience."

"You've got to sing more than one song," Opal interjected.

"You could get Caruso to come back from the grave on the 'Gong Show,' Billy said, "and if he sang at the Apollo, they would gong him off the stage. That's the whole thing in show business – giving the people what they understand and what they want.

"So this is going to be a lot of fun because our batting average had been terrific so far. When we went to Hollywood, we were the only group that got a standing ovation and we got three of them. And we had such heavy people like the Capris, the Flamingos, the Dixie Cups . . . and stuff like this, you know. And so, everywhere we've gone, I don't know why, it seem like the people . . . it's a charisma. That's something you can't explain," Billy tried to explain.

"Now that was the difference in this group and the group, you know, Parma Lee (Rainge) and them? Technically speaking, they're terrific singers and stuff like that, but it always came off, they were always saying: 'Look at what I can do vocally: Woooo, oooo, oooo . . .' he mimicked. 'Look at that. How do you like that?'

"You know, instead of singing to the audience, you know, out of love. Judy Garland wasn't a heck of a singer but she was one of the greatest entertainers because the love she had came through for the audience. She was a drug addict and she'd get up and her voice would crack and the audience would stand up and cheer and say, 'We love you, Judy . . .' I think it gets back to that. People know when you're really singing because you love it or if you're singing to make a buck."

* * * *

Before wrapping up for the day, Willie C. took great pleasure in recounting the story of how the "young, dumb Spaniels," as he called them, dealt with a problem with the transmission on the new 1954 Buick station wagon Vee-Jay Records bought them:

"Instead of buying transmission oil, we went and got that cheap oil they used to sell for a nickel? They called it 'buck oil.' We put that buck oil in the transmission and drove around the country for, man, I guess, about four or five months. We just kept buying whole cases of it. Whenever the transmission started slipping Count would pour it in."

"Count (piano player Morris Wilkerson) was a nickel mechanic anyway," said Opal.

"He said 'as long as the oil will stay in, the transmission will run," Willie C. continued. "It ran. It leaked, but it ran. And he said, 'Put some sawdust down in there and that'll stop the leak a little bit.' And it did. Next time we checked the transmission fluid, it was still up. So we went a few more miles to the next stop and it was down maybe about a quart. So Count said we'd go over there to the lumber yard and we got some sawdust. And he poured it down in there. He had a Ford and he told us to push his car with the station wagon. This was a strain on the transmission and as soon as the fluids got hot with that sawdust, that car wouldn't move no more."

"That reminds me of the time our clothes got stolen from the car in Cleveland," Opal said.

"I never will forget that," Willie remembered, laughing aloud. "We were there the same time the Cleveland Indians won the World Series, uh, October '54."

"That's when it was," said Opal. "I ended up with my uniforms because I took mine out of the car."

"Courtney always takes his clothes with him," Willie C. noted.

"Courtney's always a rebel," kidded Billy. "It's just something that . . . like Teddy was saying when we were on the plane. Everybody was sitting on the straight line because we have our seating right together. You know where he had gone? Teddy said, 'Pop, I heard of people disappearing in strange places, but on a jet plane?' Courtney would be back there in the tail section or the fuselage – anywhere – but you can't see him."

"But if you got seats that open straight across, why sit

like this?' Opal explained, scrunching his legs up in front of him. "I learned that from . . ."

"I think that's something between you and Gerald, because Gerald's just the opposite," Billy said. "It's a personality thing. Gerald is conventional and he believes in doing everything proper and correct, you know. Anticipating that your . . . Opal is more of a pioneer. He'll venture out and see something. And I think that personality thing . . ."

"That might have something to do with it," Opal agreed. "I'm not regimented at all."

"And Opal's family, you know. Well-known basketball player and stuff like that, so they had like a little family pride-type thing; and the guy (Gerald) would say, well, 'Opal thinks he's better than anybody as far as his family and stuff like that, you know.

"And it's amazing because here's a bunch of senior citizens and it's just like going back to high school. With the same little . . ."

"Same little stuff," Opal agreed.

"We have a rehearsal and he'd say, 'You want to go out in the alley? Come on; come on, nigger. I'll take you right here. The guy's on Medicare, you know, talking that shit . . ." Billy laughed.

"So, it's something that I just refuse to accept," Opal emphasized. "I'm not going to accept anything but something good for everybody. And I'm not going to allow one person . . . and I'm just a bit more outspoken than everybody else. They're diplomats. But I don't have time to be a diplomat. Either he's gonna' shit or he's gonna' sing or he ain't gonna' sing."

"I am a bass singer," Billy said. "I've been singing baritone or second tenor, you know, because I can do it. But I'm naturally a bass singer. As a matter or fact, when we won all these contests I was singing bass and people would say, 'Wow, listen to him!' So, Teddy has my identical voice. If you would hear Teddy sing, it would be very hard for you to distinguish. And so, uh . . ."

"And I sing bass, too," chimed-in Opal, to laughter all-around.

"So, it's not like one guy can stop the show," Billy went

on. "Now in Pookie's case, it's a little different. I don't care how good a guy can sing second tenor . . ."

"He does have his voice," Opal interjected.

". . . Pookie . . . it's a certain style of Pookie's that's very hard to duplicate. By him being the lead singer all the time. For instance, if Gerald sang lead all the time, then it would be a different story of having somebody to put in. But he only does it, like he'll do certain featured bass and stuff, but the main attention is on Pookie.

"So that's the whole thing," said Billy. "I just hope nothing happens to Pookie. That's where my worries come. Because I always felt about the Spaniels . . . there's Pookie and Gerald. Anybody else can be replaced like that. You could interchange the three of us with anybody, as long as they're singing correctly, you've got the Spaniels.

"But you can't take Pookie away. It would be practically impossible to take Pookie away. They tried it before. When Gerald, God bless his soul, held the group together – Even when Pookie left. And that's when he went and got Parma Lee and Donald Porter and James Cochran. Well, Parma Lee – Carl Rainge – was a terrific tenor singer. First tenor, you know. He could do it all. So he was singing lead, he was doing Pookie's thing. It wasn't the same, because people knew how Pookie sounded. That was the thing. That was the sound of the Spaniels."

"Carl had a group before," said Willie C., "and he was the lead singer. He sounded the way he sounded and they sounded the way they sounded. He sounded good, but it wasn't the Spaniels."

"Well, I'm more like on the outside," Billy responded. "But when we started, Pookie and me cut our teeth doing Ink Spots and Charioteers and Mills Brothers and stuff like that. That's why Pookie, given the proper background, this guy could go to all kinds of heights. Even now. That's the amazing thing. Nobody has lost their voice. Out of all these years, almost 40 years, the voices are still intact. It's very similar to the Hi-Los."

An acknowledged expert and student of modern music, Billy stressed that the "true sound of the Spaniels is the interplay between Pookie and Gerald, and a tight, solid background. Those three things come into play. From the time he first started singing, Pookie had a distinctive sound – even as a kid. And that sound would reach people back then.

"It's the interplay between Pookie's voice and Gerald. I remember when Gerald was a kid in school. At that time, nobody had ever heard of Jimmy Ricks. He was the first bass singer in history who popularized lead singing. He took bass and instead of singing bass in the background, he actually sang lead. And Gerald loved this guy. It was fantastic because every time Jimmy Ricks would put out something Gerald would have it and you couldn't tell the difference," Billy continued.

"It wasn't that he was trying to sound like Jimmy, but it was Gerald's natural sound. And from that, people like – I'm sure Melvin Franklin of the Temptations and all the great bass singers of today – have copied off this guy. Or they were inspired or want to emulate Gerald because he kind of set the standard. Even singing background bass. It's a distinct sound he also has that you'll know his voice. A lot of guys can sing bass, but Gerald to me sounds like a saxophone.

So that's the sound of the Spaniels. Pookie's distinct style and that ballad lead, that easy sound. Gerald's deep, you know, smooth bass and the background being tight. Together, that makes the Spaniels.

"It was the same thing with the Platters," Billy concluded. "Tony Williams . . . they must have been eight or nine leads over the years but it never was the same without him."

But Tony Williams and the Platters – singly or as a group never were a match for Pookie Hudson and the Spaniels. Not really. Not among those who were able to hear both groups. Unfortunately, however, that did not include everyone in America in the '50s.

* * * *

"Well Richard, I always pooh-poohed doo-wop singing because to me it kind of got away from the basic harmonies," said Billy. "In doo-wop singing it was more of a feel; you could do what you felt and I believed in strict, tight harmony singing. For instance, today a top group would be Take Six. I would rank them over any of the other groups for that reason.

"Pookie and I basically cut our teeth on the Ink Spots and Mills Brothers and things like barbershop-type spiritual singing. I rank the old singing much higher than I did than groups that would just get together and harmonize. But that was just my personal thing. I'm not saying it was right or wrong.

Do you think that if young kids today had a chance to listen to the old Spaniels stuff they could appreciate it?

"Yeah," responded Teddy. "As a matter of fact, I think they like it more. Because of them listening to nothing but midi-systems and electronic music and all these different things, the old stuff is now new to 'em. So now they get to hear to what I call "pure" music – just straight singing and maybe a couple of instruments in the background. But it's not all built around the board where you just push the button. So I think they really get a kick out of it."

"But the thing about the Spaniels that made them unique is the special ingredients," said Billy. "I believe that when you have a product to sell, certain ingredients have to be prominent. Just like a good soup or a good dinner. And with the Spaniels it was Pookie's unique sound – that relaxed ballad-type delivery that he would give. No matter what song he would sing, it would have his identity on it.

"And Gerald," he continued, "and the counterplay between the high, second tenor sound and the low bass. Gerald's identity on the bass, working together with that background. The other three guys – the tight harmony trio for support. That certain combination was just a winner and for some reason, it always worked."

While the Spaniels were first to do a number of things in early original black R&B, playing-off the bass tenor wasn't one of them, according to Billy.

"They didn't pioneer it," he explained. "Certainly there were groups before like the Ravens. Jimmy Ricks was the low bass and Gerald's idol at that time. And they had a high tenor who had a long name – Van somebody; uh, Van Loan. Joe Van Loan. But this guy could go just as high as

Jimmy could go low. And whenever you could find groups like that – with an outstanding lead and outstanding bass and a tight background – it was a successful group."

And why does the group think the whole R&B thing is back? Is it because the style have changed, or whites coming in, or what?

Billy: "People look for change. Change has to happen. I think the reason so much is going back to the '50s and '60s now is simplicity – a lot of people haven't heard it before. Those were happier days, happier times. You could take a little money and go to the store. Everybody had a car, you know, the muscle cars. And for some reason, the TV commercials all go back to the '50s."

Teddy: "I think a whole lot of it has to do with the movies and different things like that. For instance, 'Three Men and a Baby.' I'm sittin' down and I hear 'Goodnight Sweetheart.' And a lot of my friends who weren't aware of the Spaniels – now they are because of the end of that movie, with the credits rolling. And on the commercials, they're playing a lot of the old stuff. Like I say, it's new but it's old."

Billy: "When things are beautiful, they become antiques. Time only makes them more valuable. It's the same way with this. I really had to develop an appreciation for the '50s music, because there was one time I had turned the radio off. Now I listen and I can see a lot of beauty in it. Because along with that comes what the guys went through – the times you could feel the soul."

And why do you suppose the quality of the voices hasn't deteriorated?

"I can't figure it out," Billy answered. "As a matter of fact, Willie C. sounds better now, to me, than he did when he was in high school. Willie C. was always the cohesive guy in the group. He was way ahead of the gigs. Now, he's like the chaplain. Now before we go on stage, we usually have a prayer, so we remember where we came from and we know where all the blessings come from. And it's been working."

Say you do an album, they were asked, how do you get it played on the radio?

"I don't know that much about the business, but I do know that making an album and doing a lot of appearances and shows go hand-in-hand," Billy said. "I'm an old groupie and I used to follow groups like the Delphonics and the Dells and the Moments; we were on the road with them. It was a direct correlation that the amount of record sales adds to the appearances.

"If you play a town and there are 6,000 people out there – after the show, if you done your job right all 6,000 are going to be down there to get your album when the record shop opens on Monday. It works that way. Marvin Gaye was one of the artists who didn't go out; he was shy by nature and stayed in the recording studio. His record sales probably would have gone up . . ."

But what makes DJs play it?

"Pookie would probably know," Billy continued. "In the old days, it used to be things like payola. It got down to that. But the recording industry is not what it used to be. They're not the giants. It's like Hollywood of today. They could take a guy like Fabian and make him the hottest thing because they had the distribution and could get the records played.

"But nowadays, with this high-tech equipment, somebody can turn on the radio and get Michael Jackson and you can't tell the difference. You've got the whole album. Where in the old days, you had to buy the records. As a result, the recording industry is laying-off a lot of established artists. Talent scouts are almost nonexistent these days."

And the key to getting white audiences? Or maybe you should just forget about color.

"Teddy and I are working to keep our chops up over the weekend and our audience is like 98 percent white working in an area of rich whites. I've found the best thing to do is just be as good as you can be and whoever, whatever traffic comes, that's fine," emphasized Billy.

"Pookie just brought out the point that we could perform at home here in Gary and probably not too many people would show up – for a lot of different reasons. The money situation and things – and then being close to the artists, it's hard. Right now, it's hard for me to give Pookie the respect that's due him because I'm so close to Pookie. He's like my brother.

"So I was in awe when we go on the road and great groups that I admire – all of them are trying to get next to Pookie and talk to him. Wow, this guy is a powerful guy. It's going to be hard for Teddy to maybe know because he's also close to him. A lot of our people – the people who are able to buy tickets – would go and hear Luther Vandross or something that's happening now because they want to be associated with the happenings of today. But foreign people and white people are more antique collectors, you know. They hear something they like and they'll drive a long way to see original groups like the Spaniels."

*   *   *   *

"I feel pretty good about things now," said Gerald, "have no doubt in my mind. It depends upon us as a team that if we work together, we're going to be successful."

"You hear what I'm saying," Opal chimed in, attempting to clear the air. "I love him (Gerald). He don't think I do but I do. I swear I love him. You see what Michael Jordan did with the Bulls. Michael incorporated the team from jump street. In the beginning of the season he incorporated the team and Michael took a back seat all during the first part of the season. He would incorporate Pippen (Scottie) and all the rest of them. Make 'em take the shots at the beginning of the season that he knew you would have to take when it came down to the money.

"So this is what you got to do. You got to have faith in somebody else. You just don't do it by yourself."

Said Willie C: I often say a group of people – anybody can have individuals. But a team is always together and that's what I've always told the Spaniels since we started. We've got to be a team, because we're a team group. We're a team. We got to work together. We used to get on a stage and we'd say 'All for one and one for all,' and a little prayer. And we never had any problems."

"Ever since we've been back together, there is a prayer," Opal added.

"Back stage . . ." said Pookie.

"At rehearsals too," Willie C. said. "We try to keep God

in there and this keeps us loving one another. So I figure we have a great future because we all have one accord, the same accord. And we all want to be good again and to get out there and perform. And the time is right."

"I have nothing but positive feelings," Opal said. "And an example of that, last week I was offered a better job and I told Tommy (his boss) I'd have to think about it. I thought about it two or three days and I turned it down, because it would interfere. I'd have to quit singing with the Spaniels.

"I turned this down last week. I told Pookie about it and I told Willie C. I said I'm thinking about it. They said, 'Well Courtney, what are you going to do about it? I said I plan to go to the Apollo on the 10th. I plan to got to California when we go. I plan to go to Europe and I plan to go with the Spaniels.

"It's not all about money. I believe. And I'll be very honest. I believe in Billy. I believe in Pookie. I believe in Willie C. I believe in myself.

"Now when Gerald and I make peace with ourselves, I will do everything in the world for Gerald. But we've got to make our own peace. You say be very candid. I turned money down because I love the group. And love is a whole lot deeper than a dollar and a cent. You understand this?

"Now we're working," Opal went on. "Now we're going to work. And I told Pookie, I said Pookie, we've got to have Gerald. We're got to have Gerald.' It was my idea to come by and talk to you (Gerald). And you said that's the way it's going to be. We're going to be one group like we used to be. I don't see nothin' but love, I don't see nothin' but togetherness. And it can't be nothin' but good luck."

What specifically, is it going to take for the group to succeed today? they were asked.

Said Pookie: "It's going to take a lot of perserverance. It's going to take a lot of knocking on doors, telephone calls. Basically, it's going to take us – like Courtney was saying, it's going to take love. Because we've got to be able to support each other, to support the group. And when we go out, we've got to represent ourselves as being businessmen, being artists, being here to do a job. To do the job that we know how to do – the best way we know how to do it. Not like other people do it.

"That's another thing. We don't get to the point we want to emulate anyone. All we got to do, is do the Spaniels as the Spaniels. And you say look, man, that's what makes us special, because we are different.

And when you succeed, will you be representing all those other groups who fell by the wayside?

"Yes, we will," Pookie responded. "And the way to do that also is — and they would be glad for it to happen — is that we carry ourselves . . . If we go out as a bunch of drunks, if we go out as a bunch of drug addicts, if we're not going out as entertainers, it ain't no use in going out there."

"Richard, another thing," Billy interjected, "I don't want this to go by without thinking about this. We are the oldest group — to my knowledge — you've got to correct me if I'm wrong. But we're the oldest group singing with the original members. You've got four — four guys who were with the original group who were recording in 1953, and the new guy who is actually older. I'm a prehistoric Spaniel. So I don't think you have another group out there that has four original members who were recording in that era."

That, in itself, is significant indeed.

* * * *

"I feel like Willie C.," Gerald said. "Give me that last five minutes man. Let's do 'Heart and Soul' before you go."

And then, Willie C.'s wife, Zola, called down that it was time for work, bringing to a conclusion a historic, marathon interview with the original Spaniels — still intact 38 years after they started. Men ranging in age from 54 to 58.

Following is exactly how the day ended:

"OK, Willie's got to get ready to go," I said. "Can I hear one song or whatever? For the tape?"

"Yeah," said Willie C.

"Could we get by 'Heart and Soul?' Billy asked. "Let's do something that we . . ."

"Well I told the man that ya'll can sing 'Heart and Soul,' Pookie said. "Now ya'll gon' make a liar out of me."

"No, no, no. We'll do it. We'll give it a shot," Billy said.

"Maybe you can sing two of them . . ." I chimed in.

"I ain't talking about him," Pookie added. "I'm talking

about Gerald. I told Gerald. See, I think this is for Gerald."

"We'll do it for Gerald," said Opal.

"See, Gerald told me that ya'll couldn't do it, and that's why he wants to do it," Pookie laughed.

"Well we'll sing 'Heart and Soul,'" said Opal.

"I been tellin' the man that ya'll can do it," Pookie re-emphasized.

"Let's find out," Billy said.

"I want to hear 'Heart and Soul,' then if you feel like it, I want to hear 'Baby, It's You,'" I said. "But that's up to you."

"Alright, OK," said Billy. "Let's give 'em both to him."

"Since you didn't sing it at Radio City that night," I added. "You know I wanted to hear it."

"What's that, 'Heart and Soul'? Opal asked.

"Naw, 'Baby, It's You,'" I replied.

"OK, let's give it to him," said Billy.

"I want to hear 'Heart and Soul,' too." I added.

* * * *

"Myyyyyy heart and souuul . . ." boomed Gerald's bravura bass. He then paused and asked: "That key sound alright?"

"Yeah, that sounds good," said Billy.

"Heart and Soul is everybody," Gerald knowingly noted – proceeding to lead the casually attired, completely relaxed, born-again Spaniels a capella through his signature smash.

Following my singular round of applause, with a resounding "Awwwright," I said: "Now do 'Baby, It's you and I'll let you go Willie."

"Yeah, I got to catch my ride," he replied.

Now it was Pookie's turn to lead on the song that sent the Spaniels soaring while still in high school in 1953. One chorus only, because Willie C. had to get to the steel mill.

When "Baby, It's You" ended, I thanked them for doing it. But in my heart and soul, I knew I also was thanking them for doing all the others. Including, of course, "Goodnight Sweetheart, Goodnight."

The Spaniels live!

FOURTEEN
Reflections

"The Spaniels had the high harmony and the lowest bass – Gerald Gregory – I've ever heard on records. I busted a speaker on his 'So Deep Within.' And they had the most wonderful lead singer, Pookie Hudson. He had this beautiful floating voice over the high harmony which gave them a sound all their own. I have most of their records." – Warren Tesoro, Colony Records, 49th and Broadway, New York City.

There's no middle ground when it comes to the Spaniels. Everyone who's ever heard them loves them. And that means millions. This includes music lovers from coast-to-coast who know the real thing, as well as old friends from Gary – a hometown that has never really done right by the group.

Take Warren Tesoro, himself a member of several rhythm and blues vocal groups and a man countless New Yorkers turn to by name when they're on the prowl for vintage R&B records. Of the Spaniels, the knowledgable Tesoro said:

"The group is totally unique. They have a sound all their own. I don't know how Gerald (Gregory) gets down there. It's almost as if wind is coming out of his voice at the same time. He sounds like a baritone sax or a bass sax."

Tesoro said the Spaniels were "very much revered in my Williamsburg (Brooklyn) neighborhood when I was growing up. I knew about them long before I got into the record business. I've been singing in groups all my life, starting right there in the projects.

"And listening to them helped inspire me."

Tesoro said the first tune he recalls hearing the Spaniels do was 1958's upbeat version of "Stormy Weather" – before ever having known it was recorded in classic style by Lena Horne. And he expressed surprise at Pookie's stated feeling that he is not real comfortable singing fast songs.

"Well, he's a wonderful writer and a wonderful singer. He's a great ballad singer, he's a great blues vocalist. He's got that range, still today. And he sings those upbeats great, man. I love him when he does those. And he can really sing the blues too, like 'Baby, It's You.' He's got a style all his own.

"It's just amazing that they were able to capture a bluesy sound like that on 'Baby It's You' when they were so young; just in their teens, I understand. They sounded like seasoned blues men. I put the Spaniels right up there with the top groups of that time – Spaniels, Five Keys and Drifters were the three best, in my opinion."

* * * *

Milwaukee's Richard Berry first heard of the Spaniels in 1953, owing, he said, to the close geographical proximity of Gary and it's initially regional Vee-Jay label. As a result, he was able to see the group perform in Chicago as well as Milwaukee during the '50s.

"I think the thing about the Spaniels was that you can listen to many groups – like the Midnighters with Hank Ballard, and the Royals, and the Five Royals and the Five Keys – and sometimes the groups would become confusing. But something about the Spaniels was unique. And that was Gerald Gregory, the bass, and James (Pookie) Hudson, the lead singer. You could never mistake the Spaniels for any other group.

"Here in Milwaukee, we'd hear the Orioles on the Federal label and the Moonglows on Chess Records. Most of the aspiring groups we had here would always try to sing like the Spaniels. Not like the Moonglows, not the Five Royales, not the Midnighters, not the Orioles but like the Spaniels. They were so unique. The harmony was good and the lead singer was great.

"And the El Dorados, with Pirk (Pirkle Lee Moses Jr.)

singing lead, also were real good, said Berry. But they couldn't sing the slow tunes like the Spaniels because I don't think they had the harmony. The Spaniels had harmony, kind of like the Orioles with Sonny Til. They had the closed-mouth harmony and also the open-mouth harmony. They were quite superior in that they could harmonize both ways. And of course they had great emphasis on the bass. Many groups had a bass that was synthetic. The Spaniels had a true bass and could do authentic bass leads.

"They also had something else in their music," Berry went on. "They had a feel for humor, like in 'Play it Cool.' If you're black and you went to church, you know that piano intro came right out of church. And when you hear the lyrics about cigarettes and alcoholic beverages and the message they sent you, you just cracked up. It was so funny."

Berry was asked his initial impression of "Goodnight Sweetheart, Goodnight" in 1954.

"I was 16 at the time and we all had groups then," he replied. "We all tried to be singers and tried to imitate what we heard, because we were so impressed. And I was blown away. There were so many groups at the Lapham Park Social Center and just about all of them were doing Spaniels' songs like 'Goodnight Sweetheart' and fracturing their throats trying those opening bass notes.

"The rip-off by the McGuire Sisters really happened because they (the Spaniels) were regional on a small label.

"It's very important to note that music in those days was stolen. Even now, you hear 'Goodnight Sweetheart' on TV commercials.

"And the Spaniels were very limited. They had no distribution on Vee-Jay. At best, they would be heard in Indiana, Wisconsin, northeastern Illinois, parts of Michigan and perhaps Ohio.

"And it's amazing, all these years, that the original Spaniels are back together again. Because in the old days, most of the groups, like the Spaniels, had original music of their own. And the great sound really hinged on the harmony of the groups. Just imagine with their sound quality then, with their musicianship, if the Spaniels had the audio and sophisticated recording techniques you have now.

"It's also a shame," he said, "that they were never able to appear on a big TV show like Ed Sullivan's because they were from the Midwest and had no distribution. So we never know how great they could have become. Maybe now, this kind of stuff will change for the better."

* * * *

And how do people in the Spaniels' home town of Gary feel about them in the 1990s?

According to solid citizen Larry McWay, "nothing could be finer . . ."

President of Gary's 500-member U.S. Steelworkers Union of America Local 1014, McWay's organization is the second-largest steelworkers local in the United States. And U.S. Steel's plant in Gary is the nation's largest.

"When I hear the Spaniels sing records from the golden days, it's always 11 o'clock on Friday night in the summertime," McWay enthused. "Spaniels' music has inspired and created more romance than anyone in history. It helped create more black babies . . .

"Where I lived, we heard Spaniels' records on WDIA in Memphis – the soul capital of the nation. I also heard them on WWCA in Chicago – 'Livin' with Vivian' disk jockey show, which played all the music of the day."

McWay said he came to Gary in 1969 – "looking for the Spaniels. But it's just too bad the place of their roots never looked hard enough for them.

"The Bible often said a man is not recognized properly in their own land – and it's the same with the Spaniels in Gary."

On the other hand, 81-year-old (in 1991) S.W. (Mickey) Smith, proprietor of the Royal Barbershop at 112 W. 25th Ave., brings a bit of a different perspective to the legendary Spaniels and the vocalizing counterparts of the early 1950s.

"I remember 'em well when they started because I was managing a spiritual group, the Royal Quartet," said Smith, who likes to be called Smitty.

"That's the reason this shop has that name. And this is a place where musically inclined people would stop off to get their hair cut and talk about their work."

Smitty, who came to Gary from his birthplace of Pine

Bluff, Ark., feels that his popular local gospel group is one of the reasons Gary ended up producing several well-known vocalizers, such as Michael Jackson and the Jackson Five, the Dells and, of course, the Spaniels.

"All forms of music has its origins," chimed in Billy Shelton, "and gospel was pretty much that for rhythm and blues. You'd find the kids on the corner singing the latest Soul Stirrer songs and the legendary groups all were booked in Gary by Smitty. They inspired many of the young people who went in different directions. But it started here."

"And the Spaniels are still great today," Smitty said. "I just heard 'Goodnight Sweetheart' on a TV commercial last night . . . for Dodge. But we always appreciated 'em here in town, from the time Vivian Carter gave 'em a boost on her disk jockey show. We knew they would succeed. It didn't surprise us."

*   *   *   *

According to Ernest Warren, who opted not to return when the original Spaniels were reunited in 1991, the main reason the Spaniels failed to cash-in properly at their peak was a lack of exposure.

"We were having problems at that time with our records going on white stations," he said. "This just didn't happen. If we had been played on the stations like they do today, with mega-hits back then, we would have been the uh . . . I would say we'd have spearheaded some great things. But our records just weren't played."

And how about now? Would the old tunes be accepted if they were released all over again today?

"I know they would be accepted," he said. "That's without a doubt because some of them – especially 'Goodnight Sweetheart' – I heard it on a commercial yesterday.

"I was sitting in my den and a fellow was visiting and I told him, 'You just heard my voice.' And he said, 'Aw, you're kidding.' He didn't believe it. And then I pulled out one of my old tapes and played it, and showed him that it was us that really made that commercial. It's allowed that they were using our voice on that commercial because we have no recourse to get any money from them."

Ernest said his biggest regret was that "we never did really get the opportunities and the chance to have the kind of life . . . the people didn't do, you know . . . I don't think they really backed us the way they (Vee-Jay) should have. Either they were incompetent or . . . I don't know what it was. If they had been Motown — people with a knowledge of music . . . that's probably one of the things I regret most. That we never did hit Motown. But they came a little late for us.

"And I would imagine they (Motown) considered us over the hill by the time they were really doing their own thing. And I would say we would challenge their groups when it comes to ability and singing."

How would he compare the songs of today and his day?

"Ours is more touching," he said, "more down to earth and in line with what was really happening as far as life was concerned. All this stuff that's going on now is just vulgarity, really. It's not music.

"One thing I was listening to when I played that tape, that if we had the help . . . we had only one . . . it was on one record, I would say, two records, that we had the person recording it that knew what he was doing with music. That was on 'Baby, It's You' and 'The Bells Ring Out'. Those two records . . . they . . . the A&R man . . . he knew what he was doing and things that were missing. He had them put it in and he actually was arranging on the spot for us . . . for some of the music. So after those records it was kind of cut and dried, you know, and extemperaneous and it really wasn't together; really wasn't no musical rehearsals with the group to really get the best technological sound or mixing and so forth. We didn't have that."

What about the Rhythm and Blues Foundation award?

"I thought it was a great honor," Ernest said, "and I thought it was about time. But I also was a little apprehensive because I don't think, uh . . . it kind of disappointed me in a way because I was looking for a little something, a little more than what really happened.

"I'm talking about . . . being a little more organized, a little more together. It just wasn't professional. Nobody even sang."

Ernest was correct in his assessment of the 1991 awards program, held at a swanky New York nightclub called Tatou. How can you give out music awards without having someone sing, especially when you have so much great talent assembled? Fortunately, that situation was corrected for subsequent R&B Foundation presentations.

*   *   *   *

Among R&B afficionados in general, and the legions of Spaniels' fans in particular, the relative quality of the originals honored by the R&B Foundation, and the Porter-Rainge-Cochran second group always has been argued. And rightly so. Both were great in their own way.

Says Pookie: "It was two different styles. The first group was a feelin' group. We felt our way through the harmonies, we felt our way through the songs and things and basically, we sang straight from the heart. The second group was more technical. They sang parts, everybody stayed on their part.

"Whereas in the first group, each person in the background might change voices right in the middle of the song. Like Courtney would sing top tenor, the next thing you know he be singin' baritone; Ernest be singin' top tenor; Willie C. might sing tenor and Ernest might sing the baritone. And it would all be done in the process of singing.

"With the second group, we went to rehearsals and everybody had a part to sing and we had it organized. We had a precise way of what was gon' be done. Didn't nobody do no changes; everybody knew the part that was theirs."

Which group did he, as lead singer, enjoy the most?

I basically liked both of 'em, but I liked the first group for some reason for the feelin', because everybody was feelin' what we was all feelin'. You know, it was one thing.

"I liked the second one because it was beautiful. I mean, they sang correctly; the harmonies were great and, what can I say, and they was soulful. But I just feel the first group was more soulful because they based their singing from the heart, not from some music to sell.

"But the second group was the better singers," Pookie acknowledged. "They had more vocal talent, they were more harmony-oriented. The imagination wasn't there, but they didn't have to have as much imagination. All they had to do was the vocal truth. Whereas the first group, everything we did was through imagination. We imagined what we wanted to hear and that's what we tried to do to tell the truth."

I respectfully noted that the second group's version of "Baby, It's You" in 1958 was a perfect example. It was good, but it can't compare with the classic, original 1953 recording.

"Yeah, that's right," he agreed. "The more technically correct second version took something from it."

Had the R&B Foundation at the Smithsonian not insisted on the original Spaniels, would Pookie have taken the working (second) group to New York for the awards? After all, it was the second group who made most of the records.

"I don't think so," he answered very thoughtfully. "If they had just said they wanted the Spaniels, then I probably would have taken the other group. Because we, at that time, was singing. I had come back and the group I had put together wasn't Courtney and them, it was Carl Rainge, Donald Porter, Gerald Gregory, and then we had Billy Shelton. And I would have taken them.

"We were having a little shaky problems and maybe that would have helped us get our, I figured, you know, like get our feet back on the ground like we wanted to," he noted.

And if that happened, would he be mounting the Spaniels comeback with that group?

"See, that's another thing I don't know, because I've gotten so many knocks about the group. About them personally. I don't know, because I was ready to get rid of the group just about two weeks before we (the originals) went to New York. I not only was ready to get rid of 'em, I was ready to get out of the group. Because it got to the point that I was bein' told what to do, and what they didn't want and how they wanted it and carryin' on. And my ideas didn't matter.

"And what I was tryin' to do was rebuild the group and put us in a position to get to do some things they want to do. But you have to rebuild first, really. As far as older records, yeah, they know us, but what they (the working second group) wanted to do . . . they was askin' me to ask people for outrageous money and , uh, groups that got records don't ask for. And they felt they should have got that. So I felt like, if ya'll feel that way, ya'll get a group and ya'll ask for the money if you want to, and I'll get a group and I'll ask for what I want to, and that way we don't get in the way of each other.

"So it just got to the point that I just feel that I'm at an age that I need to run what I think is going to be beneficial not only to me but to those that are with me. And if you don't agree with that, then we don't need to be together."

If you had to replace Gerald Gregory because of his drinking problems or his acting up, who would you replace him with?

"Either with Billy Shelton or his son, Teddy Shelton. Right now it would probably be Teddy Shelton. And he could still play the guitar. He could sing and play."

But what about the reaction to the Spaniels without Gerald? Could this hurt you?

"No, because I done had too many groups, No. 1. And this is not braggin', but everywhere I went they tell you, 'If you ain't bringin' Pookie Hudson, you ain't bringin' the Spaniels. I don't care who you got. So basically it's just me. And I've had other groups, and every time another dude that sing the bass and say 'Do do do do dooo . . .' the people jump up and scream. They didn't care if it was Gerald Gregory or not. All they know is the song."

Does he feel the Spaniels are finished with all the drinking and drugs, except for keeping Gerald on the straight and narrow?

"Oh yeah. What we definitely need now, to help speed it up, is some innovative marketing, some TV shows; we need more jobs, more gigs; we need to be put in front of the people more.

"All of this should come to a head in the next year. We'll put the Spaniels in the light so we'll be able to entertain and make the people happy.

"We're going to have our say," he said, "and have control and all those things in place that need to be, to make sure we don't go back to the '50s as far as finance and as far as bein', uh, correct as a group."

Any jealousies or bad feelings over the group now being

billed as 'Pookie Hudson and the Spaniels' rather than just the Spaniels?

"No. I explained that situation. I explained what that was. I told them (the reformed originals) before we started. I called it Pookie Hudson and the Original Spaniels for the simple reason that if Carl (Rainge) and them decided they wanted to put a group together, I want the distinction so the people know who Pookie Hudson is and what group he's in. So if there is a choice, they accept that. They won't be gettin' nobody thinkin' Pookie Hudson is there, and he ain't there."

* * * *

Pookie was asked about the storied emotion of the late Vivian Carter, despite the bad financial situation between her, Vee-Jay Records, and the Spaniels.

"Aw, she truly, loved our music, " he sighed. "There's no doubt about it. Like I said, I never saw her face dry at any of our sessions. When we come out of a session, she had been cryin' just by sittin' there listening to us sing. She was victimized like we were and some others were – but on the right side, where the money was."

It must have taken a lot of work to cultivate the smooth sound that Vivian loved so much – even on the uptempo stuff.

"Oh, yeah, it took a lot of practice, but it was nothin' that we was lookin' for. We just sang what we sang and sang what we felt, and that's what came out. But it took a lot of rehearsal and a lot of singin' and a lot of feelin.'

"Also, a lot of takes," he continued. "This was mainly when somebody messed up. When we first started singin', they didn't have but two tracks, so when you did it wrong, you had to do it again . . ."

Does Pookie feel the Spaniels have gotten a fair shake from the public over the years? Is the public fickle? Have they forgotten?

"Well, I just have a thing . . . I feel that we as black people, we do not have the heroes like white people have. Like the white people, they got the Bob Hopes, the Frank Sinatras. Even to the point they got the blacks coming over like Lena Horne and Sammy Davis Jr. Those people were able to continue doing what they loved and want to do because they were accepted by people. We black people only accept you basically by your last record. And if your last record is not really concrete . . .

"We were lucky," he went on. "Now a lot of (our) records didn't really make it, but we were still recognized as a group. But I know a lot of groups, and a lot of individuals, after that first record – if didn't nothin' happen then – they were dead after that. But this is what happens with black people. We just don't hold onto, or have, those type of heroes, or whatever you want to call 'em."

Is it true the Spaniels were one of the originators of the phrase "doo-wop," which the music has come to be known by?

"We were the originator," Pookie emphasized. "It was just a phrase we used as a harmony line. At that time, most groups were singin' straight harmony – just hummin' and whatever. We got into what we called 'answering,' where the group would answer the lead singer. They would use made-up phrases like 'doo-wop' which we did. Good examples were in records like 'False Love.' And 'Painted Pictures' was another."

And nobody ever used "doo-wop" before you did?

"Not to my knowledge, they didn't. But this shouldn't be confused with our record 'Doo-Wah.' That wasn't doo-wop. It was close to it. We thought about doo-wop. We had been singin' doo-wop before then but we figured we had overused the phrase doo-wop so we went to 'doo-wah.' As a matter of fact, we called the song 'Doo-Wah.'

* * * *

In the golden days, some famous show business names appeared on Spaniels' shows, including Redd Foxx and Flip Wilson. Some even opened for the group – that's how popular the Spaniels were.

"It happened at the Apollo, the Regal (in Chicago), the Uptown in Philadelphia, the Howard Theater (in Washington)," Pookie said. "They were the emcees, basically. They come up and do their little act and bring the acts on. They were great to us.

"In fact, Redd Foxx sat us down one time. At that time we

had some yellow suits that we wore and people really seemed to enjoy 'em. He said, 'Man, look, ya'll too good a group and need to tone down and get into that love thing, and ya'll need to cross over into the white thing. But we was too dumb to understand what was goin' on.

"That was just before he (Foxx) really started gettin' famous. I guess it was '58. But we didn't take his advice, but he sure told us. No doubt about it. And Flip was there – a very congenial dude. Then there was another one with a dummy; not Willie Tyler and Lester. He's been in some movies now. A little short dude. Him and Jim Brown had a fight one time. Stu Gilliam. I thought he was the funniest man. In fact, they had a chitlins' circuit tour at the time and we were at the Apollo and we were going to the Royal (in Baltimore) and the Howard and then down to Virginia.

"We rode with him because we had parked our car in a no-parking zone and went to somebody's house to sleep. We got up and the car was gone – towed. And we didn't have the money to get it out. I mean we'd just finished at the theater, just got paid and didn't have enough money to get our car out. So we rode with him and sent somebody back to get our car after Vee-Jay decided to let us have the money to get it.

"We told 'em it wasn't nothing we could do about it since we didn't have no money to get it. So we'd let it stay there. That's how we felt about it. But it was a new car so they gave us the money to get it out. Matter of fact it was Doo-Doo, and he went to get it for us."

In all the intervening years, Pookie said he and the group have not talked to any of the stars-to-be they appeared with.

"I ain't heard nothing from nobody but Flip," he said. "One time he was emceeing Johnny Carson's 'Tonight Show' – substitute host, you know – and said he wondered what happened to Pookie Hudson and the Spaniels. But that was about it."

* * * *

One of the best things about a Spaniels' show was the occasionally intricate, always enjoyable dance routines – the acknowledged leader of which was James (Dimples) Cochran, a member of the second group.

"He was a great choreographer," said Gerald. "We didn't start off really dancing. What it was, Pookie, as you say, he got two left feet, and his style is just like that – slow, easy going. And for us to accentuate his slowness, we had to do something around it and the people liked us better that way. And we had a lot of compliments because of this. By Pookie being as slow as he is and us dancing, it made us look better. And ever since we started it, I liked it."

Speaking of dancing, Gerald regrets that the Spaniels weren't able to capitalize on 'The Twist', which was written for them by the Nightingales, a gospel group. "We recorded it but Vee-Jay didn't put it out because it was deemed too sexy. So Hank Ballard copyrighted it and recorded it. It always bugged me that we didn't copyright it."

RANDOM REFLECTIONS

One of the sensational things about Pookie Hudson is his phrasing – the way he says certain words like "love" and "baby" and "cry" – making him sound kind of like a deeper-voiced Bill Kenny.

"He's got that funny tongue," Gerald smiled.

BILLY: "The bad stuff the group had to go through made it good now. What makes it good is when you still end up together.

"Willie C. is not that much of a singer but he's an organizer. He and Gerald actually got the group started in the old days. The Boys Glee Club at Roosevelt High also included the nephew of the organizer of the Flamingos – David Morrison. Some others were Walter and John Ford – who run a successful Gary cleaning business, and Lee Simms.

"Back then, Rev. Milton Joiner of Joiner's Five Trumpets gospel group, was singing on WWCA Radio. Don Porter and James Cochran also sang with them."

Did the Spaniels ever get the recognition they deserved in Gary?

WILLIE C.: "No, we never got the recognition in our earlier years. It was just taken for granted that you guys are just singing around here in Gary."

OPAL: "We still don't get it."

POOKIE: "We'd hang a lot, too. We stayed on the corner

with them dudes and we drank the wine with 'em and carryin' on, so when it came to performances we'd say, well, 'We're singing tonight.' They'd say, 'So, what do you want us to do about it?'"

BILLY: "You were too close. Like when the Three Bees would be at the Barber's Playhouse and we jumped out from behind the Christmas tree. I think 'I Don't Know,' by Willie Mabon was popular and we were entertaining the Roosevelt students, basically. Now here they paid to go to hear some music and they're seeing the same group that's been walking up and down the halls. And they'd say, 'Aw God, not them!'

"When you're too close to people you can't appreciate 'em right."

WILLIE C.: "You know, it's a strange thing, we used to go to Gerald's father's candy store every evening because a lot of times he had to work. It would be slow. When Pookie would come up with the words to a song, the background just fell in. We never practiced it. He just started singing and we just . . . That's the reason I say doo-wop, like Billy said, is what you feel; you don't have to learn no chorus, you don't have to learn nothing. You just feel it and it blends. That was the difference between the first group and the Rainge group."

GERALD: "That's why it's so important for a group to be close."

WILLIE C.: "We never had a problem getting a background for a song. One person would just start singing and we'd all blend in. We'd know where to change, we'd know just what to do with each other."

POOKIE: "That's the time we all thought alike, you know. That's what happens with each generation. If you notice, you hear some music here, then all of a sudden it starts spreading out. That's only because for some reason or other with each generation, whatever is going to be predominant seems to spread without even . . . It's like it's there.

"Like with our thing, we started singing and the next thing you know all them groups just started popping up and singing; and doing it the way we do it.

Now the Flamingos were there. But there weren't that

many groups copying when the Flamingos came out. But they were singing that straight harmony. You know, that straight, pretty harmony."

OPAL: "With high top . . ."

POOKIE: ". . . which came before them because everybody else was singing that straight, pretty harmony; Orioles . . . except for the Clovers. The Clovers were doing a lot of repeating. Five Keys . . . all the rest were basically straight harmony groups. We came in, we started doing the answering thing. We did some harmony. But our basic thing was the answering where the group would answer the lead singer. They wasn't doing that, you know, like 'Baby, It's You.' What made 'Baby, Its You' so different was the answering and the channel."

OPAL: "Who came up with that bass? How did that come up? Junior Coleman?

POOKIE: "Like Willie C. said, Coleman used to play that all the time. That was his line. But it came from that song, 'I'm gone, da dom da dom da dom, I'm gone,' by Shirley and Lee. Junior used it in all his songs . . .

WILLIE C.: "All his songs . . ."

POOKIE: "What happened was that Count (Morris on piano) came in and Count changed it around (Dom, dom da dom da dom, dom da dom da dom . . .). Count changed it around to that."

WILLIE C.: "Junior couldn't play nothing but straight chords anyway. That's what his problem was . . ."

POOKIE: "Basically it was all the same thing. That was coming out of California at the time. . . Little Esther . . ."

GERALD: "In 'Baby, It's You' – Do, do, do, do, do, baby; Do, do, do, do, do, baby . . . that was easy, just keeping the song going. Because most of the songs in those days were in that vein. We'd do a thousand numbers, a thousand tunes in which they'd have that run. So that was nothing."

OPAL: "But the backgrounds . . . the only constant thing back then was Pookie, Gerald and Willie C. Ernest was on top, one time. I'd sing baritone and next time we'd switch around. Now this (Willie C.) was the mole. He stayed one place. Willie stayed. He'd never switch.

"But on 'The Bells Ring Out' you'd hear Ernest on top. I

come back down. 'Goodnight Sweatheart' the same. 'Baby, It's You' is the same way. Because I sing Billy's part. I sing baritone. But when the chorus comes out you hear me 'woo hoo hoo hoooo . . .' I switched all the way back up again. This is because we all were together – and feeling. This is how we felt. We felt what was easy."

WILLIE C.: "If you know what the next guy is going to do . . . you know his part too . . ."

OPAL: "But we do that today."

About how many takes would it require in the studio?

OPAL: "Sometimes at Universal Studios it would take forever."

POOKIE: "Aw, man, we used to stay in the studio all night long. They didn't write the music down and we'd go on and rehearse with the band in somebody's basement – 'The Little King' we called him at that time – Al Smith. We rehearsed in the basement all day long, all week. And as soon as we go to the studio, didn't nobody know nothin.' Because they done lost all of it. So we had to rehearse it all again."

BILLY: "Those days it was different, too. You didn't have the high-tech studios. You only had one mike. If anybody made a mistake, you couldn't isolate him. And now, a guy doesn't have to know how to sing. He can sing flat through the whole thing and they can just speed up the tape to bring him on key and throw him back in.

"In those days, what you heard is what you got."

OPAL: "Today, each one of us might have a mike in the studio. but back then, we had one mike here, five gather around it; one for the band . . ."

POOKIE: "They called it a 'true-tech' studio. We had to sing. Wasn't no dials and shit. You had to do this yourself."

"Today they have live shows where they don't sing," I noted. "Madonna, with the mike on her head, will be lip-synching, right?

POOKIE: "Same thing with Janet (Jackson). Janet does the same thing. Ain't no way she gon' be doing all that dancin' and shit and be singin' like they be singin, man! Sweatin' and shit. Jumpin' up and down. You gon' tell me you don't get no interruptions in your voice? Ain't no way.

Any reason the Spaniels didn't record with strings?

"That came in with Ben E. King and the Drifters," Pookie continued. "They were the first group who recorded with strings. Way after Clyde (McPhatter). That was unheard of when we were out there. That's when they changed the whole group of the Drifters. That's when they took out Gaylord and his brother, Bubba, and Bill Pinkney and that little boy, David (Baughn) or Johnny whatchacallum (Moore) was singing lead and they just wiped that group out. They just put in a whole new group with Ben E. King with his group. They were called something else, and they just changed their name to the Drifters, and they came out with 'There Goes My Baby.'"

When the Spaniels make new albums, will it be the old sound that people recognize?

POOKIE: "That's our dispute right now. They (the group) want to do it exactly as done in the past. I can understand that because you got those people who know every word and every beat and knows what's happening in the song. And if you deviate from that then you're not coming with what they want to hear.

"Now white people will buy it. See, that's why I'm trying to go to this early morning, during the day – whenever it is – TV thing. Do about 20 songs, put it on cassette, put it on CDs and go early morning with it. Say two cassettes and one CD. And we ain't got to go to no record company. We're our own record company. And we can sell them damn things across the country.

"Then once you get that kind of money in your hands, you go and do those things you want to do. You go to the studios and do new stuff. Right now, with old stuff we want to pull out, ain't no company gon' deal with us. We can get that right on out of our minds. Ain't no record company gon' deal with the Spaniels talkin' about doin' nothin' new.

"Because like I meant to tell you, I was talkin' to Marvin and Mickey (of the Dells), and they said, 'Man, we catchin' hell. And we can't get no recording contract. That's why we're going with Gamble & Huff because they reopened their thing. They're the only ones we can find who will deal with us. Because we're too old and we're not up to date as far as they're concerned and they will not deal with us."

Would America today buy a vocal group in their mid-to-late '50s?

POOKIE: "They haven't been doing it. Now, when you put money in your pocket, you can take all the chances you want to. And you might as well go out there and do it yourself and you might be able to . . . They do not want to be bothered with you, see, and you got to remember this: It's the youth that's runnin' these companies. It's the dudes that never heard of us in their life. You say Spaniels, and they say . . .

"Like the dude, he was talking to people at the Arsenio Hall Show. He was . . . other than that broad that takes care of the business. They're youth. They never heard of the Spaniels. Who? What the hell they do? He had to get to the lady that has the final say and she was the one who said, 'Aw, yeah, the Spaniels. We'll take a look at them.'

"But as far as what's happened with this music, the thing today has turned around so that the white people know more about our music than the black people know about it. We, as black people don't carry our history. Especially about music.

"We are a one-record community. In other words, if you've got a good record today, everybody knows and loves you. And tomorrow, if you put out a record and it don't do nothin', you're dead. They just don't . . . we don't care.

"If you put a Sammy Davis Jr. down here or a King Cole at this particular time in life, we wouldn't go as blacks, because we don't attend those type of things. We'll attend these artists that got that one hit, or two or three hits, we attend his thing. Like at Merrillville (Ind.) at the Holiday Star Theater. You can count on one hand the blacks that go to these shows."

Why is there so much interest by whites in the revival of R&B?

BILLY: "As far as the whites go I believe, like the song says, 'Ain't nothin' like the real thing.' And you can't fool young people any more. They want to go back to the original sound. You can doctor it up but it always ends up in the original bracket. And I think the young people of today want to hear the pioneers – the people who actually started it, and I believe we are going to be seeing more of this. My son said a lot of young people never heard it before. It's new to them and hearing it like it was originally done is going to be the thing now.

"Teddy feels great doing it because I think they've run out the rap music thing, and the synthesizers and all the electronic things have run their course now. It's a thrill for them to hear it like it was originally done, and he feels great to be part of this revival.

"Of course, he knew about Pookie and all of them on a first-name basis when he was growing up. Pookie is more like his uncle because I used to talk about him all the time, and how we used to sing in school. I believe he got a respect back then for this kind of music."

When the group decided in 1991 to really give it another full shot with the originals, what kind of shape were the voices in?

POOKIE: "It didn't really affect me at the time. My voice was a lot stronger; it carried more. I was basically singing in the same range. In fact, it was lower."

BILLY: As you get older, your voice drops. That's why a bass singer is at his peak when he's like middle age, around 40. And people like Frankie Lymon, their careers were ended because they had that voice change. Dimp (Cochran) the same way. Dimp used to sing . . . he was a first tenor. I mean he could get up high natural and his voice dropped to baritone.

"But with Pookie, it was just the opposite. When I first started singing with Pookie, he was what you call a baritone; I'd say like a baritone-second tenor. He'd sing at the high register of baritone and come on down. And now, from what I heard yesterday morning, he hit that high C, and that's a legitimate first tenor. And I happen to know – that's why I asked him – he doesn't sing falsetto. Whatever he sings is natural. That made him capable of singing first tenor, although he may never do it because he has a tendency to sing where he's more relaxed. And that surprised me."

POOKIE: "Like 'Danny Boy.' On the record 'Danny Boy'

(Canterbury – 1974) I didn't hit the high part 'cause I couldn't get there. Now I can get there. I can hit the parts myself now. At one time, I couldn't. 'I.O.U.' the same thing. I couldn't hit that tenor part – so Carl (Rainge) did it. Looks like as the years progressed, my voice got higher."

BILLY: "Carl's voice dropped, on the other hand."

POOKIE: "Yeah. "Cause he was a natural first tenor for a long time."

BILLY: "He was one of the best first tenors I ever heard. Natural."

What was the part on 'I.O.U.' that Carl hit?

POOKIE: "'IOUuuu . . .' He'd sing that part."

BILLY: "Now you can do that."

POOKIE: "Yeah."

Did Pookie do solos as a kid when they came and got him to sing with church choirs?

POOKIE: "Basically, they had me singing solos in the choir. In other words, they'd sing back behind me and I would sing the words."

Would they introduce him by name?

"No. I was another choir member. But nine out of 10, they knew I was comin', you know, so people come to church and sit there and listen. I would do this with all the churches. They would all come and get me. I was 14, 15 years old. Around the time of the Three Bees."

BILLY: "We used to do little things, too, the three of us – me and Pookie and Calvin. At the Y. Remember the show they had? And a lot of white churches in those days, which was unheard of. All the 'houses.' And we were known for our tight harmony. Our voices – the timbre of our voices was so close that was why . . ."

POOKIE: "Yeah. We had this girl we used to sing be-hind . . ."

BILLY: "Yeah, Beverly . . . She could sing, too."

POOKIE: "Yeah. She used to sing, 'Fish gotta swim, birds gotta fly . . .'' We had background. That was real nice."

BILLY: "That particular song tickles me because of the arrangement of the song and there was just one note of the song that we weren't sure. The background . . . all the rest of it was beautiful. We sang the song and everybody at school was screamin' and we couldn't even hear ourselves. Until we got to this one part that we weren't sure of and you could hear a pin drop. Everybody got quiet."

Pookie was then asked about the songs he's written that have never been recorded.

"There's quite a few," he replied. "'She's All That I Have' ; 'Climbin' That Mountain'; 'Impossible'; 'Sweet El';' They are basically romantic and slow things, which is what I do. I don't do fast things well, so I don't try to do 'em. I've done some fast things but I've never been happy doin' 'em. I get my inspiration and my feelings from my heart for the songs I do. I like to express that and to do it, you can't do it like an express train. I mean I can't. Maybe some people can. I like for it to sink in what I'm talkin' about, what I'm thinkin' about and people can understand it."

What did he think of "Baby Come Along With Me"?

"That was one of those fast songs I wrote and I wasn't too crazy about," he said. "I wasn't particular about it. Like the thing me and Speedo wrote, 'Great Googley Moo.' It was alright. And 'Tina.' I liked 'Tina.' Things like 'Why Won't You Dance.' I didn't write 'Please Don't Tease.' Otis Blackwell wrote 'Please Don't Tease.'"

BILLY: "Who wrote 'Crazee Baby'"?

POOKIE: "Calvin Carter and some other dude wrote 'Crazee Baby.' I liked that."

BILLY: "He actually wrote something?"

POOKIE: "Well, they were together so I don't know. He had his name on it. But he had his name on 'Everyone's Laughing' too. I just wasn't particular about fast songs. I like to stick to the romantic."

Would a new Spaniels album contain a few upbeat things?

POOKIE: "I guess. That was one reason Gerald was singin' lead 'cause we tried to give all the fast songs to Gerald. I did the slow songs and he did the fast songs. It didn't make me any difference if somebody else in the group did 'em. Personally, I am not an upbeat singer. I like to take my time; I like to be able to say what I got to say so people can understand what I'm saying the way I say it."

Would you envision anything like 'Play it Cool' this time around?

POOKIE: "It's according to what we come up with. I wouldn't say no. I don't know off-hand that we would do that. The only thing I'll say about 'Play it Cool' is somebody sooner or later gon' say something about we pushin' whiskey and cigarettes in this time and age when it's a no-no."

With the market today dealing in rap and upbeat, does Teddy (Shelton) particularly like that upbeat stuff?

BILLY: "Oh, yes. That's one thing . . . the difference in Teddy and me. See, I turn the radio off. I haven't listened to the radio in years. If it's a song that I like I'll get it, but as far as the music of the last 15 years, I just haven't been into. I guess it's wrong. Since I'm still in the same business, I should be up on everything. Like a doctor, you know. I just haven't been able to force myself to listen to something I don't like to hear."

"I'm impressed that you're practicing and rehearsing to relearn," I said.

POOKIE: "That was the difference in the other (second) group. See, the other group was, 'Hey, man, we singin'. We just meet and sing. We don't do no rehearsing.'"

BILLY: "You need to get everybody to run over the songs. And that's what we're all about. Man, we sing every time we got a chance. Yeah, I hope that we never get away from that, from the basics. Because I just believe you're just as good as your last rehearsal."

"You know, when I was writing about the music fairly regularly for the New York Daily News," I said, "I got a lot of positive reaction from well-known people, like TV's Soupy Sales and Art Rust Jr., who does talk radio – mostly sports. I remember Art, especially, telling me, 'The Spaniels? Man those cats were great!' And Art was mainly a jazz enthusiast."

POOKIE: "I know what you're saying. And these particular people that we're talkin' about, you don't need no records with. Because they the ones got the money, and they don' spend it. The thing is getting them in the spots where they can go to spend their money. They don't want to go where you got all those jitterbugs and hippety-hoppetys.

They want to go where they can be cool and subdued and be themselves without being ridiculed and stepped on or reached around, and they done got your woman, that kind of shit. They don't want that.

"Them young boys do that shit. You be standin' with your woman and they be all around you. They act like you ain't even there."

"Your favorite Spaniels record?" I asked Opal.

"'Peace of Mind,' without a doubt."

"But you know, going back to the shows and the acceptance," he said, "being 75-80 percent white was very evident at Radio City Music Hall. Because believe it or not, being away from it, this is the very first time that I have had anybody – black or white – walk up to me and say, 'sign my shirt.' Guys come up with Spaniels' logos, Spaniels' pictures on their jackets and everything. All they want . . . and they're satisfied.

"Buses – there were three buses full. A little girl said, 'Sir, my mother's on the bus in a wheelchair. Would you please get Pookie up on the bus and say hello to her?' At first Pookie didn't like it. He didn't know why I asked him that and it took me about 15 minutes. But he got on and said, 'Hello everybody. How you doing? Did you enjoy the show? I'm fine.'

"And then he got off, the young girl walked up to me and she said, 'Thanks.' Now, everybody on that bus was white. And I think they're more knowledgable as far as our music is concerned. Now black people are real funny. They will not . . . I don't think they actually know. The people that know are our age but they aren't in the forefront where they can come out and talk about it.

"Now, maybe they will come out and see a show – 'Oldies But Goodies Show.' Most of them are sold out at the Holiday Star. But then again, you've got 75-80 percent white. Now in California, it was just the reverse. Here was a young black man, about 21, 22. He was a collector. And he knew every one of us. I invited him back and met everybody. But it's still a minority as far as blacks to whites.

"We make as much money now (1991) for one appearance as we were making for a whole week back then," Opal went on. "Calvin would put money in our hand. Showed us contracts and I think Pookie made a statement (on my tape) that they had duplicate contracts. Come to find out that we were playing for $2,500 and it was supposed to be $6,500. So, you didn't know. Monies, I was never concerned. I always trusted them.

"You know when I left the group, and I found out what Vivian did, I didn't make peace with her. Pookie said he made peace with her. I didn't. Because I just disassociated myself. I hate to see someone die, but . . ."

So Vivian died in 1989 and Pookie visited her in the hospital and they made up, is that right?

POOKIE: "Yeah, I made my peace with her. It was hard to understand her because she had that stroke thing and she could hardly speak and she was . . . but she was in pretty good spirits. And the thing was, so I explained to her, you know, that she did the group a terrible injustice. She got us when we were just kids and messed us around.

"'But it don't make no sense to me to sit here and thrash out old shit,' I told her. 'All it do is make you feel worse and make me feel bad. It keeps my mind focused on what I don't need to be focused on. It should be focused on the future, so I'm going to make my peace with you now and God bless you.' And she said 'God bless you.' It was just one of those things. I'm going on with my life and I'm not going to sit here and worry about whether people like me . . .

"I mean, they called me and said, 'Look, Vivian died.' No, first they said they were having a benefit or something for her and asked me if I would come, and I said 'no.' And they said, well, she passed. And like I told 'em, well, 'I can love you, but I ain't got to be with you. I ain't got to be around you. So, I love her, I'm sorry things happened to her that did happen, but she don't get no reward for what she did. You don't get those kind of rewards on earth. She might get some kind of reward in heaven, but not from me. Let the Lord take care of her."

GERALD: "I never personally had anything against Vivian."

POOKIE: "Like I said before, Vivian was a victim too."

GERALD: "Yeah, she's a victim. Because I look at it

like, look, she gave us a chance to get out there. So it was left to us to go on for ourselves. I ain't sad."

POOKIE: "But that went two ways. She gave us a chance, but it was what we did that put her in the position to do what she did do."

"You know, my favorite Gerald Gregory lead-in is 'Here is Why I Love You.'" I noted. "Why wasn't that a bigger hit?"

GERALD: "I was so sure. I thought so too. There was another one, 'Don't go, don't go-oh . . .' I also liked that one. It wasn't played for some reason. I don't know what happened at the time. I guess we're going to have to do that one again.

"I get a kick out of the way you like the bass, really. But, I'll tell you something about this bass singing, too. I met a lot of bass men, and they would run me out as far as the volume is concerned. What I find out is different is, I like to sing bass. I meet very few basses that, by my voice being a little more flexible, I can sing around it. But as far as the volume itself, you know everybody don't want to hear low all the time. That makes me have a kind of, if I may say so, uniquer bass."

"It certainly gives the Spaniels – you and Pookie blending and playing off one another – a sound you can recognize anywhere," I said.

"Oh yes," said Gerald. "And, it's a gift, too. Because I could be in a group, and I'm going to use my bass according to how they sound to get the right blend in there. That's why I think they like for me to be around, too.

"I feel I'm better now, than ever; now that I feel I've learned to sing. I didn't really know how before. It was all instinctive."

OPAL: "And believe it or not, Willie C. and Billy and I feel very comfortable on stage close together at one station, although each of us has our own mike."

"Your favorite Spaniels record?" I asked Gerald.

"'Peace of Mind.' It tells the best message we ever sang. It's as simple as that."

How about the Drifters with Bill Pinkney on bass for "White Christmas" in 1954?

"Oh, man, I'd loved to have done that," Gerald enthused.

"Sure enough. I'll tell you another one I would have liked – one Melvin Franklin (of the Temptations) did: 'I'm sending you a big bouquet of roses . . .'" Boy, that one knocked me out."

"To me, 'Bounce' would be a No. 1 hit if it came out today," I said. "You don't hear bass leads anymore."

"True," Gerald agreed. "So it could be my time, huh? Well, I'm ready. When I started, I actually had a natural baritone or even a little second tenor. Then after I lost my voice in school, it just came out with the bass that way.

"Then there was 'You Don't Move Me,' talking about Gable and Grable," I reminded him.

"That's another one I helped write, that's all. But the idea really comes from another source," he said.

How would you contrast the environment in a recording studio with a live performance?

"Well, the difference is, you can't go back on stage," Gerald said. "If you make a mistake, it's made – you've got to keep on going with it. That's where your experience comes in. How to get by and get over it. In a recording studio, you might stop a thousand times during the course of making a record."

You recall any times mistakes were made on stage by you or other group members?

"Oh yeah," he laughed, "like forgetting the words to a song. You have to do something. You just can't stand there. That's where experience comes in. I don't remember where anybody noticed it, exactly, but it has happened."

Why did the group rehearse so much in the old days? Were you trying to get just letter perfect?

"Yes. That's the reason we've been lucky enough to have hit recordings," Gerald smiled. "And we really didn't know how to sing as far as 'you got this voice and I got this voice.' We wouldn't know who was right and who was wrong, as long as the feeling was there. Now today we know voices, so it's different altogether. We know exactly where we're supposed to be."

OPAL: "Speaking of where we're supposed to be, I remember once when there we were in Texas under Roy

Hamilton on a tour, and segregated as we were, he came in with a white woman. I think that might have been one of his downfalls."

GERALD: "Like I said, I'm scared of women right now. I'm shy."

BILLY: "You remember Mickey Smith (Smitty) at the Royal Barber Shop," he asked Pookie. "He said Joe Jackson (Michael and the Jackson Five's father) sang with the Three (or Four) Bees, along with you, Billy, Calvin Fossett and William Dooley. Is this right? Calvin was tellin' me that he (Joe Jackson) sang with us for a while; that he made a few rehearsals."

POOKIE: "I don't know nothin' about that. Where was I? Well, you know, whatchacallit put it in her book – Joe Jackson's wife – that Pookie Hudson used to sing with Joe Jackson and I left when we broke up our group; I went and formed the Spaniels. That's what she put in her book. And I don't remember none of this."

BILLY: "I think if it happened, we might have had a couple of rehearsals or something. It was like that. It's nothing that I remember that we were doing shows or anything."

"Calvin (Fossett) even told me that on the phone today," I said. "He acknowledged it."

BILLY: "Well, I'd like to say this, too. Joe Jackson sang with just about every Gary group that was organized. Gospel groups and everything. Joe just loved music. He'd been around and say, 'Hey, can you use a baritone?'

POOKIE: "You're tellin' me something I don't know 'cause I don't remember that."

So much for Joe Jackson and the Spaniels.

FIFTEEN
The Future

"I think the Spaniels have really got it together now. They'll be on top if they can straighten out Gerald.

"They sing like angels. Pookie's got a voice like in heaven. Opal and Billy are back with them as they should be. It's not like the old days when, as young men, they went out and drank ." – Zola Jackson, wife of Willie C.

And what of today – the 1990s? Is it really possible for the Spaniels – that great, truly legendary kingpin of all the original black rhythm and blues groups, to mount a successful venture? Here's what each of the original 1953 group members had to say about it:

OPAL COURTNEY JR.: "The Spaniels had been held together by Pookie, Gerald, Dimp, Donald and Carl Rainge. This is when the music changed from being crude, hard, feelings to more of a regimented, harmony-type of a thing.

"Now, we got back together for this thing (1991 Smithsonian Institution Award) in New York. Pookie said, 'Courtney, I've got an idea. Do you want to sing?' And I told him I had always wanted to go back and sing. And Gerald doesn't know this. The highlight of my life.

"They were at the Claimants on 15th Avenue in Gary, and they walked up and said, 'Courtney, come on up and sing 'Peace of Mind' with us. I remember good. You know how you have something and then you . . .when I went to the service, the Spaniels got big; 'Peace of Mind' came up and all of the songs came up and you say, 'Damn, I was with them.'

page 192

"And when Pookie asked me . . . he said, 'We're thinking about getting back together. The original group. How about it?' This is something you always want to do, but if nobody actually thinks that you want to do it, you're never going to do it.

"I did not realize until the awards ceremony, getting back out on the road, going to California, going to Radio City, but my greatest moment was to perform in front of my peers – the black audience in Washington, D.C. And you know, it's nice to be remembered by people – I'm not going to say black or white. But when you look out there and you see people of your color and they are just as frenzied and love you, well . . . the Spaniels – Pookie and them – have made one hell of a reputation up and down the East Coast.

"And as a matter of fact, I broke up in that show," Opal continued. "I had to quit singing 'Peace of Mind.' Tears came into my eyes. But that song does something to me anyway. I walked away from the mike and Willie said, 'Where the hell is Courtney going?' I know Billy said, 'What is wrong with Courtney?' But I looked down at the crowd and I looked over at Gerald and, you know, peace is all that you could ever ask for. And to have peace of mind and harmony . . .

"I'm very sensitive. As a matter of fact, I've got tears in my eyes right now. Because of . . . I've always wanted peace of mind and harmony. And I'd give my last . . . people might think I wouldn't, but I'd give my last. I ask nothing in return. Because I've had teachings in certain areas and other endeavors that I've gone into in my life that allow me to not place great dollar value on things that you do.

"You do things because you come from the heart. And I'm a believer in that; Willie C. is a believer in that. But if you do it, you don't look for it. Down that line it's going to come back to you. Now the Spaniels is a second rebirth for me.

"I turned down a promotion to service manager at $40,000 a year at Gillespie Ford so I'd have time to dedicate to the Spaniels because I believe in them. I sing all day on the job with my Walkman. I know all the parts and Billy knows all the parts. So goes the background, so goes the group."

Opal also revealed that he has been urged to try and sing lead on some songs – and has the range to do so – but is content to do background, which he feels is very important.

"The only problems we may have are internal," he noted, "with Gerald. The money should be good this time. Pookie is handling it and Gerald is the only one who may question that. We have a real cohesive-type thing going.

"I've been the one in the new group to speak openly to Gerald. Willie C. is kind of laid back and Pookie is kind hearted. So in Washington, after the R&B Foundation Awards, me and Willie and Pookie met with Gerald and gave him an ultimatum. Willie C. got real upset and cussed out one of our helpers and Gerald. The potential is just too great and I refuse to let anyone spoil it. I can't stand alcoholics anyway."

Opal said Gerald brought his lady friend to his (Opal's) office at Gillespie Ford and talked about the Porter, Rainge, Cochran (second group) routine at a rehearsal. Opal, who was on the phone to a customer, blew up when Gerald said how good the second group was – so professional, how they hit the notes, etc.

"Gerald's behavior is why I left the group the first time," he said. "His real test is always on the road where the drinks are available. We are for the group. Gerald is for Gerald. We wouldn't have been able to go through the rehearsal session you attended properly with Gerald present."

Opal believes everyone in the group is supposed to have a function. Teddy Shelton is musical director, guitar player and backup singer, but Opal said the second group criticized him at the Star Theater in Merrillville, Ind., and in Florida. He said they also complained that they didn't have their whiskey set-up backstage like the Dells. In East Chicage in 1983, at a Knights of Columbus gig, they were all drunk, Opal said.

"And yesterday (July 22, 1991 during a group interview at Willie C.'s house in Gary) something happened and I'm going to tell Pookie. If you noticed, Gerald had resolved himself to not drink a beer. And he drank only one. Afterward, when he reached over, Pookie didn't hand it to him.

He sat right there in that chair and didn't drink. Just think about that. And Pookie should have left it alone.

"Pookie said 'You think I'm going to buy it and give it to you?' He should not have offered it to him. Pookie has a soft nature. I'm firm. Hey, the man drinks. Hell, it might be a catalyst. This was a test for Gerald and Gerald didn't pass the test.

"And I wanted to bring that out to Pookie," Opal continued. "I said 'Pookie, you know how Willie C. and I feel about this.' Really, I was so proud of Gerald, because he did reach over and Pookie didn't hand him the beer and he just sat there in the chair. You know, I refuse to be part of something that's going to be negative. After his performance in Washington, D.C. (in May 1991), had it been in Radio City Music Hall where we were, we wouldn't be able to go any place.

"His voice was gone," Opal said. "He was totally out of it; he was drunk; he missed . . . we started three songs without him. He started doing his thing for Gerald. People loved it. When he walked in, all his friends said, 'Hey Gerald,' you know? So we just made an ultimatum; 'Either you do it or you don't do it.'

"Gerald missed a part in 'Goodnight Sweetheart, Goodnight.' His voice was so bad, rather than 'Do, do, do, do doooo . . .' he said 'Ah say, do do do,' you know, trying to make up for it. He was in his world. He was a showman. But he wasn't a team. He wasn't the group. So it's up to here right now with Gerald. And I don't give a damn if . . . and Pookie . . . I'll tell you how it is. Willie C., Billy and I, we're together as far as how Gerald should be treated. We are together. And we told Pookie it's an ultimatum: 'Either Gerald or us.'"

"I think Pookie will stand by it. Pookie is tired of Gerald," emphasized Opal. "And we got Teddy (Shelton). Teddy can sing more bass than Gerald. Teddy is a bass. I got a spiritual record here with Teddy on bass and I'm going to let you hear it. We're blessed in having Teddy. Not only does Teddy do a good job as music director, but he can sing, which is a plus.

"Anybody can sing that ('Goodnight Sweetheart') opening. That part sings itself. A girl (Do do do do dooo . . . at a pretty high pitch) can sing it. And if Pookie comes in with his voice in the background, anybody can sing it. You know people said we can't do without. We can do without. Because there was a lot of times that Pookie said that Gerald was not in there. And Billy can sing bass.

"I'm looking for good things, without a doubt. I think the trial and error period is still there, where we have to prove ourselves like a new group. Because a lot of people haven't touched the Spaniels for years. Right now, we're not concerned with the new stuff. It's just a matter of the old stuff. Like you brought up to Pookie yesterday on the words to 'Goodnight Sweetheart': 'It's not your daddy, Pookie, it's your father.' People understand that and they miss it, especially whites.

"Blacks grew up with R&B – they took it for granted. They're so used to it, while whites had to slip to hear it. Their parents wouldn't let them hear it in the house. That's why whites seem more interested in it today and pay such close attention.

"On 'Baby, It's You,' if you don't hear that 'Woo, woo, woo, woo . . . if you don't hear that in the song, you know, hey, that's the reason that people come," he said. "People are now reverted back to the originals. And I love it because it's like I said yesterday, it's like rebirth. And things are similar: Like a Carter (Vivian) and a Carter (Richard), the Flamingos, and the Flamingos and the Spaniels. And we're back together. And we're going to do good things."

* * * *

ERNEST WARREN: "I'm not part of the group now, by my own choice, but I was honored by the Smithsonian thing with them. I feel that for me to return to the group would be a conflict with my work in trying to get people to the Lord on one hand, and asking them to dance sexily on the other.

"Still, we tuned up at the Smithsonian Awards and sounded good. But I don't think no one could ever really take my place as far as that's concerned because that's the original. If they stay in their natural ranges and don't stretch their voices, it will be fine.

"I hope thcy can make it and they can get the due from some of the past things that they've done. I hope that that can be rectified. I don't know how, but I hope some of the heartaches and heartbreaks that was in the past will somehow be assuaged. I just wish them the best.

"If the song – 'Goodnight Sweetheart' – keeps popping up like it is, I don't see how the Rock 'n' Roll Hall of Fame can keep us out."

* * * *

GERALD GREGORY: "I feel good because we've been blessed with our voices. I think we're better than ever. I think this comes from experience; I feel good about the group, sincerely. I'm beginning to enjoy my lead singer, Pookie, even more. Like one of the fellows mentioned, I can't think of another group where all the originals are there.

"We rehearsed more before than we do now. Today, we know voices so it's different all together. We know exactly where we're supposed to be. And I'm realizing more today (about our popularity) simply because we were just introduced into the Hall of Fame at the Smithsonian. I appreciate it very much. But I do realize we wouldn't have gotten in there without 'Goodnight Sweetheart.' It's very much what's keeping us alive and what we are today.

"Nowadays, I notice that 70 percent of our audience is white. And they seem to know more about us than the blacks, and I can't quite understand that . . . like at Radio City Music Hall in June (1991).

"We had just not too long left California and I was very surprised at the white reception that we got. These people know more about me than I know about myself, it seems. I'm surprised when I mention the color line. I mean you would think that us being black that the blacks would know more about us. And they (the whites) were very enthused and I haven't gotten over yet how deep they know about us. They even have paraphernalia, and some of the records that are collectors items.

"I was looking at Newsweek magazine where one of our tunes, the first one – the number you like best, Richard, 'Baby, It's You' – written by Pookie and James (Junior)

Coleman, is a collector's item. It was selling on a 78 (rpm) for $900. I said, What?' That makes me feel good.

"I'm looking at that audience still out there waiting for us and I'm very grateful for that. So the sooner we can get an album out, the better. I've got some new material I've been having in my mind quite a while, and I've talked about it with my lead singer, Pookie. He said, 'No, not now. People want to hear our old material just like they heard it before.' And that kind of surprised me too – to do the same material that we've done – but that's what the people want. So that's what we have to give them if they want it.

"He (Pookie) wants to do all the new material on another album completely. I wanted to kind of interperse it. You know, something different. But we'll find out the best way to do it."

Did he ever think the original Spaniels would get back together?

"I never gave up. That's the reason I left the other groups. I had a chance not too long ago to be with the Coasters, but I was born to be a Spaniel. It's just in my heart. The people always ask: 'Where's Gerald.' I didn't get back in because the fellas wanted me back.

"I didn't realize it would be this group, though, the original. And you can't really call our baritone (Billy Shelton) – he's the only new one – you can't really call him not an original because he's the one who trained my lead singer. So he kind of fits in. We're all from the same high school."

How does he view Pookie as a lead these days?

"To be frank with you, I never cared that much for Pookie in the beginning, as far as a lead singer – as far as my choice of lead singers. I always liked that strong lead, like say the O'Jays' type of lead, or the Dells' type of lead. Me personally. But now in my later years, I'm beginning to listen to Pookie a little more, and he's beginning to sound better to me. Yeah, he's better than he used to be. And I'm enjoying him more and more myself."

It's too bad they didn't let someone sing at the Smithsonian R&B Foundation Awards, right?

"Uh-huh," Gerald agreed. "Or at least I should have did my five notes (the 'Goodnight Sweetheart' opening)."

"I see the future's looking good," he went on. "I believe that as long as we try to do things in a correct manner the way we know how and the way we should, I have no doubts the group is going to go over again. And I'd like to give all the encouragement I can to my fellow singers that I've been with, as much as the new ones, and I can't forget the other groups either, because I know they're pulling for us. And I want so much to come through. That inspires them too.

"Like at this last (Smithsonian) Awards, I was so glad to see the Dells there. And the Clovers, our granddaddies, as I call 'em. I'd like very much to feel that I'm part of the ones that are not in the limelight now. It makes me want to come through even more so I think it'll make them feel better."

Later in a private telephone conversation, Gerald had this to say: "I want to thank you for those nice things you said about me and Zola at Willie C.'s house. I appreciate it. There's no personal problems I can't handle and overcome if I can sing again. And I will be singing again. I can cold-turkey alcohol like I cold-turkeyed drugs. I don't need it. All I need is singing.

"I suffer today because of not growing up with my children. Thank God they're beautiful now. I'm a granddad, but every now and then I catch myself suffering in my reminiscing, because I didn't grow up with my children."

* * * *

POOKIE HUDSON: "To get over today, we have to go back to the old stuff, clean it up and put it out, because this is what they want to hear. Those companies are after youth. They not looking for no old, gray-haired niggers coming out singing.

"I see great things for us. All we need is to keep on pushing and putting together these things like the history of the workings of the group; get our rehearsal thing so when we do appear before people we can show we have the class and that we can sing and that we can entertain. And bring back those memories and add some new memories. And let people see there is no sin in being old; the sin is dying young."

Why are the Spaniels mounting a rebirth now instead of five years ago or 10 years ago?

"People wasn't ready for it then. I think they're kind of getting fed-up with the whoopin' and the hollerin', the screamin' and carrying on. A lot of these people that were for that type of music are getting ready to come into an age where they are a little more settled.

"People with the money are the ones that are looking and listening for something they can really sit back and relax to," Pookie said. "And that's the ones who are keeping us alive – the baby boomers who came along when we did and can afford to buy these albums on TV and this type of thing. If we depend on kids, we'd be in trouble.

"So we are for those people who really believe that this was a true form of music and it entertains and it fills you with love. And that's what it's about."

Will it take new tunes, old tunes sung different, or the same?

"A mixture of both; to put new tunes together and to be able to present our old material the best way that we can. People want to remember it. We can't sacrifice our distinctive sound. It's like the statement you made when you caught me changing the words (on 'Goodnight Sweetheart'), singing 'daddy' instead of 'father.'

"I mean, people catch that, as if somebody was listening and interested in the music. And like you said, a lot of people sit there and can tell you word-for-word what it is. And if you vary from one of them words, they'll tell you right quick, 'Look, man, you didn't sing that right.' And those are things we're going to have to watch and do more carefully. I'm going to have to do more carefully. But the timing is right for us now.

"When we were able to come together at the R&B Foundation Awards and talk, and for everybody to lay it on the line and say 'this is what I want to do,' we knew it was right. If you don't talk, you never know. If nobody hadn't said nothin', it would've been the same situation. We'd have gone on and got the award and everybody went their separate way. But we were able to get some comaraderie and we said, 'Hey, man, I been wanting to do this for years.'

Any new songs in mind?

"Oh, yeah, I have a few songs," said Pookie, "and Willie

C. just wrote a tune and we rehearsed some things. And Gerald too, he says. We all have little things we want to do. I have 15 or 20 songs I wrote."

How will you go about getting a recording contract?

"That's another story. That's something we definitely got to have a good lawyer and a good agent to deal with it. They just don't give them out (recording contracts) much anymore. You really got to have something to offer. This is why with your book and the Arsenio Hall Show and we get, say, a couple of nationwide TV things, we could take off. Especially if we put all this together with the gigs and things we do – like the Apollo, which is a benefit but it's supposed to be a lot influential people involved. Sometimes it takes this for something to come about that will make everything else happen."

Arsenio Hall set for a date?

"No, not yet. Right now (at this writing), they're reviewing material that has been sent to them on the Spaniels. But at least we got that far. We've even talked to Oprah Winfrey, but they showed no interest at all."

How would the Spaniels co-exist with rap?

"We don't have to be in the same spot. Where rap would be accepted we wouldn't. Where we would go and things we would do, rap wouldn't be accepted. To me, it's like heavy metal. I see a lot of it on TV. I don't hear too much about them (rappers) being around, but when they go the places they go, they draw thousands of people. But there's some places if they were to go, they wouldn't draw flies."

Pookie's opinion of Motown and other '60s sounds?

"I thought that was great music. I enjoyed the Temptations, I enjoyed the whole Motown thing. I thought they had great writers. I'm beginning to find out they basically had the same situation we had as far as Motown was concerned. I was listening and talking to Dennis, Eddie (Kendricks) and David Ruffin before he died. They got a little thing they do. And they were saying that basically 'we got the same problem. They didn't give us our money and they didn't give ya'll your money, you know. It all went to Motown.' They feel they been beat. They probably didn't get beat as bad as we got beat, but they feel they got beat out of a substantial amount.

"I would like to hear more of the unfamiliar (to the white public) Spaniels' songs at your gigs," I noted.

"When we do a show by ourselves, we can do that. But usually when we do a show like the Apollo (with a lot of other groups), first thing they say is they want us to do four or five songs and these are the four or five songs we want you to do. And basically, they always want the same ones: 'Peace of Mind,' 'Baby, It's You,' 'Goodnight Sweetheart,' 'Danny Boy' and 'Stormy Weather.' They pay us, so we just go on ahead."

"As you know, I attended a background rehearsal this morning and Gerald was not there," I said. "They said he is not comfortable with you handling the business. How do you feel about that?"

"He's not comfortable with it. Gerald wants to be in the process and have a say in what we're doing. Only problem I have with that is Gerald still lives in the '50s and this is the '90s and you have to go about things different.

"I have my shortcomings," Pookie admitted. "I have to go to people I know that are on top of what's happening to-day to find out what direction I'm going in. Gerald don't have anyone to go to. He's not really made that many friends and he ain't been out that long, and the people that he knows are not qualified to guide us."

How much do you feel the group has to work during the year to become viable as a moneymaker?

"At least 10 months," he said. "I don't mean every day, but at least 10 months of weekends to make a living out of it. The last part of this year (1991) look better that the last four or five years. Now, with the change in the group – the attitude and things, this group is hungry and they want to do it.

"The other (second) group was more cocksure of them-selves. They just felt that they were Hollywood and didn't have to do nothin' but just go sing. These fellas here work, the ones now – Willie C. and Courtney. They work; they work hard, and this is something they want to do and they want to do it very bad."

* * * *

WILLIE C. JACKSON: "Things look bright, a lot better now that in the past. I see the audience, especially in the South. Wherever we go now we're being accepted just like the white people are. You get your due respect. I really didn't know anything about how the whites feel about us until I rejoined the group. It's a new experience for me.

"And the money seems to be coming right. I notice that we're getting paid well although we don't have a record right now. All the expenses and everything are taken care of. And people are appreciative of what we're doing. I jumped for joy when Pookie asked me to come back this time."

What kind of sound would you need on a new record?

"Definitely we must have a new sound, but the identity of the Spaniels would be there with Pookie singing the lead-in. This would be necessary, but I think we have come up to date. But, we would still have our identity with James (Pookie) Hudson because his voice is unique and when you hear it, you know that it's the Spaniels.

But can today's younger audiences identify with it?

"They would identify with it. It has been done with other groups. I notice the Dells are keeping in touch with the younger people. Now that they're older, they're changing their style a little bit. But they still have that 'Marvin' sound, that Dells sound too. But the arrangements are more of a beat for today's type of music.

"To reach the younger people today, to get their attention, you must have something for 'em to listen to. Because a lot of 'em don't want to hear . . . they might get tired of listening to our songs."

Willie C.'s opinion of today's music – 'rap,' etc.?

"We came through the rhythm and blues era and the rock 'n' roll era and I feel that I have lived this type of music. The 'rap' sound is hard for me to grasp. I guess it's just a little bit too much for me. I couldn't handle it. I would say it would be more like somebody just talking. Fast poems. Just talking fast. I don't think that is music. I really couldn't tell you why it's so popular. I guess it's the generation of this time.

"But you know, talking about younger people and the

Spaniels, we had a little young girl 7 years old write us a letter – and one (age) 11 – and they said how they enjoyed our music. Now this was really surprising to the whole group. Their mother and father had evidently played some of our records for 'em so we sent 'em an autographed picture. They responded and said they really wanted to see us. Whenever we're in the town where they live, they want to come out and really meet us and shake our hands and get our autographs. Now these are young people.

"We were at a banquet the other night and a young girl 20 years old came up and said she really liked that song 'Play It Cool,' and she said something that Gerald had said before: 'Do you know that you are the original rapper?' Like I say, maybe these young people are beginning to understand it and grasp this type of music."

Can you see kids getting excited about a group of 58-year-old men?

"No, not about us," Willie C. noted. "But maybe about the music. They wouldn't be. I don't think they'd want to date us or anything like that, but I think the interest would be there."

* * * *

How do two of the Spaniels' wives see the future for the group?

ZOLA JACKSON, wife of WILLIE C.: "I want the best for him. He's been a decent husband and father. He's been a good provider for his family. I'm satisfied the way things have worked out. If Willie had stayed with the group, he couldn't have taken care of his family right. Now, if this is what you want to do, I say 'go for it, honey.'

Zola beamed with pride over the Spaniels' R&B Foundation Award in February 1991 – a ceremony she attended in New York. And she said their two sons, (32 and 30 at this writing) are very proud to read in the papers about Willie C.'s career after all these years.

"The kids are wonderful; they're blessed. They're millionaires to have a father like him.

"Most of the Spaniels have grown up and learned about life," she continued. "Opal Courtney changed dramatically. Gerald Gregory is a drunk; he needs AA but feels he can do

it by himself. They may have to drop him. He could hold
you down if you don't get rid of him; pluck him out.

"You'd think that when Gerald got hit in the eye with a
beer can, he'd stop drinking. But Gerald still drinks with
this man in his 30s. He mistreats his woman Tanya, he lives
with and who provides for him. His talking about the Lord
and all is getting him confused.

"He says he can do it alone; all he needs is Jesus Christ
in his life. But he can't do it by himself."

Zola said she doesn't want Gerald "disrespecting her
house." She said Tanya goes through a lot with him.

Zola said she told Gerald she wouldn't stay with him being treated like that. Tanya told her she put him out once,
and will do it again."

Zola said she overheard Gerald berating Tanya in their
house when she was there to take her shopping. "He came
into the room drunk but sobered up when he saw me."

"The group should put their foot down and make him get
treatment.

"Gerald is the best person in the world when he's not
drinking. But when he is, look out!" she emphasized.

"The group told him he was giving them a bad name and
if he didn't straighten out they weren't going to include him.
He's fooling himself. When they were younger, they were
said to be a bunch of drunks. They don't need that anymore.
They don't need Gerald drinking on corners with young
dudes."

(Tanya died subsequent to this writing.)

"When easy-going Willie C. gets upset with him, you
know it's bad," Zola said.

"Gerald hasn't learned from his mistakes; he won't admit
it. The Spaniels have been on different trips and he's been
embarrassing them.

"There were problems with airport ticket clerks in Philadelphia and Washington after the R&B Foundation trip in
New York."

Zola said Gerald had gotten drunk at rehearsals at she
and Willie C.'s home, and she has told them they can't rehearse there with him in his drunken state.

"He becomes an ugly drunk," she said. "The demon

comes out in him – howling like a mad dog. Sometime people get the Lord and the demon mixed up; the demon comes in the Lord's clothes sometime.

"When he gets like that you have to babysit with him. He needs to get help for himself."

* * * *

MAMIE HUDSON, fourth wife of POOKIE: "Pookie seems more determined now (1991). When I agreed to marry him he said: 'Well, I guess I have to go out and work.'"

She said the phone bills at home average $150-$200 a month because of Pookie's ritual of calls all over the place to rekindle interest in the group. She feels the original group's outlook is positive – the four others will keep Gerald in line. They're retiring from jobs and have a second chance. They now can be totally involved. No longer do they have to worry about raising their families and their pensions.

"I don't think they'll let anything hinder them. They can concentrate heavily. They're more mature and realize how big it can be this time. They've learned from previous experiences and can take the risk. They're not totally dependent on singing to pay the house note. And it lets them travel in their later years, which is a bonus."

Mamie said she now feels she is helping Pookie in staying away from drink and drugs, but Gerald won't admit he has a drinking problem. "Pookie is OK," she smiled, "but still, you never know what may click. Pookie is Gerald's downfall. He loves him so much he just can't say no to him. He keeps giving him more chances.

"Gerald depends on Pookie; they should have been married. It's hard to imagine the Spaniels without Pookie and Gerald.

"As singers go, original R&B voices like the Spaniels were pure, unenhanced and unencumbered compared to many of today's singers and rappers. And people are beginning to realize that, which is why I think they'll do well."

Mamie said rapper MC Hammer's 'Have You Seen Her?' is an attempt to recapture the Chi-Lites sound and influence, and with it, pay tribute to original black rhythm and blues personified by the Spaniels.

*   *   *   *

Finally, the oldest member of the current Spaniels, Billy Shelton, who started with Pookie Hudson in The Three Bees, talks about the future of this legendary vocal group:

"Man, I have such good feelings, you know, about the way things are beginning to take off. Before, the group was only doing like, what, four or five shows a year, which is not enough for you to keep in demand. At the time, they were floating a lot. They didn't rehearse. They had one guy (Donald Porter) that lived in Boston.

"Man, the fact that you are here. That has done so much for us PR-wise. Here is a great writer that came out to write a book about us. Just that right here. And the radio interview you did with Pookie; you being there at the Steelworker's Union with me. People in Gary are a special breed. If you can get something going in Gary, you'll get it going anywhere. This is a stressful town . . ."

"I told him that already," Opal jumped in.

"Michael Jackson would still be singing up and down the street if he hadn't left Gary. But these people are negative, that's all. "I told him the same thing a few nights ago, man."

"I grew up here, man," said Billy.

"Last year (1990), the Spaniels had an opening in the group because, like most groups, there were big changes in personnel over the years. So they needed a baritone singer and I was considered. And I really felt honored that they would ever think about me after all those years. And so when they called I was very happy to hear that and I got back with the fellas.

"My son (Teddy) had played with the group before as a musician. They had used him on different things and remember, by him being my son he grew up listening to the Spaniels. So he was pretty familiar with the music. He was working with bands at the time and they needed a key musician who could control the various bands and cue them in.

"I think my son is the best guy that we could possibly get totally, all-around, although there are other very qualified musicians. So when I mentioned it to him, he was very happy that the group also needed a musician. So my son and I are together anyway. We perform together. By being part of the Spaniels, it keeps us together. That way, I can enjoy his company, you know, be around him.

"No, it was no way I ever thought it (the Spaniels' success) would get this good," Billy continued. "There were so many dynamic groups in those days singing, I never thought the Spaniels could reach the point that they did. But it happened because of guys like Gerald and Pookie and Willie C. and Opal who really paid the price. They went out there and they were determined. They didn't give up. They became No. 1; at one time they were the No. 1 rhythm and blues group. And not only was I proud of the guys, Gary was proud of them.

"The truth will begin to come out," said Billy. "The truth will always come out, if it takes a thousand years – sooner or later. The movie 'Three Men and a Baby,' probably did more for the career of the Spaniels than anything else I know. Guys like Tom Selleck and Guttenberg and dancing . . . these guys never . . .they were too young to have heard the Spaniels, but what the Spaniels created was so great that time couldn't kill it; couldn't slow it down.

"So it went on through . . . like with the McGuire Sisters, it went on through Sha Na Na and a lot of these other groups, and in 'American Grafitti' and other movies that came out. So they wanted to use the song in 'Three Men and a Baby,' and somebody probably said, 'Hey, let's do this. Let's cut through all the rest.' This song has been done by so many, let's go back and get the original recording. Somebody had to say that. And it ended up that they got the original recording, which happens to be these very guys right here.

"I think there's a movement now," Billy went on. "The world is aware of what's going on. Movies like 'The Five Heartbeats' could be the story of the Spaniels. I wasn't with these guys when they were on the road, but see, they went through hell. I came up during those years traveling South. I think that the world is ready now. They want to give the credit due to the originators. Cut out all the middlemen and go back to the originators.

"I heard the group when disco was popular, for instance, with Donna Summer and them. They changed 'Goodnight

Sweetheart' into a disco – without the bass line. I think some instrument was doing it. It just wasn't the same. It was like desecration."

Billy's first show with the Spaniels was Oct. 13, 1990, at the Sunrise Musical Theater in Sunrise, Fla. Also featured were Chubby Checker, Sam Moore, Lou Christie, Little Anthony, Tommy Roe and the Angels. After all the years, they ended up together. And he loved it.

"Last year," he said, "there was a lot of talk about the Spaniels being inducted into the Hall of Fame (the R&B Foundation). And that was fine. Nobody deserved it more. But really, what we've got to do now is look ahead. I feel the future of the Spaniels is international travel, international support. I think we can remember the past as lessons, you know, but that's the only time we bring it up. Where we can go back, and it should make us closer. But we should concentrate on the future.

"Here I can walk into a group that is already established, which makes me lucky. I'm really lucky. I wouldn't want to work with a bunch of fellas any different. I've sung with 200 to 300 groups and now I'm back with the guys I started with. And it's really a great feeling. I have nothing but good feelings for the future. Really, Richard.

"It's our plan now to have the best of both worlds. The main thing is to sound like we did, because that was the beauty of it; that's what the people want. But at the same time, little things where you could hear a guy singing flat or sharp or catching his breath, or hear a sax going off on a solo in the wrong key or something. We can tighten up those things and have everything high-tech as far as the delivery, but take the sound back to the original.

"To be successful, we can't overlook anything. And the key to all of this is us being able to respect each other, love each other, go back to the basic things. We're like brothers. And be good. Put the time into rehearsal where we're giving a finished quality performance. I think if we get to that point, everything else – commercials, TV shots like 'The Tonight Show,' trips abroad – all of these things are going to happen."

"I understand that in February 1991, there was an argument during a rehearsal in Willie C.'s garage," I said, "and Opal invited Gerald to go outside and settle it. I am told that Pookie said Gerald would have to leave the group if he didn't change. How do you feel about it?"

"Gerald is one of the best bass singers of all time and I don't want to compete with him," replied Billy. "I don't need to. His mature authoritative bass on 'Baby, It's You' was accomplished with one background mike, and he wasn't able to stand as close to the mike as he should have. That's how great he is."

I pressed: "But how far can you string along a disruptive influence, as Gerald might be, despite his great talent and dynamism?"

"Well, Richard, I've learned in life . . . you know, I've never been successful in life and I wondered why all these years, what stopped me," he said. "I found out because I would string along with things I knew weren't right. If I'd stopped at that point, fate would work different for me. So now, whatever years I have left are going to be quality years. I'm not going to waste one minute doing something that's going to stop my career or be detrimental to the group.

"And so, I feel this way: If everybody's caught-up in the group, we sould all be focused in the same direction. And if a guy falls short, my first thing to do is everything I can to help get him back on track. And if he doesn't let me help him, then, it's just simple. I have to disassociate myself from that person or those people. That's my philosophy.

"I've only been following that philosophy the last couple of years, but I find that everything's been falling into place. I've been making money, getting close to being successful. Just get away from people who are not kosher and get close to people who are.

"My thoughts of the Spaniels of today is that everything is happening at the right time with the right personnel," Billy went on. "Within this group we don't have ego conflicts. And out there under pressure it's rough because we turn on each other. That's the only . . . you know, we pick fights with each other because of the outside pressure. But with this group it's a little different. We have a love for each other that goes way back to high school. When I'm with these guys it's like going back to Roosevelt. And nobody can get the big head or be too big because we're too close for that.

"The group is based on the wholesome idea of the cohesiveness of each individual and we've got a team now," he emphasized. "Where one is weak, the other will stand up. But at the same time, we all know we have to give our best. And so it's going to be a lot of fun.

"When we went to Universal Studios in Hollywood – our first performance together with the original group – Willie C. told me it was like history repeating itself. It was like an omen because the headline group was the Flamingos. And Willie C. said the Spaniels' first big show was at White City in Chicago and the Flamingos also was the headline group. So it was like going back."

Listening to the Spaniels today really is like going back – back to a better musical time. A time when talent flourished on street corners all over black America just waiting to be discovered. The legendary Spaniels personified that talent. Lucky for us, they were discovered. And their music will never die.

Here's looking at you, kids:

James (Pookie) Hudson, Gerald Gregory, Willie C. Jackson, Ernest Warren, Opal Courtney Jr., Carl Rainge, James (Dimples) Cochran, Donald (Duck) Porter, Billy Shelton and Teddy Shelton.

You were the greatest. And you still are.

DISCOGRAPHY

The legendary Spaniels recorded exclusively for Vee-Jay Records in their hey-day from 1953-60. Following are releases (singles unless otherwise noted) for the label — many of which became big hits on the rhythm and blues charts:

1953: Baby, It's You/Bounce – Vee-Jay 101
The Bells Ring Out/Housecleaning – Vee-Jay 103
Goodnight Sweetheart, Goodnight/
You Don't Move Me – Vee-Jay 107
Doo-Wah (released 1955) – Vee-Jay 131
Since I Fell For You (released 1956) – Vee-Jay 102
1954: Let's Make Up/Play it Cool – Vee-Jay 116
1955: Don'cha Go – Vee-Jay 131
Painted Picture/Hey, Sister Lizzie – Vee-Jay 154
1956: False Love/Do You Really? – Vee-Jay 178
Dear Heart/Why Won't You Dance – Vee-Jay 189
Baby Come Along With Me – Vee-Jay 202
You Gave Me Peace of Mind/
Please Don't Tease – Vee-Jay 229
1957: Everyone's Laughing/I.O.U. – Vee-Jay 246
You're Gonna Cry/
I Need Your Kisses – Vee-Jay 257
I Like It Like That (released 1959) – Vee-Jay 310
1958: I Lost You/Crazee Baby – Vee-Jay 264
Tina/Great Googley-Moo – Vee-Jay 278
Stormy Weather/
Here is Why I Love You – Vee-Jay 290
Heart and Soul/
Baby It's You (new version) – Vee-Jay 301
Trees (released 1959) – Vee-Jay 310
1959: 100 Years From Today/
These Three Words – Vee-Jay 328
People Will Say We're in Love – Vee-Jay 342
Red Sails in the Sunset (released 1961)
– Vee-Jay LP 1051
1960: I Know/Bus Fare Home – Vee-Jay 350
Lovely Way to Spend an Evening
– Vee-Jay LP 1002
Little Joe, Posse, So Deep Within,
Baby Sweets – Vee-Jay LP 1024

OTHER SONGS ON OTHER LABELS
1956: Jessie Mae – Solid Smoke LP 8028
1957: Lucinda – Charly CD 222
1958: I'm Gonna Thank Him – Solid Smoke LP 8028
1959: Automobiles – Charly CRB 1114
1974: Danny Boy; She Sang to Me – Canterbury EP 101
1991: Santa's Lullaby – Street Gold Cassette 1352
1993: I Know, I Know; One Day At a Time;
Zing – JLJ CD

One Day at a Time/Someone – JLJ 2324